D1047417

Office

2007 HANDBOOK

Office
2007 HANDBOOK

Rob Beattie and Ian Whitelaw

LONDON, NEW YORK,
MUNICH, MELBOURNE, DELHI

EDITORS Elizabeth Watson, Martha Evatt
SENIOR EDITOR Peter Jones
MANAGING EDITOR Adèle Hayward
MANAGING ART EDITOR Kat Mead

DESIGNER Vicky Read
SENIOR DESIGNER Sara Robin
CREATIVE TECHNICAL SUPPORT Sonia Charbonnier
PRODUCTION EDITOR Jenny Woodcock
PRODUCTION CONTROLLER Wendy Penn

Produced for Dorling Kindersley Limited by
crosstees.eyes, The Lazy J Ranch,
Vancouver Island, Canada
EDITORIAL MANAGER Ian Whitelaw
EDITORIAL CONSULTANT Rob Beattie
SENIOR DESIGNER Andrew Easton
EDITOR Julie Whitaker

First published in Great Britain in 2008
by Dorling Kindersley Limited,
80 Strand, London WC2R 0RL

A Penguin Company

2 4 6 8 10 9 7 5 3 1

This edition copyright © 2008 Dorling Kindersley Limited

Microsoft product screen shots reprinted
with permission from Microsoft Corporation.

All rights reserved. No part of this publication may be reproduced,
stored in a retrieval system, or transmitted in any form or by any means,
electronic, mechanical, photocopying, recording, or otherwise,
without the prior written permission of the copyright owner.

A CIP catalogue record for this book is available
from the British Library.

ISBN 978 14053 3344 3
Printed and bound in China by WKT Co.Ltd

See our complete catalogue at
www.dk.com

ABOUT THIS BOOK

The Office 2007 Handbook is an easy-to-follow guide to five of Microsoft's® key programs–Outlook®, OneNote®, Word, Excel®, and Powerpoint®. It also introduces the Office Live web hosting service.

THIS BOOK WILL HELP YOU TO GET the most out of Microsoft Office, whether you are a complete novice or an experienced user who knows Office but is approaching the 2007 version for the first time. In a series of seven chapters, *The Office 2007 Handbook* helps you to become proficient in five key Office 2007 programs on a computer running Windows Vista and Windows XP, giving you the confidence to get up and running and to investigate the programs in more depth. It also explains how to set up your own web site using Microsoft's Office Live Small Business service.

Each chapter is divided into sections that deal with specific topics. Within each section you will find subsections that cover self-contained procedures. Each procedure builds on knowledge you will have accumulated by working through the previous chapters.

The sections and subsections use a step-by-step approach, and almost every step is accompanied by an illustration showing how your screen should look at that stage. The book contains several other features that make it easier to absorb the quantity of information that is provided. Cross-references are shown within the text as left- or right-hand page icons: and . The page number within the icon and the reference are shown at the foot of the page.

As well as the step-by-step sections, there are boxes that give additional information to take your knowledge beyond that provided on the rest of the page. Finally, at the back, you will find a glossary explaining new terms, and a comprehensive index.

For further information on computer software and digital technology, see the wide range of titles available in the *DK Essential Computers* series.

CONTENTS

OFFICE 2007 ESSENTIALS

THROUGHOUT THIS BOOK we will be looking in detail at specific core programs in Microsoft® Office 2007– OneNote®, Outlook®, Word, Excel®, and PowerPoint®, as well as Office Live, a website facility provided by Microsoft. Each program has its own functions, tools, and commands, but certain features are common to all the programs, and we will be looking at these in this first chapter. We begin with an overview of the key Office programs and at the combinations of programs contained in the various Office suites. We then look at those aspects of Microsoft's Vista operating system that relate to opening and closing programs, changing views, and moving between programs. Finally, we explain the new look Microsoft Office toolbar–the easy-access Ribbon.

INTRODUCING OFFICE

Microsoft Office includes some of the world's best known desktop applications. Here we look at the core programs that are the subject of this book and at the Office suites that feature them.

THE CORE PROGRAMS

In this book we have chosen to focus on five of the Office programs and Microsoft's Office Live Small Business web site hosting service, as we consider these to have the broadest appeal to the widest range of users, from the youngest student to the most serious professional. The selected programs have a high level of integration, allowing you to move text and images, pages and graphics seamlessly between them, supporting each other and helping you work and create efficiently.

OUTLOOK 2007

● Outlook (not to be confused with Outlook Express) helps you organize your communication, time, and information by giving you all the tools you need to manage your e-mail, calendar, contacts, and tasks, putting them all at your fingertips. It also integrates closely with OneNote 2007.

ONENOTE 2007

● OneNote is the ideal tool for gathering information of every kind for a school project, an article or book, a PhD thesis, or a report. Using notebooks, sections, and pages, the OneNote screen helps you pull together text and images, web sites, jottings, and even sound bites in an easily organized format.

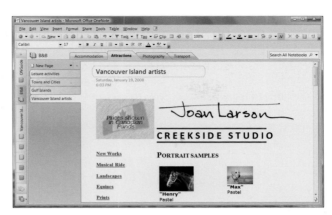

WORD 2007

● Well known and well respected, Word is a powerful word processing and page design program. In its 2007 incarnation, it has an even greater range of features and tools than previous versions. These include useful Building Blocks of pre-designed content, and "whole-document" font Styles and Themes that improve the look of all aspects of the design. The new Ribbon toolbar, with its tabbed groups of commands, arranges tools in a logical way and puts them all within easy reach.

EXCEL 2007

● Like Word, the latest version of Microsoft's spreadsheet program uses the Ribbon toolbar, part of the Office Fluent user interface, and includes the document Themes feature. As well as being ideal for creating and formatting speadsheets, Excel enables you to sort and analyze data using a host of functions, and to present it clearly and visually as a table, graph, or chart. Excel spreadsheets can also include images and graphic illustrations.

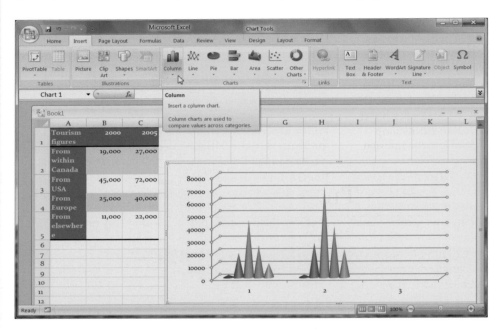

POWERPOINT 2007

● Synonymous with clear, eye-catching presentations, PowerPoint's 2007 version benefits from the same design and toolbar elements as Word and Excel—notably the Ribbon and document Themes, which contribute to a coherent design feel— but now also has the facility for saving and re-using your own custom slide layouts.

OFFICE LIVE SMALL BUSINESS

● This is Microsoft's web hosting service, offering (free for the first year) the web space and all the tools you need to create your own web site, complete with a free domain name, e-mail accounts, and the ability to monitor activity on your web site. It isn't directly related to the Office suite of programs, but it offers a no-frills shop window on the Internet.

THE OFFICE SUITES

There are more than a dozen programs in the complete Microsoft Office range. Some are designed specifically for big businesses, but most have a very wide application and are popular with home users, students of all ages, academics, journalists, and people in all kinds of work. Visit **http://office. microsoft.com** to see the full range.

WHAT IS IN WHICH?

● The various editions of Office contain different combinations of programs to suit every user. Word and Excel are in all editions. PowerPoint is in all except Office Basic, while Outlook is found in all except the Home and Student suite. OneNote is only included in the Home and Student, Ultimate, and Enterprise suites, but it's a program that's well worth installing.

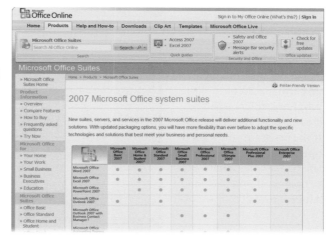

BASIC TECHNIQUES

In Windows Vista and all the Office programs there are common ways of opening, closing, and viewing programs and files. Here we look at some of the most useful.

OPENING AND CLOSING

All the programs in Microsoft Office are highly integrated, with the possibility of transferring data, objects, and pages between different applications. It is useful, therefore, to know how to open other programs and files whenever you are working on screen. Here are some of the ways in which to do this.

USING THE START BUTTON
● The **Start** button, located at the bottom left-hand corner of the Vista desktop, opens the Start menu and provides several ways of opening programs. Click here to begin.

SELECTING ALL PROGRAMS
● The Start menu opens, displaying a list of programs, folders, and locations on your computer. If the program you want to open is on the list in the left-hand panel, click on it to open it. If not, click on **All Programs**.

● From the program list that appears on screen, select the Microsoft Office folder and click on it.

● Click on the program you want (in this case Outlook), and it will open.

RECENT PROGRAMS

● When you next return to the Start menu, you will find that the program you opened has been added to the bottom half of the program list. You can now open the program from here by clicking on it.

OPENING THE START MENU WITH A KEYSTROKE

You can open the Start menu at any time, even when you are working on an open document, by using the Windows logo key (located between the [Ctrl] and [Alt] keys at the bottom left of your keyboard). If you change your mind, hit the same key again or simply left click back on the open document to close the menu.

PINNING TO THE START MENU

- If you don't open this program again for a while, however, it will eventually be dropped from the list as the panel becomes filled with more recent programs and items. To prevent this from happening, the program can be pinned to the Start Menu.
- With the Start menu open and the program icon visible, right click on it and select **Pin to Start Menu** from the pop-up menu.

- When you next open the Start menu, the program will appear in the top part of the left-hand panel and can be opened from here.

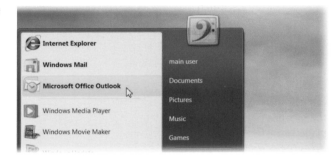

ADDING TO QUICK LAUNCH

- Programs that you use all the time can be made even more accessible by adding them to the Quick Launch toolbar to the right of the Start button. To do this, right click on the program and select **Add to Quick Launch** from the pop-up menu.

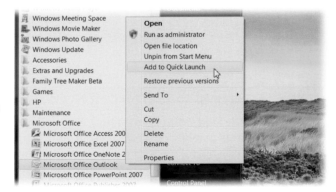

● The program icon appears on the Taskbar–the bar along the bottom edge of the screen–in the Quick Launch menu and can be opened from here.

● If the program does not appear and you see a double chevron instead, the Quick Launch toolbar does not have enough space. Place your cursor over the handle to right of the chevron and the cursor turns into a double-headed arrow.

● Click and drag to the right. The Quick Launch toolbar expands to make room, and the program icon appears.

REVEALING THE HANDLES

If the handles are not visible in the Taskbar, it needs to be unlocked. Right click on any empty space in the Taskbar and untick the check box next to **Lock the Taskbar** in the pop-up menu. The handles will then appear.

OPENING A FILE

● There is no need to start a program in order to open an existing file. The program in which it was created will open if you simply double click on the file.

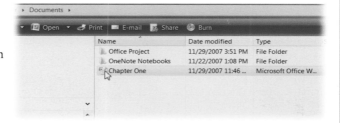

CLOSING A PROGRAM

● To close any Microsoft Office program, click on the red **Close** box at the top right-hand corner of the document screen.

CHANGING VIEWS

When you have several files or programs open and you want to move between them, Windows Vista offers a range of ways to do this. These include changing the size of the window in the foreground, hiding all open windows to return to the desktop, and displaying all the active windows so that you can choose between them.

CHANGING THE WINDOW SIZE

● When a document is open, the size of the document window can be made any size you like by clicking on one of the corners and dragging it to expand or shrink the window. This can be useful when you want to see the contents of more than one window at once, but fewer commands are available in the Ribbon in a smaller window.

MAXIMIZING THE WINDOW

● To expand the window to occupy the whole screen, click on the **Maximize** button in the top right-hand corner of the window.

RESTORING DOWN

● To return the window to its original size, click the same button again.

MINIMIZING THE WINDOW

● To remove the document window from the screen without closing the program, click on the left-hand button of the three.

● The window disappears, but can be reopened by clicking on the document name in the Taskbar.

SHOWING THE DESKTOP

● You may need to go to a folder on the desktop, such as the Main User folder, when several windows are open. Instead of closing each window individually, click on the **Show desktop** icon on the Taskbar and the open windows will minimize.

● If you change your mind, you can reopen the windows by clicking again on the **Show desktop** icon.

SWITCHING BETWEEN ACTIVE WINDOWS

● When more than one window is open and you wish to switch between them, there are several ways to do this. The first is by clicking on the **Switch beween windows** icon to the right of the Show desktop icon.

● The background Vista desktop becomes dimmed, and all the open windows are now clearly visible in this overlapping three-dimensional view.

● Click on the window you want to work in and it will move into the foreground.

● Alternatively, click on the relevant window panel in the Taskbar at the bottom of the screen. The window will open.

● A third way is to hold down the [Alt] key and press the [Tab⇆] key. All active windows are displayed. With the [Alt] key still held down, keep pressing [Tab⇆] until the window you want is highlighted. The title of that particular window (in this case the PowerPoint document second from the left) will be displayed above the row of windows. When you release the [Alt] key, the chosen window will open.

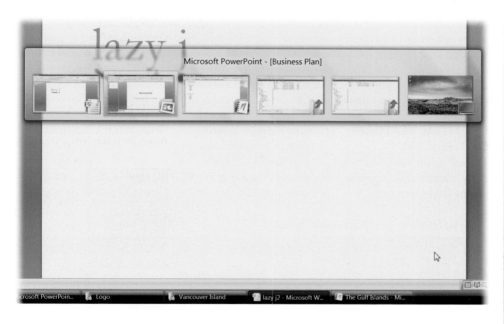

SCREEN RESOLUTION

You may find the screen shots shown here are not identical to what you see on your computer screen. This is because not all computer monitors are set to the same resolution–the number of pixels on the screen. A higher resolution, gives more detail, but at a slightly smaller size. To change the resolution, go to **Control Panel** in the Start menu and select **Adjust screen resolution**.

THE RIBBON TOOLBAR

One of Office 2007's greatest strengths lies in the easy control that the new Ribbon toolbar, part of Microsoft's Fluent interface, offers. In this section, we look at the main features of the Ribbon.

INTRODUCING THE RIBBON

In previous versions of Office programs, it was necessary to navigate your way through sequences of menus and sub-menus in order to find the options you wanted and carry out various commands. Office 2007's Ribbon changes all that. The same commands are still here, along with a host of useful new ones, but most are now only a click or two away, whatever it is you want to do. Word, Excel, and Powerpoint all use the Ribbon toolbar, and so does the e-mail composing window in Outlook.

ESSENTIAL FEATURES OF THE RIBBON

We will be looking in detail at the commands available on the Ribbon in each program in subsequent chapters, but some features are common to all the programs that use it. The window shown here is from Word, but the layout of the Ribbon is broadly the same in Excel, PowerPoint, and parts of Outlook, as we shall see in the following pages.

Office button   *Quick Access Toolbar*

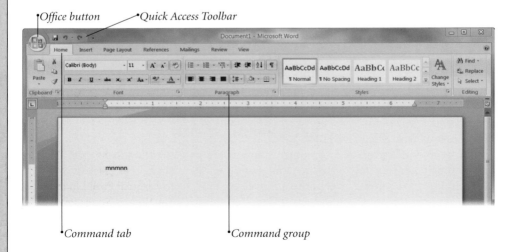

Command tab   *Command group*

THE OFFICE BUTTON

All of the commands, such as opening and saving documents, that were available through the File menu in earlier versions of Office programs can now be reached easily and quickly by clicking on the Office button at the top left corner of the window.

VIEWING THE FILE MENU

● The panel that opens contains options to open a new file, open an existing folder or file, or save the current file, as well as file commands that are specific to the particular program.

● In this example, the Word file menu includes options for printing, preparing the document for distribution, sending it by Internet fax or e-mail, publishing it to a blog, and closing it.

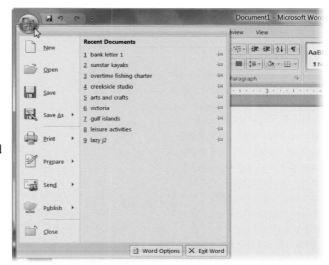

● Commands that have an arrow next to them have submenus that are revealed when you hover your cursor over them. You can then select from a list of options.

● Here we see the choices for sending a copy of the Word document to other people in various forms.

THE QUICK ACCESS TOOLBAR

The Quick Access Toolbar, to the right of the Office button, is the location for frequently used commands. By default, three icons are already there–**Save**, for regularly saving your work, **Undo**, to remove an unwanted change, and **Redo** for when you change your mind again. Other commands can be added as you wish.

CUSTOMIZING THE TOOLBAR

● To add commands that you find yourself using frequently, click on the downward-pointing arrow to the right of the Quick Access Toolbar to bring up the Customize menu. Here you will find a short list of common commands that you may want to add. Click on any to add to the toolbar.

● For an even more complete set of choices, move your cursor down to the bottom of the list and click on **More Commands**.

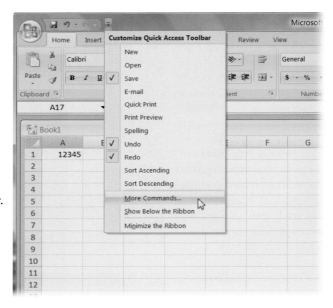

● In the dialog box that opens, you can choose from an extensive list of popular commands by selecting one and then clicking the **Add** button between the two panels. The command will then be added to the panel on the right, which lists the commands on the Quick Access Toolbar.

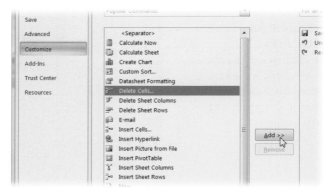

● For an even greater range of choices, click on the arrow next to **Popular Commands** to open the full list of available commands and command sets 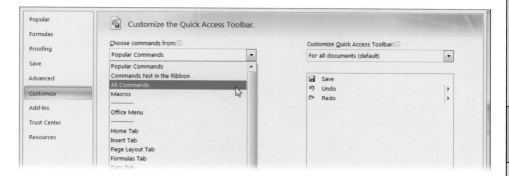. ● Note that many of the commands are specific to the program in which you are working. In this instance, we are looking at the Excel Options.

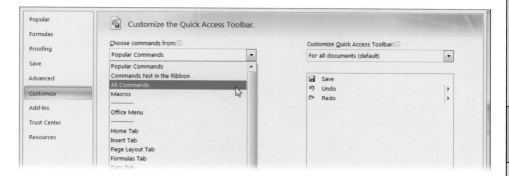

ADDING TOOLS FROM THE RIBBON

● Any of the commands on the Ribbon can be added to the Quick Access Toolbar by simply right clicking on the particular button (here we have selected **Delete**) and then clicking on **Add to Quick Access Toolbar** in the drop-down menu.

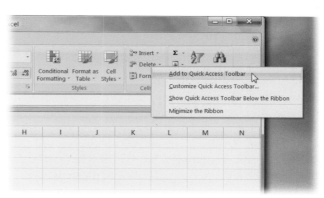

REMOVING COMMAMDS

● To remove a command, right click on the icon and select **Remove from Quick Access Toolbar** in the drop-down menu.

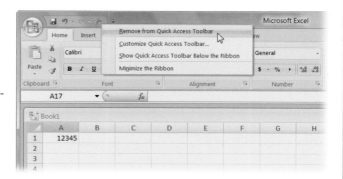

27 Command Sets

22 Introducing the Ribbon

EVEN QUICKER ACCESS

● To move the toolbar even closer to your working area, open the **Customize** menu again  and click on **Show Below the Ribbon**.

● The toolbar now appears below the Clipboard tools.

THE RIBBON COMMANDS

All the commands and tools that you may be accustomed to from previous versions of Office programs–and many more besides–are available in the Ribbon. The commands are grouped under a series of tabs that are opened by clicking on them.

Each tab contains sets of commands relating to specific aspects of the task. Some command sets have additional drop-down dialog boxes, and there are also command options that automatically become available in certain contexts.

COMMAND TABS

● A row of tabs runs along the top of the Ribbon. Clicking on any of these opens a separate range of commands. The tabs are different for each program, but they have generally been designed so that, as your work proceeds, you will tend to move along the tabs from left to right.

● The **Home** tab, on the left, is displayed when a file is opened, and here you will find most of the tools that you need to start your project. In the Excel Ribbon, these tools are for inputting data and formatting the contents of cells.

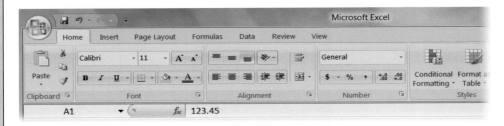

 **Customizing**
24 **the Toolbar**

● Clicking on the next tab displays a further range of tools. In Excel, the second tab gives us the options for inserting tables, charts, hyperlinks, text boxes, and other elements.

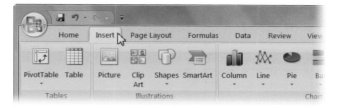

COMMAND SETS

● Each tab is subdivided into groups, or sets, of commands that are related to a particular aspect of the document. In the Outlook New Message window, for example, the first tab–**Message**–includes sets called **Clipboard** (commands for cutting, copying, and pasting) and **Basic Text** (commands for managing text fonts, size, style, and alignment).

CONDENSING THE VIEW

● When the size of the window is reduced beyond a certain point, or a very low screen resolution is used, the amount of detail displayed in the Ribbon is decreased. Here, for example, the labels next to the **Cut**, **Copy**, and **Format Painter** icons have disappeared, and the **Names**, **Include**, and **Options** sets have each been reduced to a single icon. Each of these sets can be opened by clicking on the arrow beneath the icon.

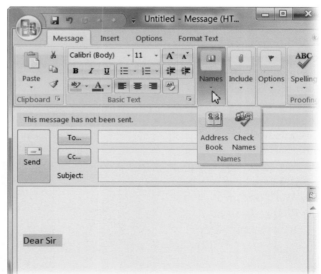

● You can check the identity of any button by hovering the cursor over it and waiting for a moment. A screen tip appears, telling you its function and giving you the keyboard shortcut if there is one.

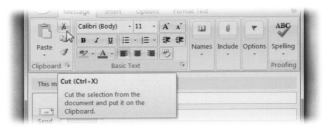

DIALOG BOXES

● Command groups that include additional tools not displayed on the Ribbon have a small arrow at the bottom right corner.

● Click on one of these to see the full range of tools in that set. Clicking on the arrow in the Outlook Basic Text set, for example, opens the **Font** dialog box.

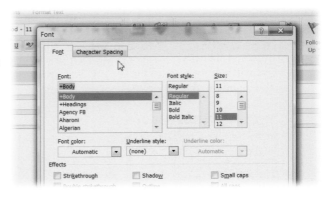

CONTEXTUAL COMMANDS

● Many of the commands in Office programs are only needed in particular circumstances. Rather than cluttering the toolbar by making these available all the time, the programs cleverly display them automatically in the right context. Here, for example, a picture has been selected in a Word document, and the **Picture Tools** are immediately available.

WHO NEEDS A MOUSE?

If you have difficulty in using the mouse for physical reasons, or you just prefer using the keyboard, you can achieve almost everything in Office 2007 by using keystrokes instead of the mouse. Here we look at mouse-free ways of navigating the Ribbon toolbar. In this example, we have the opening slide of a Powerpoint presentation on screen, and the text of the presentation title is highlighted.

ENTERING COMMAND MODE

● If we use any of the letter keys now we will simply overtype the highlighted text, so begin by pressing the Alt key. We are now in command mode, and each of the command tabs, as well as the Office button and the tools on the Quick Access Toolbar, now has a number or letter in front of it. These are the Access keys for the commands and tabs.

USING THE ACCESS KEYS

● We want to change the font size of the title text, so we have typed the letter **h**. (Although the onscreen Access key is capitalized, the lower case letter works too.)
● The Home tab has opened, and we see that almost every command has its own Access key or keys. Type **fs** to access the font size settings.

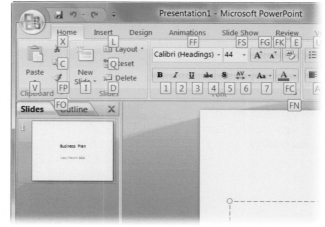

- The current font size, which is 44 point, is now highlighted. Any numbers that we now type in will replace this figure.
- Type in **60** in its place.

 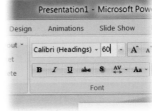

- When we hit the [Enter ←] key, the size of the text in the document becomes 60 point instead of 44, and our keyboard has returned to text mode.

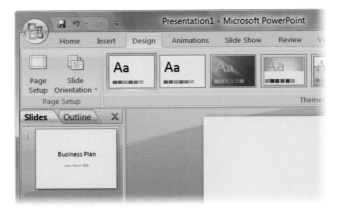

USING THE ARROW KEYS

- Instead of using the Access keys, we can move around the Ribbon by pressing the arrow keys on the keyboard. Begin by pressing [Alt] to enter command mode, and then press the [→] cursor arrow on the keyboard twice to highlight the **Design** tab.

- Press the [↓] key to go into the tab, and then use the [→] and [←] keys to move along it. Here we are highlighting the **Themes** command set.

- To open the Themes set, press the Enter ↵ key or Spacebar. The range of built-in themes is displayed.
- Use the arrow keys to move through the different themes. As you do so, Office's Live Preview feature shows you how the slide would look using each particular theme.

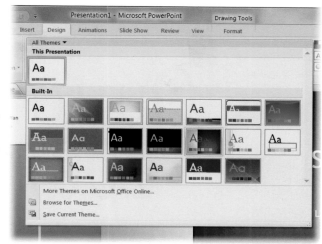

- To implement the chosen theme, press the Enter ↵ key or Spacebar, the Themes set closes, and the slide now has the new theme design.

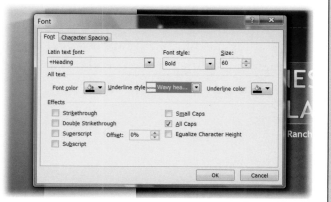

NAVIGATING DIALOG BOXES

- With a dialog box selected, you can use the Tab ⇄ key to move around the box, the ↓ and ↑ keys to change values in panels (such as font size), the Enter ↵ key or Spacebar to select options, and the Esc key at the top left of your keyboard to close the box.

OUTLOOK® 2007

ANY WINDOWS USERS WILL BE FAMILIAR with Outlook Express, the e-mail program that's included with every copy of Windows. Fewer people will have used Outlook however, the more sophisticated version that adds a calendar, task management, and contact manager to e-mail. Although originally conceived as a tool for larger businesses, Outlook also has much to offer the individual who has a busy personal or family life, or who is involved in running a small business. In this chapter, we'll explore how you can use Outlook to plan a strategy for re-launching a bed and breakfast business, planning meetings with suppliers and trips to local places of interest, creating a list of useful contacts, and liaising via e-mail.

OUTLOOK ON SCREEN

In this section, we'll introduce Outlook, the Office program that's designed to make it easy to organize all your appointments, tasks, events, contacts, and e-mails.

WHAT IS OUTLOOK?

Although it began life as a program primarily designed for use in larger businesses, where the ability to share information via networks is vital, Microsoft Outlook has developed into something that anyone can use to organize their diary, keep track of appointments, handle important tasks, as well as sending and receiving e-mails.

WHAT CAN IT DO?

● The Calendar can be used to make lunch dates, keep track of school holidays, schedule trips to the doctor, remember birthdays, etc.. You can color code entries to distinguish between business, personal, and family commitments.

● Use Tasks to handle those jobs that may need days or weeks to plan, for example, business projects, family reunions, weekend trips, even tax returns.

● Use Contacts to keep details of friends and business associates at hand.

● Use Mail to handle all your business and family e-mail needs.

NOT OUTLOOK EXPRESS?

Outlook should not be confused with Outlook Express, the e-mail program introduced with Windows 98 and included with all versions up until Windows XP; in Vista, its place has been taken by Windows Mail. Outlook Express, like Outlook, is for sending and receiving e-mails, but it does not include any features for handling tasks or appointments.

KEY OUTLOOK FEATURES

● UNIFIED INTERFACE

Microsoft calls this the Office Fluent user interface, and it means that once you have discovered how to work with one part of Outlook, you'll discover that you already know how to use other parts almost straight away. Aside from the standard Windows controls, Outlook uses the new Office 2007 Ribbon toolbar, which we saw in the last chapter, to access many of its commonly used features. This feature helps you to learn faster, and your will find that you can progress with confidence more easily than ever before.

● CATEGORIES

Categories are simple color codes that you can "attach" to almost any Outlook item, including tasks, contacts, appointments, and e-mails. You can give each color code a name (for example, photography, leisure, homework, or holiday). This makes it easy to organize and display any relevant information that shares a particular category,

whether it's an e-mail, a lunch date, a deadline, or someone's name and address. Outlook comes with six color categories already set up, and you can add a further nineteen if you wish.

● ALARMS

You can add an alarm to almost anything that you wish, whether it is an appointment, to remind you to reply to an e-mail, a deadline that needs to be met, someone's birthday or your wedding anniversary, and so on. You can also have Outlook notify you when you receive an e-mail from a specific individual or one that is tagged with a particular category.

● TASK INTEGRATION

Tasks are now integrated into the Calendar view, so they appear at the foot of the day that they are due to be completed (though this can be changed so they appear on the start date instead). E-mails can also be flagged in the same way as tasks for a follow up, so that you're reminded to reply at a later date.

● INSTANT SEARCH

Outlook lets you search for any kind of information stored in any of the main modules–Calendar, Tasks, Mail, and Contacts and, courtesy of its "word wheeling" feature, begins to display answers from the very moment that you type in the first characters of your search.

● ELECTRONIC BUSINESS CARDS

Contacts can be used to create attractive and distinctive electronic business cards, which you can then swap with other Outlook users via e-mail. This feature saves having to type in all contact details by hand.

● ATTACHMENT PREVIEW

Whereas previous versions of Outlook made you open an e-mail attachment before you could see what it contained, Outlook 2007 lets you preview the contents before opening it. This is not only safer, but also allows you to see the attachment in the context of the entire message.

OUTLOOK IN ACTION

Although Outlook comprises four main modules, it's likely that most people will turn to Outlook either to send and receive e-mail using Mail (see previous page) or to plan their time by using Outlook's Calendar. Although the Contacts and Tasks views are extremely useful–as we'll see later in this chapter–the calendar is the most intuitive of Outlook's features and, thanks to the new integrated tasks pane at the bottom of the Calendar screen, it can now display all the crucial parts of a personal or business schedule so that you can see your commitments at a glance.

FEATURES KEY

❶ **Button Bar**
Use to access Outlook's main features.

❷ **The Menu Bar**
Click on any of the items here to open a menu that offers further functions.

❸ **Day, Week, Month**
Click here to switch between day, week, and month views.

❹ **An Appointment**
Any appointments will appear here.

❺ **Working/Full week**
Click here to switch between the work week and the full week views.

❻ **Help**
Type a question here to open Outlook's help feature.

❼ **Search Box**
Allows you to search for anything in the calendar.

❽ **Task Window**
Create any tasks here.

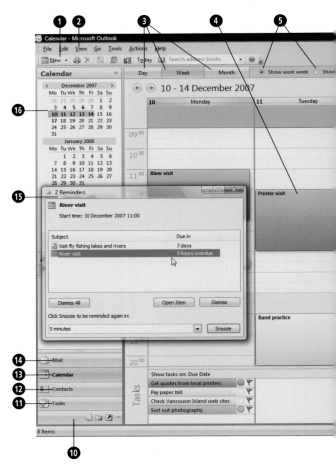

E-MAIL PROTECTION

If you use Outlook for sending and receiving e-mails, it's important to buy and install antivirus and antispyware software to protect yourself from fraud and viruses. There are a number of excellent third-party products available that can help you to stay safe, and Microsoft also offers plenty of help. To visit Microsoft's web site, make sure you have an Internet connection, then click on the **Start** button, choose **Control Panel**, then **Security**, then **Security Center**, and finally click the **Get the latest security and virus information online from Microsoft** option in the left-hand column.

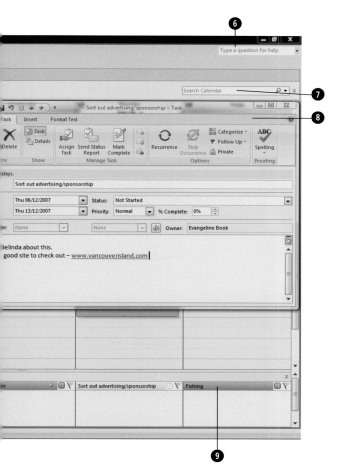

FEATURES KEY

9 A Task
Tasks appear at the bottom of the day they're due to be completed.

10 Extras
Any programs that Outlook doesn't have room to display appear here as miniature icons.

11 Tasks
Click here to switch to the Tasks view.

12 Contacts
Click here to open the Contact Manager.

13 Calendar
Click here for the Calendar.

14 Mail
Opens the e-mail program.

15 Reminder Box
Notifies you of any due appointments, tasks, etc..

16 Miniature Calendar
Highlights the current week and allows you to jump from date to date.

CALENDAR

The Outlook Calendar is an excellent way to keep track of a busy social life, run a business, or monitor a specific project with milestones and deadlines.

VIEWING THE CALENDAR

Although the Outlook Calendar comes ready to use "out of the box," it will be worth spending a little time setting it up so that it works exactly the way that you want it to. In this section, we will be showing you what the Calendar's different day, week, and month views look like, and how to move easily between them.

SWITCHING TO THE CALENDAR

● Outlook usually starts in **Outlook Today** view which displays a summary of that day's appointments, tasks, and e-mails.

● Switch to Calendar view by moving the cursor down to the large **Calendar** button toward the bottom of the left-hand column and clicking on it once.

DAY, WEEK, AND MONTH VIEWS

● By default, the Calendar opens to the **Day** view where you can see the current date, the day divided up into hourly sections, and the current time indicated by a little horizontal orange line in the hours column to the left of the main window.

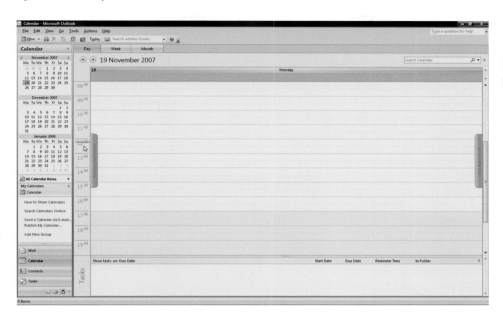

● Let's switch to the Week view and look at that. Move the cursor over the **Week** button at the top of the main window and click it.

● The view changes to show the default working week, from Monday to Friday, with each day represented by a column.

● Note that two new options have appeared above the main Calendar window. These options allow you to switch between the working week (as shown in the previous step) and the full week.

● Move the cursor over the radio button next to **Show full week**. Click on it and Outlook will then display the weekend as well as the week days.

● Next, switch to the monthly view by moving the cursor over the **Month** button at the top and clicking that button.

● Outlook displays the current month in full. The larger your screen, the more Outlook can display. Note that next to the **Month** button Outlook displays three new radio buttons– **Low**, **Medium**, and **High**. We will look at these later once we've added some appointments.

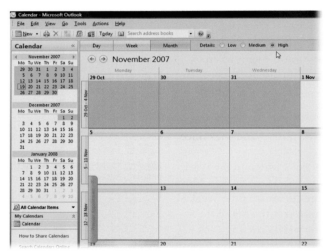

ALTERNATIVE TIME ZONES

If you work with people in a different time zone, use the time zone feature to make sure that you don't disturb their sleep. Choose **Options** in the **Tools** menu, then click **Calendar Options**. When the dialog box opens, click the **Time Zone** button and put a tick next to **Show an additional time zone**. Choose a time zone from the list and then keep clicking **OK** until all the dialogs have closed. The new time zone will appear in a strip at the side of the existing calendar.

Adding a
Complex Task

Customizing the Calendar

By default, Outlook's working week begins on a Monday and ends on a Friday, while each day starts at 8.00am and ends at 5.00pm. Changing these defaults to reflect the way in which you work is very easy and the calendar can be adapted to display different start and end times or working days, part-time work, and so on.

CHANGING THE WORKING DAY

● Switch back to the Week view by clicking on the **Week** button.

● Next, move the cursor to the **Tools** menu where Outlook keeps many of its most important commands. Click once to open it, slide the cursor down the menu to **Options**, and click once to select it.

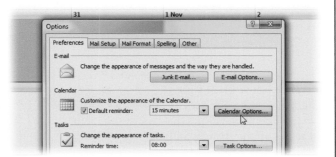

● This opens the main Outlook Options dialog box, which contains settings for E-mail, Calendar, Tasks, Contacts, and others.
● Click the **Calendar Options** button to continue.

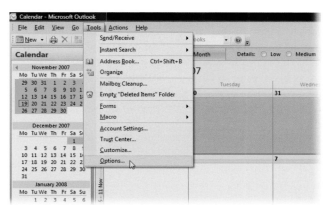

● Currently the working day begins at 8.00am and ends at 5.00pm. To change the times, move the cursor to the arrow next to 08:00 and click once to open the drop-down list. Then move the cursor down to a new start time–in this example it's 09:00–and click there once to select it.

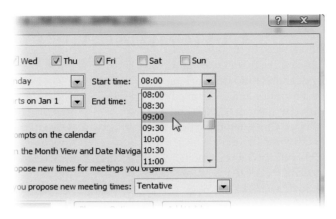

CHANGING THE WORKING WEEK

● In the same way, it's also possible to tell Outlook which days to display as part of the working week.
● In the example that we've been using so far, it's a conventional working week with Monday to Friday ticked, but Saturday and Sunday excluded (by not being ticked).
● However, because ticks can be added or removed for any day of the week, it's possible to construct a calendar that displays any combination of the seven days of the week. Here Friday has been removed and if we were to click OK now, it would not be displayed in the Calendar.
● From here it is also possible to set the start of the week and the first day of the year (for example, to start on the first full week or on January 1st).

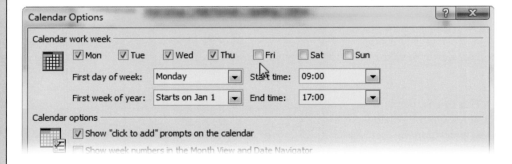

● When you've made your changes, put the tick back next to Friday, and click **OK** to accept all the changes and close the dialog box.

● This still leaves the main Options dialog open, so click the **OK** button to close it and return to the Calendar.

DISPLAYING THE WORKING WEEK

● To see our changes, move the cursor over to the **Week** button and click on it.

● Then click the radio button next to **Show work week**. The result is a five-day working week that starts on Monday and ends on Friday, and a working day that starts at 9.00am and finishes at 5.00pm.

NAVIGATING THE CALENDAR

Now that you have set the calendar up so that it displays the working week in the way that you want and the days start and finish at the required time, it's important to spend a few minutes finding your way around. Outlook provides various ways to navigate the calendar, making it easy to jump from one day, week, or month to another, so that you can find what you're looking for quickly and easily.

THE MINI CALENDARS

● Depending on your screen resolution and whether you're running the program full screen or not, Outlook puts between one and three small monthly calendars at the top of the left-hand column. Note that the current working week is highlighted in orange in the top calendar so that it's easy to see where you are at a quick glance.

● You can use the mini calendars to jump to any visible date just by clicking on the day with the cursor. In this screen, we've clicked on the first day of the following week. Outlook changes the main display so that it now shows that week in full. Note that the current date remains highlighted by an orange square.

● It's also possible to move forward or backward through the mini calendars by clicking the left or right arrow at the top corners of the first month. Here we've clicked the right-hand arrow to move forward an entire month.

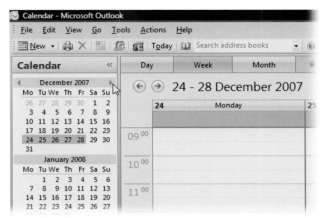

THE TODAY BUTTON

● You can always return to the current day and week (or whichever view is currently active) by clicking the **Today** button on the button bar at the top of the screen.

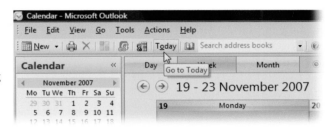

NAVIGATING THE MAIN CALENDAR

● In Day, Week, or Month view, you can navigate around the main calendar just by moving the mouse. However, as soon as you hover the cursor over a time slot in any view, Outlook will offer to create an appointment there.

● It's also possible to jump straight to a specific date that occurs outside of the current main window or any of those months covered by the mini calendars. Click on the **Go** button to open the menu and choose **Go to Date**.

● When the dialog box opens, click the Date drop-down list to open it and then use the mini calendar to navigate to the date you want.

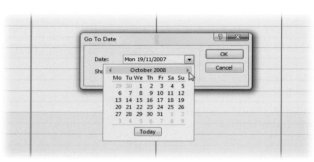

● Next, open the drop-down list next to **Show in** and choose which of the calendar views you want.

● Finally, click **OK** to jump to the chosen date in the chosen view.

QUICK APPOINTMENTS

Outlook allows you to add appointments to the calendar in any view and in various ways. At its most basic, these can be a simple one-off luncheon date or an appointment at the dentist, and Outlook makes these easy to create, adjust, and edit. We will explain how these Quick Appointment work in this section.

ADDING AN APPOINTMENT

● To add a quick appointment, hover the cursor over the time and day that the appointment is going to occur. In this example, it's on a Tuesday at 1.30pm. After a moment, Outlook displays a grayed-out box that reads **Click to add appointment**.

● Click once on the bar to turn it solid and make the text disappear. Outlook places a flashing cursor in the new empty box.

● Type in some text to describe the appointment. In this example it's **Lunch with Ian**. Then press the [Enter ←] key.

APPOINTMENT LENGTHS

● Currently this lunch appointment only lasts half an hour, which won't be long enough. To increase the time allocated quickly, move the cursor over the bottom of the appointment box until it changes from the cursor arrow shape into a double-headed arrow.

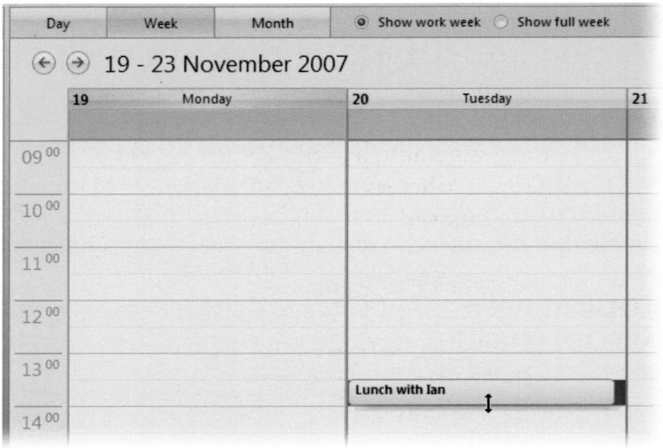

| Day | Week | Month | ○ Show work week ○ Show full week |

19 - 23 November 2007

● Next, click and hold down the left mouse button and then drag down to increase the duration of the appointment. Altering the length of appointments like this is quick and logical.
● Equally, if you find that an appointment is too long, click and drag until it's the correct length again.

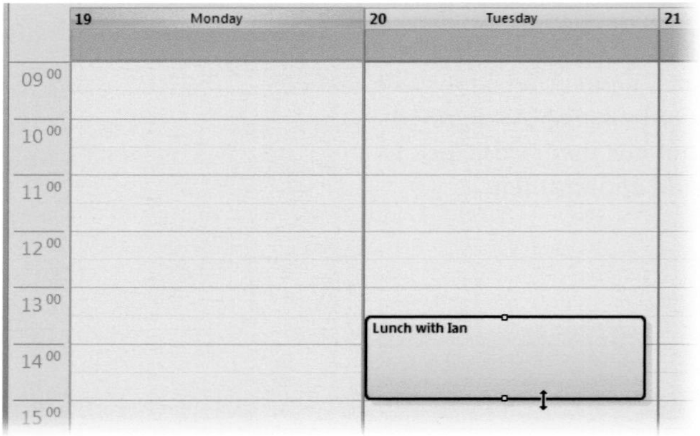

MOVING AN APPOINTMENT

● Having created an appointment, it's easy to move it to a different day. In Week or Month view, just click on the appointment and then, still holding down the left mouse button, drag it onto a different day as shown here.

• In Week view it's possible to re-schedule the appointment when you move it to another day simply by dragging it into a different position, whereas an appointment moved in Month view will remain in the same time slot.

• You can also drag an appointment out of the main window completely and drop it onto any of the dates in the mini calendars on the left of the screen. Note that the cursor has a small dotted rectangle below it. This indicates that you are dragging something into a new position.

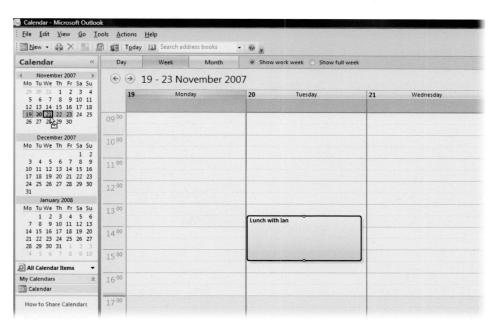

SETTING ALARMS

When you create an appointment (or a task), you can assign an alarm to go off at a pre-determined time to act as a reminder. How does this actually happen? Outlook will display a small pop-up window with the name of the task or appointment and when it's due; if you've told it to, it will also play an alarm sound to attract your attention. In the same dialog box you'll see several options, including the ability to dismiss the item, to snooze it (if you're not quite ready to deal with it), or to open it so that you can postpone it for longer. Alarms such as this will pop up over any Windows program that you're using, so there's never any danger of missing an important appointment or task.

Complex Appointments

Outlook can also handle more complex appointments. For example, a repeated anniversary such as a birthday or an event that spans a number of days. Outlook can organize your appointments into different categories, and it is also possible to attach alarms to them. Appointments can be set to recur whenever necessary and can be given an importance rating, depending on what needs to be done.

OPENING AN APPOINTMENT

● To see the full range of settings that Outlook makes available to you when a new appointment is created in Calendar, double click on the appointment that we created in the previous section. This Appointment window will appear.

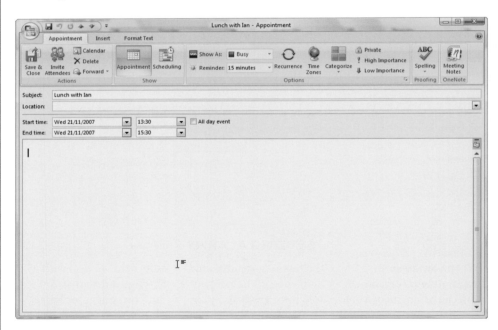

● The main Appointment window has three tabs along the top–**Appointment**, **Insert**, and **Format Text**. On the next page we'll look at the Appointment tab in detail. The Insert and Format tabs are almost identical to those used elsewhere in Microsoft Office; this is a good example of how the consistency that's been designed into Office helps you to learn the different programs more quickly.

THE APPOINTMENT TOOLBAR

● You can access all of the key features that you need to create a complex appointment directly from the Appointment toolbar, which appears by default when you double click on an existing appointment or double click on an empty slot in the calendar.

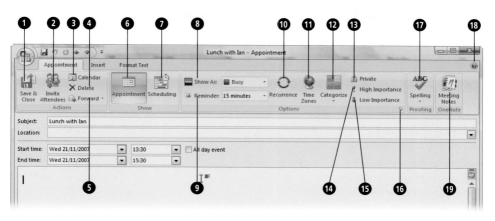

FEATURES KEY

❶ Save and Close button
❷ Invite Attendees
Useful for sending out invitations via e-mail.
❸ Calendar
Switch back to the calendar.
❹ Delete
Delete the appointment.
❺ Forward
Forward the appointment.
❻ Appointment
Displays the view shown here (only useful when the Scheduling view next to it is active).
❼ Scheduling
Useful for setting up meetings when calendars are shared by others, for example on an office network.

❽ Show As
Displays the appointment as Free, Tentative, Busy, or Out of Office.
❾ Reminder
Indicates when Outlook should remind you of an appointment. The default is 15 minutes.
❿ Recurrence
Allows you to create an appointment that repeats on a regular schedule.
⓫ Time Zones
Useful when creating appointments with people in different time zones.
⓬ Categorize
Add a color category to the appointment.

⓭ Private
Keep appointment private so others can't see it.
⓮ High Importance
Flag an appointment as a high priority.
⓯ Low Importance
Flag the appointment as a low priority.
⓰ Alarm
Assign an alarm sound to the reminder.
⓱ Spelling
Check window contents for spelling mistakes.
⓲ Help
⓳ Meeting Notes
Opens OneNote if installed.

◿ 40 **Alternative Time Zones**

EDITING AN APPOINTMENT

● Let's add a location for this appointment–a local restaurant in this instance–by typing its name into the **Location** line, underneath the subject.

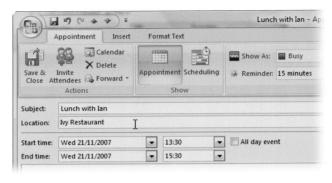

● Now, because the restaurant is a 15-minute walk away from where we live, we're going to increase the reminder time a little, so click once on the arrow next to the **Reminder** button on the toolbar to open the drop-down menu like this, and then pick 30 minutes from the list.

● We want to remind ourselves to take some local photographs along to the meeting to show Ian over lunch. To ensure that we don't forget our photo album, we will type a brief reminder for ourselves into the main window.

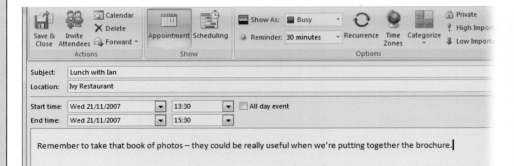

SAVING AN APPOINTMENT

● Finally, click the **Save & Close** button to finish editing the appointment and return to the main Calendar view.

ALL DAY APPOINTMENTS

● Sometimes you will have an appointment on a specific day but not at a specific time. Most people call this an event, but Outlook treats it as an all-day appointment and reserves a special place at the top of each day in the Day and Week views.

● To add an all-day appointment, click once in the bar at the top of a day. The bar turns dark blue, and a panel appears with a blinking cursor.

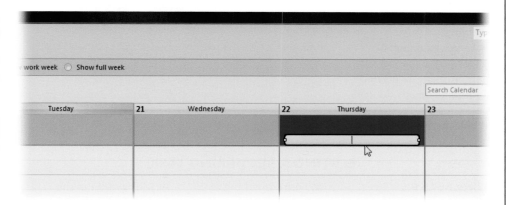

● Type in a name for the all day appointment—in this example it's **Day Off**—and then press [Enter ←] to add it to the Calendar.

● You can also turn any timed appointment into an all-day event by double clicking on it and then putting a tick in the box next to **All day event** in the Appointment window.

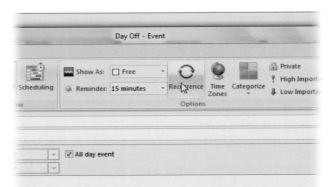

RECURRING APPOINTMENTS

● The third main appointment type is one that repeats regularly, for example, a birthday. You can either create a recurring appointment from scratch or modify an existing appointment. Both involve opening the Appointments window.

● In this example, we have opened the Day Off appointment we created a moment ago by double clicking on it. Next we click the **Recurrence** button.

EDITING A RECURRING TASK

Because Outlook "sees" recurring tasks as part of a sequence, you have to be careful when you edit them. For example, here we've shown we're taking every Thursday off from work. So, what happens if we realize one week that we need to work on Thursday after all in order to catch up with something or other? We don't want to change the entire sequence, because the following week we intend to be back in our old routine of taking every Thursday off. We just want to change that single event and leave the others as they are. If that's the case, we can just double click on the day-long event in the calendar and when the **Open Recurring Item** dialog box appears, click the radio button next to **Open this occurrence** and click **OK**. This opens the Recurring Event window, but any changes you make here will only affect this occurrence of the item.

● This opens the **Appointment Recurrence** dialog box, which, by default, assumes that the event will recur every week on the same day, forever. The dialog box has all the options you need to create appointments that recur daily, weekly, monthly, or yearly; it can handle all-day events or those that start and finish at a particular time, and it's also possible to specify the number of recurrences of a particular event or end it on a particular date.

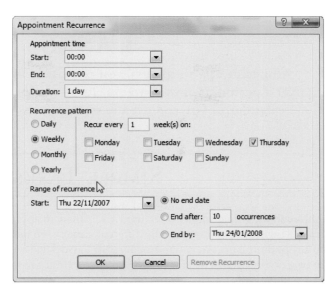

● When you've finished, click the **OK** button to confirm the details.
● In the appointment view you will now see that the appointment is shown to be a **Recurring Event** at the top of the window.
● Details of when the appointment recurs are shown below the **Subject** and **Location** panels.
● Click the **Save & Close** button to return to the Calendar view.

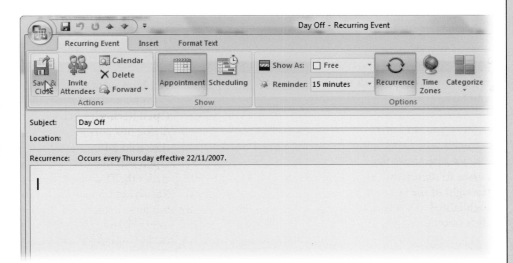

TASKS

Alongside appointments, you can create tasks that may occur over a period of days or weeks. Tasks can be added directly to the calendar or you can use the special Tasks view to add them.

SIMPLE TASKS

Although the two terms are often used interchangeably, tasks are actually different from appointments. An appointment tends to be a one-off event, whereas a specific task will typically take longer to complete than an appointment, and indeed, there may even be a number of appointments associated with completing the task. In this section, we will show you how to work with simple tasks in Outlook.

ADDING A SIMPLE TASK

● If you're not still in Week view, then click the Week button to display it. By default, Outlook displays a small Tasks window beneath each day as shown here.

● Note that Outlook displays a little tip next to the cursor that says **Click to add task**.

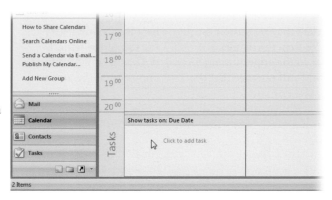

● Since you wouldn't normally add a task before today's date, move the cursor to tomorrow (to the right of the column highlighted in orange) and click once.

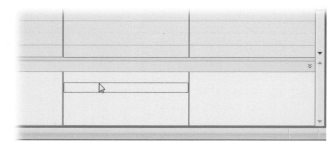

● Type in the name of a particular task–for example, **Call Colin**.

● When you press Enter ⮐, Outlook adds the task to the Task Pane at the bottom, complete with a flag and an empty tick box.

ADDING A DEADLINE

● Currently, the task can be marked as completed by simply left clicking the flag, but at the moment, there's no obvious deadline.

● Move the cursor over the flag and then click on it once with the right mouse button. Outlook displays a series of commonly used deadlines such as **Today**, **Tomorrow**, **This Week**, and so on. By default, new tasks are deemed to be due the following day.

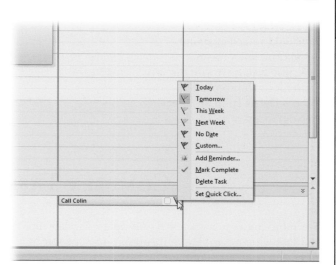

CHANGING A DEADLINE

● To change the deadline, simply right click on the flag and then click on one of the other choices from the pop-up menu. In this example, we've changed the deadline to **This Week**.

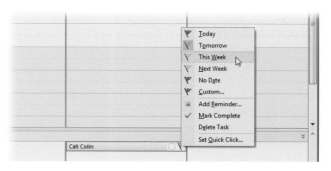

MOVING A TASK
● If you've added a task on the wrong day, pick it up with the cursor and move it to the correct place. Outlook displays a red line to indicate what's going on.

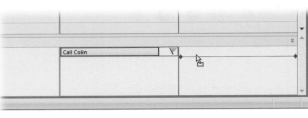

● To finish moving the task, let go of the mouse button.

DELETING A TASK
● Should you change your mind completely about a task, just click on it with the right mouse button and choose **Delete** from the pop-up menu.

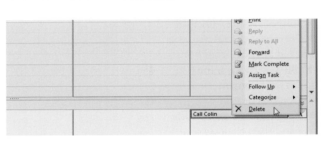

COMPLEX TASKS

For more complex tasks, you'll want to use the Task window as it has more options to offer. Although some of these features relate directly to using Outlook with other people in an office, many are also appropriate for use by individuals.

OPENING THE TASK WINDOW
● In Calendar Week view, open the Task window by double clicking in an empty slot in the Tasks panel sometime after today's date.
● The key features of the Task window are explained on the opposite page.

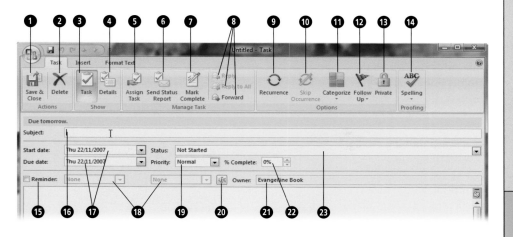

FEATURES KEY

1 Save & Close button

2 Delete button

3 Task

Displays the view shown here (only useful when the Details view next to it is active).

4 Details

Allows you to add extra information about a task.

5 Assign Task

Send an e-mail to someone, assigning them the task.

6 Send Status Report

Send an e-mail summarizing the status of the task.

7 Mark Complete

"Ticks" the task, marking it as finished.

8 Reply, Reply to All, Forward

All commands used to acknowledge tasks that are being shared by a group.

9 Recurrence

Set up a repeating task.

10 Skip Occurrence

Ignore this instance of a particular repeating task.

11 Categorize

Add a color category to the task.

12 Follow Up

Set a deadline to follow up this task.

13 Private

Hides the task so others in a group can't see it.

14 Spelling

Check the spelling of any notes in the main window.

15 Reminder

Sets an alarm when the task is due.

16 Subject Line

The details that you key in here will appear in the task subject column of the To-Do list.

17 Dates

From here, you can give the task a start and due date.

18 Reminder Details

Set a date and time here for the task to be completed.

19 Priority

Set a Low, Normal, or High priority for the task.

20 Alarm Sound

Change the alarm sound associated with a task.

21 Owner

Defines who is responsible for the task.

22 Complete

Shows what percentage of the task has already been completed to date.

23 Status

Show whether the task has been started, is in progress, is deferred, and so on.

ADDING A COMPLEX TASK

● In the Task window, type a name for the task in the **Subject** line.

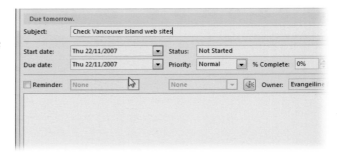

● Outlook automatically sets the start date as today's date, but we need to set the due date. Open the drop-down mini calendar by clicking on the arrow next to the **Due date** line and pick a date by clicking on it.

● Move the cursor over to the **Priority** line and click on the arrow next to it. A drop-down list will appear. In this instance, select **High**.

● Then, move the cursor over to the spin box next to complete and click the "up" arrow once to indicate that the task is 25% complete. Note that the text box next to **Status** has changed from **Not Started** to **In Progress**.

● Add some explanatory text in the main window and then put a tick in the **Reminder** box. By default, the alarm will go off at 9.00am on the day the task is due.

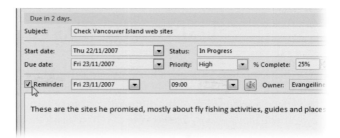

● Finally, click the **Save & Close** button to add the task to the calendar.

● The task now appears in the pane at the bottom of the calendar view, on the day that it's due, complete with a bell icon indicating that an alarm has been attached to the task.

TASKS, DUE DATES, AND THE CALENDAR

By default, Outlook displays tasks on the calendar on the date they should be finished–the due date. This clearly works for those people who prefer to focus on when something needs to be completed. However, if you're the kind of person who thinks that knowing when you're due to start something is as important as knowing when you're due to finish it, you'll be pleased to know you can alter the way that tasks are displayed in the calendar in Week view. Just move the cursor down to the **Show tasks on** text label that sits above the **Tasks** at the bottom of the screen. Click on this text with the right mouse button and then select **By Start Date** instead of **By Due Date**. You can also elect to have Outlook remove completed tasks from the calendar when they're finished.

USING THE TASKS VIEW

In the Tasks module, Outlook allows you to create complex tasks and then manage them effectively, courtesy of the different views. It will allow you to display your tasks as a simple list, divide them into categories (more of which later), or even display them on a calendar-based timeline. These features will help you to keep on top of tasks that may take place over several weeks or even months.

SWITCH TO TASKS VIEW

● With the Calendar still displayed on the screen, slide the cursor over and down to the bottom left of the screen where there's a large, rectangular **Tasks** button. Click it once.

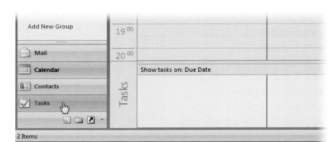

● Depending on how your copy of Outlook has been set up, or if you've experimented with the Tasks view before, your screen may have a different display. To make it match the one shown on these pages, click the radio button next to **Simple List** in the **Current View** column on the left of the main window.

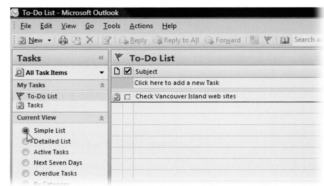

ADDING A NEW TASK

● So far we only have one task in the list. Looking above that you can see Outlook has added a **Click here to add a new task** hint in the text box. Click here to type in a new task.

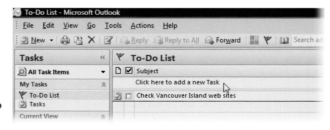

● Type in the task–in this example, it's to remind us that we need to visit the rivers and lakes we'll be mentioning later in our B&B brochure. This is a useful type of task to demonstrate, because it will take a couple of weeks to complete.

● Press ⌊Enter ←⌋ to add the task to the To-Do List.

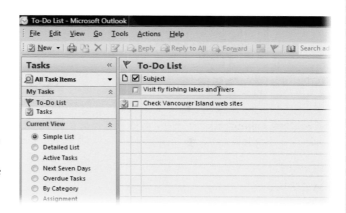

SETTING DEADLINES

● By default, Outlook sets new tasks to begin on the day they're created, but in this example we want to plan ahead a little, so let's change that. Double click on the task you just created in the To-Do List to open the Tasks window.

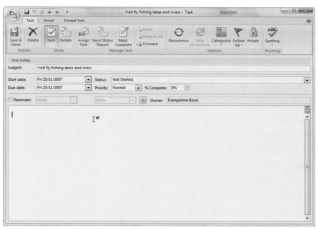

● Set the start date for a couple of days time by opening the drop-down menu next to **Start date** and picking the day from the little calendar. For this example, we're going to choose next Monday.

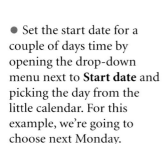
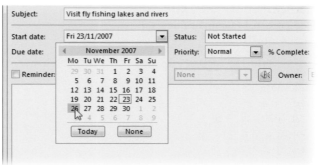

● Note that Outlook also re-sets the date the task is due to the same date. Since this task is going to take a couple of weeks, we're going to open the drop-down menu and pick a date in two Mondays' time instead.

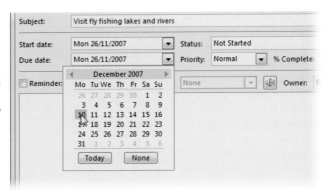

● Next, we're going to set an alarm to go off halfway through the task so that– if it turns out that we're running late–we'll have time to catch up. So, put a tick in the **Reminder** check box and then open the mini calendar next to it and pick a date for the alarm to go off; in this example it's half way through the task.

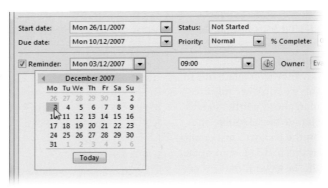

● By default, task alarms go off at the beginning of the day, but we want to re-set this to later on, so we've opened the drop-down list and chosen 11.00am as the alarm time.

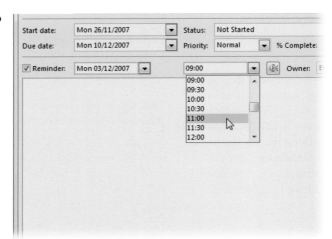

- Finally, click the **Save & Close** button to confirm the deadlines associated with this task.

OVERDUE TASKS

- Now let's move forward in time to a point after our first task should have been completed. In the Tasks view, we can see that Outlook flags this overdue task in red.

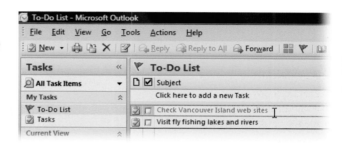

COMPLETING A TASK

- Sometimes, you'll complete a task and simply forget to tick it off. Fix that by moving the cursor over to the empty check box next to the task and putting a tick there by clicking on it once with the left mouse button. Outlook puts a line through the task to indicate that it's completed.

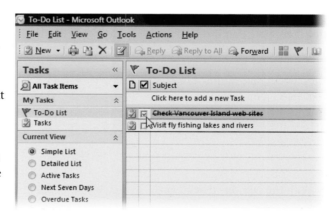

RESCHEDULING A MISSED TASK

- Sometimes, you'll miss a deadline because there's wasn't time to complete the task for one reason or another. If that's the case, you can reschedule it.

- Click once on the box again to remove the tick from the task so that it becomes active–and late– again. At this point we could double click on the task to open the detailed Task window.

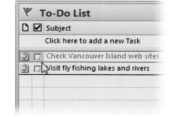

● However, as we only want to change one thing about our task–the deadline–there's an easier way.

● Slide the cursor over to the flag and click on it with the right mouse button.

● Then move the cursor down to the **Custom** option and click on this.

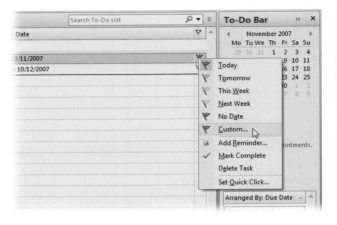

● When the dialog box appears, click the drop-down list next to the **Due date** line to open the mini calendar and select a new due date. Note that the original due date is highlighted in yellow and the current date outlined in red. Select a new deadline by clicking on it once.

● With the new due date selected, click **OK** to close the dialog box and re-schedule the task.

CHANGING THE TASKS VIEW

● So far, we've only used the Tasks module in its simplest form. If you look at the list on the left-hand side of the screen, you'll see that there are a total of 13 different views available; we've been using the top one–**Simple List**.

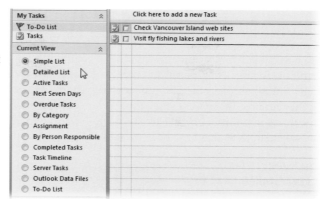

● Let's switch to a different view. Move the cursor down to the **Detailed List** and then click on the radio button next to it.

● Now have a look at the main list in the middle of the screen and see how it has changed. The tasks themselves are still in place, but there is now more information about them on display, including their status, how complete they are, which category they belong to 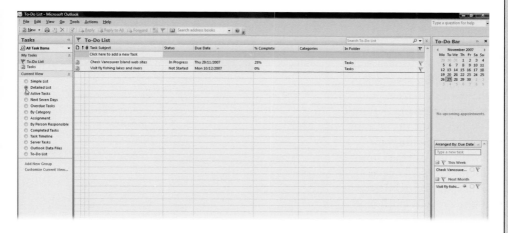, and where they're stored (useful if you're keeping track of lots of different tasks that span different projects).

Task Categories

CUSTOMIZING OUTLOOK TODAY

We have already briefly mentioned Outlook Today , the special summary that Outlook displays the first time it starts. In the Outlook Today view you'll find upcoming appointments that are stored in the calendar, tasks that have been created either in the Calendar or Tasks view, as well as electronic mail messages that are waiting in the Inbox to be read, in the Drafts box waiting to be edited, or in the Outbox waiting to be sent the next time you connect to the Internet.

OPENING THE CUSTOMIZE DIALOG

● To change the way that the Outlook Today front page appears on your screen, make sure that you click the **Mail** button in the list on the left and then select **Personal Folders** by clicking on it once.

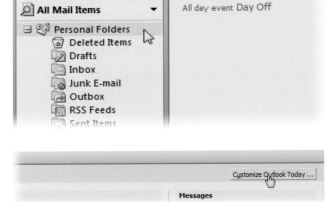

● Next, move the cursor over to the **Customize Outlook Today** link and then click on it once.

ALWAYS START OUTLOOK TODAY

● Here it's possible to make a number of changes to the way that Outlook displays the opening screen.
● Start by ticking the empty box in the **Startup** section to ensure the program always displays the Outlook Today screen whenever it opens; this is useful because it gives you a snapshot of the days and weeks ahead.

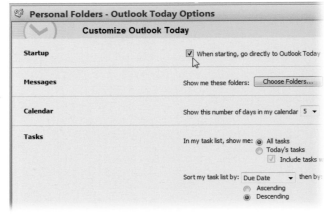

38 **Switching to the Calendar**

CUSTOMIZING THE CALENDAR

● Open the drop-down list in the Calendar section to specify how many days ahead you want the program to display.

CUSTOMIZING TASKS

● From here you can also elect to show today's tasks or all your tasks and also sort them by the date they're due.

CUSTOMIZING STYLES

● Choose a look for Outlook Today by opening this drop-down list and choosing from one or two columns as well as a special **Winter** or **Summer** look.

● Click **Save Changes** to confirm your edits, or click **Cancel** to ignore them.

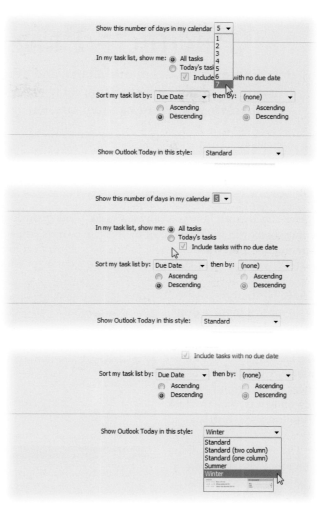

PROJECT PLANNING

By combining tasks, appointments, and events together logically, Outlook's Categories feature makes it possible to manage projects involving different participants, various deadlines, etc..

THE TASK TIMELINE

We've already seen how you can view tasks either directly in the calendar or by opening the Tasks module itself. In this section, we're going to look at the Timeline view, which will reveal even more about what's going on with a particular project. Used in conjunction with Categories, this is a surprisingly powerful feature.

TASK TIMELINE

● To make it more realistic, we've added a number of new tasks to the list using the techniques described in previous sections. To display them in a different, more revealing way, click the **Task Timeline** radio button.

● The resulting view allows you to see visually when particular tasks start and finish. The date range runs along the top and the tasks are indicated by the solid blue lines below. Here the timeline shows our tasks in Week View. Try switching to Day View by clicking on the **Day** button.

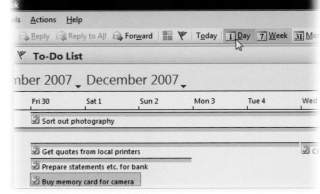

● The result is a more detailed view, showing all the tasks that are currently running.

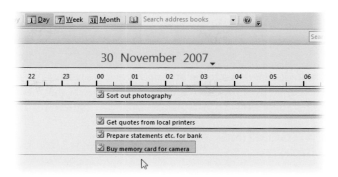

● To get a broader snapshot of how tasks are spread out over a longer period of time, click the **Month** button on the button bar and you will see this view. Use the scroll bar or the scroll arrows at the bottom of the screen to move back and forth.

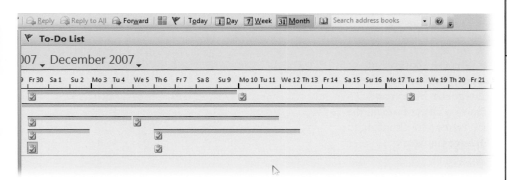

● To see which task each individual blue bar represents, hover the cursor over it and a descriptive tag similar to the one shown here will pop up.

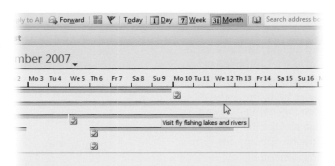

TASK CATEGORIES

Outlook allows you to assign categories to tasks and appointments. Essentially color codes, these allow an at-a-glance visual picture of the different kinds of tasks and appointments that are coming up, helping you to plan more effectively.

CATEGORIZING A TASK

• Let's begin by switching back to Week View so we can see our tasks more easily. Then double click on a particular task to add a category.

• When the Task window opens, click once on the **Categorize** button and choose a category from the list. Here we're choosing the **Orange Category**.

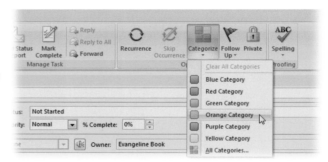

• The first time you use a Category, Outlook lets you replace the generic color name with one that has some meaning. You can also change the color at this time by opening the drop-down menu.

● In this example, we're happy to stick with the orange color, but we will replace the generic name with one of out own– **Photography** (from now on we will use this category for all tasks to do with photography).

● Click **Yes** to finish adding the category.

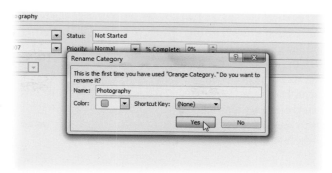

● Note that the Task window now shows a long orange bar with the word Photography in it.

● Click the **Save & Close** button to finish categorizing this task.

● Switch back to the detailed view by clicking on the **Detailed list** radio button in the left-hand panel. In the To-Do List, you will be able to see that our task is now clearly tagged with the orange photography category.

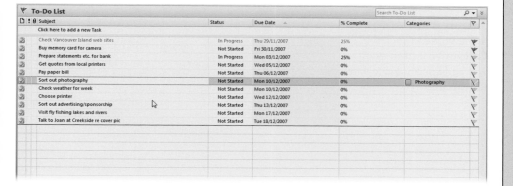

● Here we have added two more categories–**Printing** in blue and **Research** in red–in exactly the same way as in the previous steps. Having multiple categories like this will help us to keep track of the project as it proceeds.

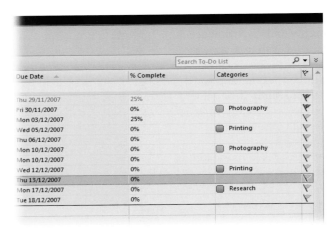

ADDING ADDITIONAL CATEGORIES

● Now, one of our tasks here actually overlaps between two categories– photography and research– so we're going to add both. Here we've double clicked on the task to open it and then clicked the **Categorize** button. We're now ready to choose **Photography**.

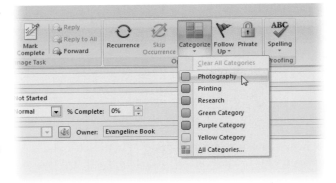

● Having assigned one category to the task, we're going to click the **Categorize** button again and add a second category– **Research**.

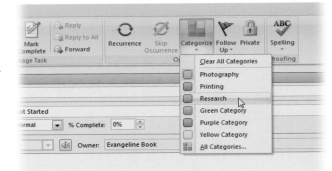

● Click the **Save & Close** button and you'll now see the task with two categories next to it. Visual tags like this will help to keep you better organized.

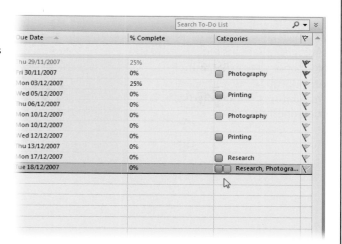

CATEGORIZING APPOINTMENTS

● Switch to Calendar view and then click the **Week** view button at the top.

● Use the arrows to move to a week that has tasks in the bottom panel and several appointments in the main window.

● We will now use the palette of categories that we have created to add the same category tags to some of our appointments.

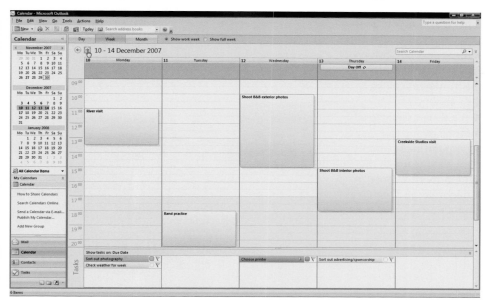

● Find an appointment and then click on it with the right mouse button.
● Choose **Categorize** from the pop-up menu and select the appropriate category for this appointment.

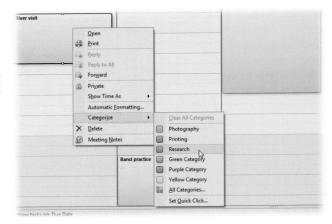

● Here's the result. The selected appointment has changed from the default color to the one that's associated with the selected category.
● We can now categorize our various appointments in the week in exactly the same way as our tasks, so they stand out clearly in their different colors.

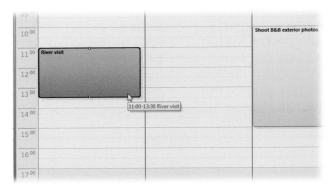

● It's also possible to add more than one category to an appointment. Simply right click again on the appointment, choose **Categorize**, and then pick another category.

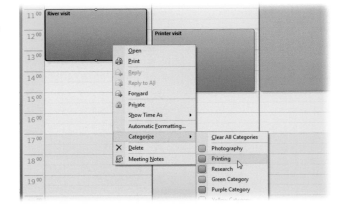

- Outlook changes the color of the appointment to reflect the category we've just chosen but puts a little square at the bottom right to indicate that it also carries a second category.

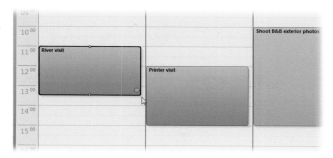

THE TO-DO BAR

- When you've finished adding categories to those appointments that need it, click on the **Tasks** button in the left-hand column to return to Tasks view.

- Let's look at the **To-Do Bar** on the right-hand side of the screen. This displays the current month as a clickable mini calendar and a selection of upcoming appointments, color coded to reflect their categories, as well as a selection of upcoming tasks, which are also color coded.

- Appointments and tasks can all be edited directly from the **To-Do Bar** by double clicking on them or by right clicking on them and selecting an option from the menu, as we are doing here.

CONTACTS

**As well as organizing your appointments and tasks,
Outlook can also help you keep on top of your address book,
courtesy of its contacts manager. Here's how it works.**

CREATING A CONTACT

Although it's possible for other Outlook users to e-mail you their contact details in a form that the Contacts program understands, you'll need to enter most peoples' information by typing it in yourself. In this section, we'll look at how to type in the details required to create a new contact.

OPENING CONTACTS

● Whichever part of Outlook is currently displayed, switch to the Contacts manager by clicking the **Contacts** button at the bottom left of the screen.

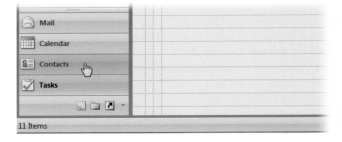

CREATING AN EMPTY CONTACT

● If you haven't already created any contacts, the window in the middle of the screen will be empty. Just double click below the text at the top to create a new contact.

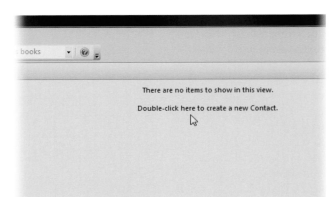

● Outlook displays the empty Contact window, waiting for you to fill in the details. Start by clicking on the **Full Name** button.

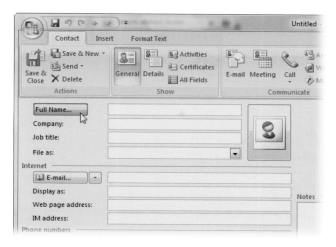

ADDING A CONTACT

● Initially, Outlook displays an empty **Check Full Name** form like this so you can type in the person's contact information.

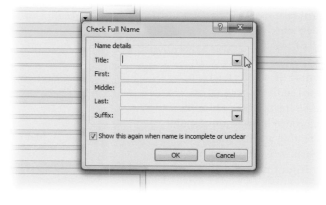

● Fill it in with the relevant information, leaving those parts of the form blank that you don't want to include or don't have the information for, until it's finished. Move to different parts of the form, either by clicking there with the left mouse button or using the Tab⇆ key. Then click **OK** to add it to the main contact form.

● Outlook adds the information you just typed into the form. To add the name of the company this person works for, click once in the **Company** name field and start to type.

● Complete the rest of this section of the form and then use the [Tab⇄] key to move to the Internet section and do the same there. Note that Outlook turns the web page address into a hyperlink that, when clicked will take you to the actual web site.

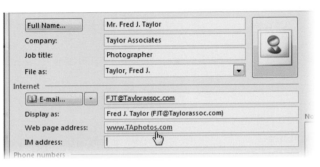

● Before we move on to finish the contact, have a look at the other side of the screen, where Outlook has been busy automatically creating an electronic business card that includes the information that we've typed in so far.

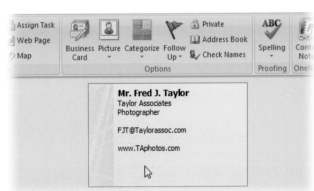

ADDING A PHONE NUMBER

● To include telephone numbers, click on the first button–**Business**–under the **Phone numbers** heading as shown here.

● Outlook displays the
Check Phone Number
dialog box. The first thing
to do is open the drop-
down list and select the
country in which you live.
In this example, we're
choosing Canada.

● We're going to fill in our
contact's area code and local
number as shown here and
then click **OK** to continue.

● Click on the button for
the next phone number
field—here it's **Home**—and
when the dialog box opens,
type in the number, using
the same format but
omitting the area code.
Then click **OK**.

● If you use exactly the same
format, Outlook assumes
the number has the same
area code as the first phone
number. When you return
to the main contacts card,
you'll see that Outlook has
filled in the area code.

ADDING AN ADDRESS

● Type in any further phone numbers and then click on the **Business** button in the **Addresses** section of the contact form.

● When the **Check Address** dialog box opens, fill in the relevant details by clicking in each field in turn and typing in the information. In the first field–**Street**– you can press Enter ↵ to move to a new line. When you're finished, click **OK** to close the dialog box and add the address.

SAVING THE NEW CONTACT

● With all the details complete, click the **Save & Close** button at the top left-hand corner of the window.

TAKING NOTES

Although not a fully-fledged sales and marketing tool, Outlook does allow you to open the Contact Window and type in notes relating to that person. Although this can be as simple as noting down the last conversation you had with them, the note area is also sophisticated enough to recognize web and e-mail addresses that you type in. It turns them into hyperlinks that, when clicked, will launch the web page or start Outlook's e-mail program with the message already addressed.

EDITING A CONTACT

It's not always possible to enter all the information you need for a particular contact there and then. Sometimes you will need to add information at a later date.

Also, you might not need to enter the same level of detail for every contact. Whatever your needs, Outlook will let you create, edit, and amend contacts.

● By default, Outlook displays your contact as a business card.

● However, it's clear from looking at this card that some of the information we entered in the previous steps isn't visible–for example, there's no address.

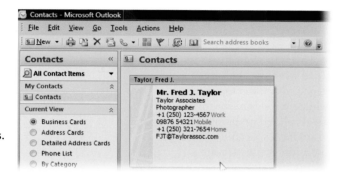

We can fix this by editing the card. Right mouse click on the card and choose **Open**.

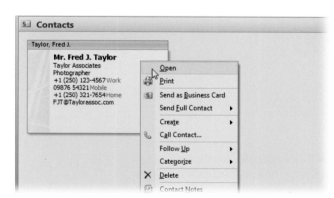

CONTACT NOTES MENU OPTION

If you don't see this option at the bottom of the menu when you click to open a business card, it's because you don't have OneNote, another Office program installed. This isn't a problem, but as you will see 📄, you should consider getting this program because OneNote is really useful for collating information.

● By comparing what's on the card with what's in the form, it's clear that there is simply too much information to fit on the card. To make the necessary changes, make sure the contact window is open, right click on the business card and choose **Edit Business Card**.

● This is the **Edit Business Card** window. The card itself is displayed top left, while the fields in the form are displayed underneath. From here, we can see that the address and web site details are missing.

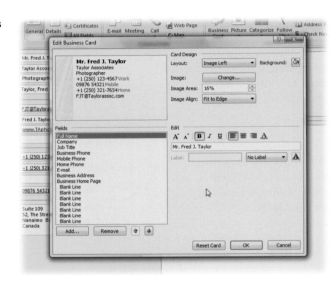

● To create space for the missing information, let's remove some unnecessary details from the card. (Note that these details will remain stored as part of the contact information.)
● We know that Fred is the owner of Taylor Associates, so begin by highlighting the **Company** field.

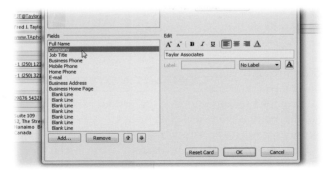

● Move the cursor down and click the **Remove** button to erase this from the card.

● We can now see that simply by removing the Company name we can fit the entire business address on the card.

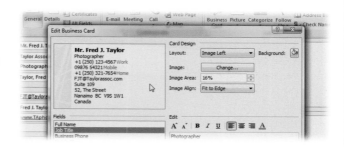

● It's still a bit cramped though, so we've gone ahead and removed the **Job Title** and **Home Phone** in exactly the same way. Now we need a space between Fred's name and the rest of the details, so we'll click on the **Blank Line** field.

● Keep clicking the little "up" arrow button under the fields box. With every click, the blank line will move up a line on the card. Here we've clicked the button once to move it above the home page line. Note how it's introduced a blank line on the business card.

● Keep clicking upward until the blank line sits underneath the name on the card. Then click **OK** to close and save the changes.

ADDING A CONTACT PHOTO

● Before we finish editing this particular contact, we're going to add a photograph that we took recently at a social event. Start by moving the mouse over to the empty photo slot and then click on it once.

● Use Windows' file commands to navigate to the folder where you have stored a picture of the person and then double click on it. In this example, the photo has been stored inside Windows' Sample Pictures folder.

● Outlook drops the photo into place.

● If you find that this first photo fails to appear in the card, double click on the card to open the Contact window and then right click on the card. Choose **Edit Business Card** and then click on **Reset Card**. Click **Yes** in the dialog box that appears, click on **OK**, and then add the contact's picture again.

CATEGORIZING A CONTACT

● Contacts can be categorized in the same way as appointments and tasks. With the contact window still open, click on the **Categorize** button and then choose the one you want to associate with this contact. In this example, it's **Photography**.

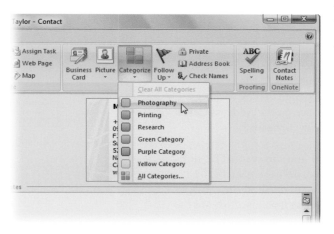

● Click **Save & Close** to finish the job.

VIEWING CONTACTS

Once you've entered a number of names and addresses into the Contacts module in Outlook, it's possible to view and organize them in various different ways. In this section we'll look at how to arrange your contacts in the best possible way, so that you can make the most of them, depending on what you want to do.

CHANGING THE CURRENT VIEW

● Here we've added some extra contacts in varying states of completeness to demonstrate Outlook's Contact views more clearly. If you haven't made any changes since the last section, then you'll be in Business Cards view. Change that by clicking once on the **Address Cards** view beneath it.

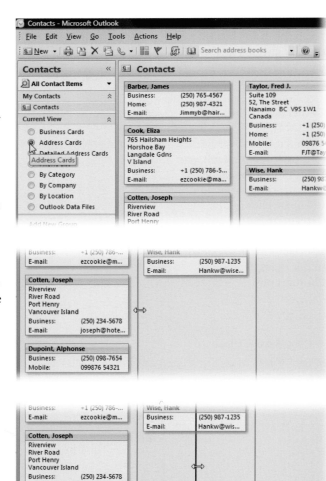

● You can see that it's not possible to see all of the detail on all of the cards, so move the cursor over to the first vertical blue line until the arrow changes to a double-headed arrow as shown here.

● Hold down the left mouse button and then drag the cursor to the right to increase the width of the columns.

● Here's the result – the wider columns allow more of the information to be displayed at once.

● If you thought that switching from here to the Detailed view would automatically use the new wider columns, you'd be wrong. Click **Detailed Address Cards** in the left-hand column and you'll see the cards are squeezed into the old narrow view.

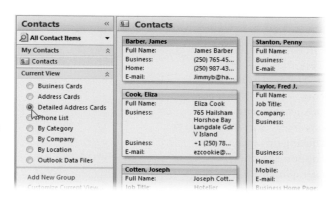

● Fix this by clicking on the first vertical line and dragging to the right again to increase the column width as you did a moment ago. The result is much more readable.

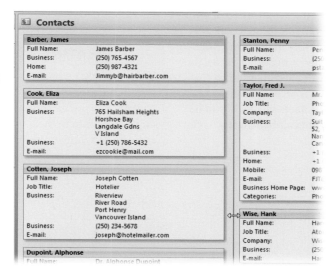

• The next view down is probably one of the most convenient. The **Phone List** condenses all the information into a simple table, similar to an Excel spreadsheet, and allows you to see a good number of your contacts at once.

ORGANIZING THE PHONE LIST

• By default, Outlook lists your contacts alphabetically by surname. However, it's possible to sort the list by clicking on any of the column headings. For example, clicking on the **Business Phone** heading once with the left mouse button will sort all of your contacts by area code.

• Note that if you return to any of the other views, they will have maintained their own organization, so contacts there will still be listed alphabetically.

CREATING NEW CATEGORIES

We've seen that you can assign categories to a contact, but you can also create new ones in the same view. While in the **Phone List** view, right click in the **Categories** column and choose **All Categories** from the pop-up menu. When the dialog box appears, click the **New** button, type in a category name, and assign it a color. You can type in any name you like, and Outlook supports 25 different category colors. Click **OK** to confirm the new category and then click **OK** again to close the dialog box. To access the new category, right click in the **Categories** column and choose it from the list.

CUSTOMIZING THE PHONE LIST

● Although one of the advantages of the Phone List is that it allows you to see more information about more contacts than some of the other views, there are still good reasons to adjust the way it's displayed.

● To reduce the size of any over-wide columns, start by placing the cursor on the line dividing the column headings so that it turns into a double headed arrow.

● Click and hold down the left mouse button, and drag the line to the left to decrease the column width.

● Release the mouse button when the line is in the correct position and then repeat for any other columns that are too wide. This will allow you to fit in more information or reduce the size of the entire program window so you can fit more on the screen.

	File As		Business Phone	Business Fax	Home P
	Stanton, Penny		(250) 098-7654		
	Dupoint, Alphonse		(250) 098-7654		
	Cotten, Joseph		(250) 234-5678		
	Barber, James		(250) 765-4567		(250) 98
	Ritner, Linda		(250) 876-6543		
ociates	Wise, Hank		(250) 987-1235		
ociates	Taylor, Fred J.		+1 (250) 123-4567		+1 (250
	Spring, Alice		+1 (250) 567-4321		
	Cook, Eliza		+1 (250) 786-5432		

	File As		Business Phone	Business Fax	Home P
	Stanton, Penny		(250) 098-7654		
	Dupoint, Alphonse		(250) 098-7654		
	Cotten, Joseph		(250) 234-5678		
	Barber, James		(250) 765-4567		(250) 98
	Ritner, Linda		(250) 876-6543		
ociates	Wise, Hank		(250) 987-1235		
ociates	Taylor, Fred J.		+1 (250) 123-4567		+1 (250
	Spring, Alice		+1 (250) 567-4321		
	Cook, Eliza		+1 (250) 786-5432		

	File As	Business Phone	Business Fax	Home Phone
	Stanton, Penny	(250) 098-7654		
	Dupoint, Alphonse	(250) 098-7654		
	Cotten, Joseph	(250) 234-5678		
	Barber, James	(250) 765-4567		(250) 987-4321
	Ritner, Linda	(250) 876-6543		
ates	Wise, Hank	(250) 987-1235		
iates	Taylor, Fred J.	+1 (250) 123-45...		+1 (250) 321-76...
	Spring, Alice	+1 (250) 567-43...		
	Cook, Eliza	+1 (250) 786-54...		

● Alternatively, right click on any column heading and choose **Best Fit** from the drop-down menu and Outlook will automatically adjust the column widths as best it can.

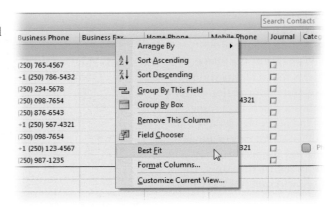

REMOVING A SINGLE COLUMN
● Sometimes a column is completely unnecessary. In this example, none of the contacts in our list have fax machines so the **Business Fax** column is redundant. To remove it, right mouse click on the column heading and choose **Remove This Column** from the drop-down menu.

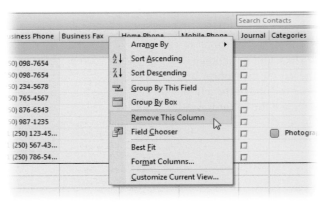

EDITING COLUMNS
● To put the Business Fax column back, or to add another column, right click on any column heading and choose **Customize Current View** from the pop-up menu.

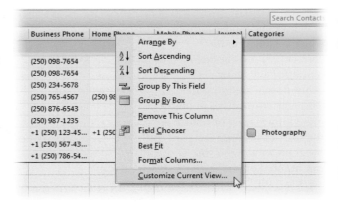

● Outlook calls column headings "Fields," so to add or remove them, click the **Fields** button at the top of the dialog box.

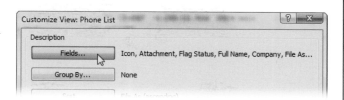

● The available fields are shown in the column on the left and the current fields are shown on the right. Columns can be added or removed by highlighting them in either list and then clicking the **Add** or **Remove** buttons in the middle. Here we're removing the **Journal** column.

● Click **OK** to close this dialog box and then click **OK** again to close the Customize View dialog box. The Journal column has now disappeared.

● To re-instate a column, repeat the process in reverse. Alternatively, right click on a column heading and choose **Customize Current View**. When the dialog box opens, click the **Reset Current View** button and Outlook will return the phone list to its original state. Just click **OK** when the Confirm dialog box appears.

E-MAIL

In this section we're going to look at how Outlook's e-mail features integrate with the calendar, tasks, and contacts, helping you to plan and work more effectively with other people.

SENDING E-MAILS

Since most tasks and appointments involve other people in some way or another, it's important to take advantage of Outlook's organizational features when you're using e-mail. In this section, we'll help you to understand how to send e-mails to the people in your contacts list, how to send the same e-mail to more than one person, and how to schedule e-mails that don't need to be sent straight away.

SELECTING A CONTACT

● Here we've created a new contact for a local guide and we're going to e-mail him to see if he'll come with us to visit a nearby river. We've already entered his e-mail address into the contacts manager, so all we have to do is right mouse click on his name and choose **Create** and then **New Message to Contact**.

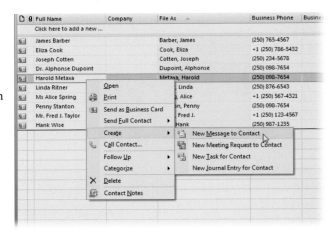

GETTING STARTED WITH E-MAIL

This section assumes that you already have an e-mail provider set up and that you are familiar with sending and receiving basic e-mails. If not, then we highly recommend that you read Dorling Kindersley's *The Computer Book: Windows Vista Edition*, which explains in plain English how the process works.

WRITING AN E-MAIL

● Outlook opens the Message window with the contact's e-mail address already filled in and the cursor positioned in the **Subject** line. Type a subject for the message in here.

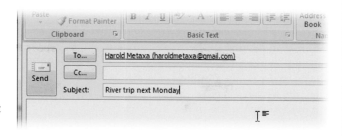

● Then click in the body of the Message window and type the text of the message.

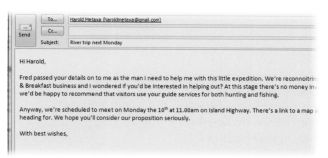

ADDING A LINK

● Next, we're going to send our guide a link to a map that shows where we're planning to meet. So, we've loaded Internet Explorer and typed in **http://maps. google.com** and pressed Enter ↵ . With the map page open, we've typed "Coombs" into the empty box at the top and then pressed the **Search Maps** button.

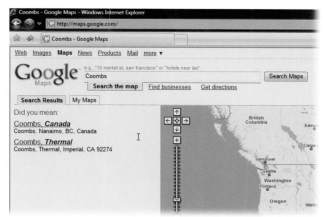

● Since we want the Coombs in British Columbia, Canada, we're going to click on that.

• That opens a map of Vancouver Island with Coombs in the middle. By positioning the cursor near the green arrow and double clicking, we can start to zoom in to the precise spot we want.

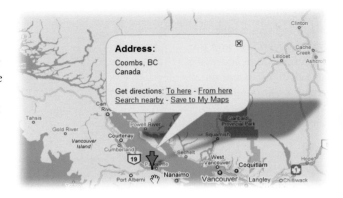

• Now we're getting very close to the view we want, it's time to switch from the Map view to the **Satellite** view by clicking the button shown here.

• We've continued to zoom in by double clicking with the cursor until we can see individual roads and houses.

• Then click **Link to this page** and this box will appear. Right mouse click on the highlighted text and choose **Copy** from the pop-up menu.

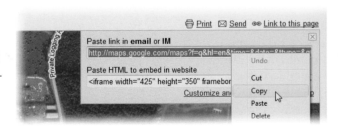

● Switch back to the e-mail, move the cursor after the last letter and press [Enter ↵] a couple of times to create two line spaces, right mouse click, and choose **Paste** from the menu.

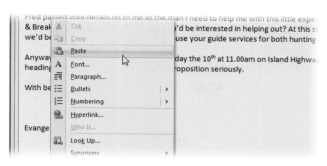

● Here's the link to the map, pasted into the e-mail.

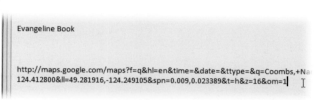

● To finish, click on the **Send** button.

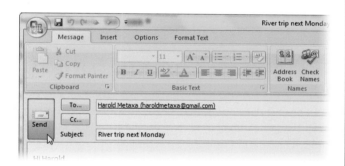

RECEIVING THE E-MAILED MESSAGE

● Here's the e-mail that we sent, having arrived in the recipient's mailbox and been opened. The Internet address that we pasted into the message is now an active hyperlink, and when the recipient clicks on the link like this, their browser will take them to the site.

● The map opens automatically in a new window, and from here it can be printed out.

DISTRIBUTION LISTS

As a project develops, it may be useful to send the same e-mail to several people at once. This will not only save you time, it will also ensure consistency because everyone on the list will then get exactly the same information. Thanks to the use of distribution lists, Outlook provides a simple way to achieve this.

CREATING A DISTRIBUTION LIST

● The best way to do this is to click on the little arrow next to the **New** button on the button bar and then select **Distribution List** from the pop-up menu.

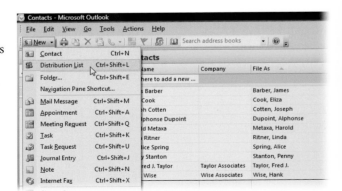

● To add e-mail addresses to the list, click the **Select Members** button.

● This opens up a dialog box showing the contents of your contacts book.
● To add people to the list, hold down the Ctrl key on your PC's keyboard and then select their names by clicking on them with the left mouse button.
● When you've chosen everyone, click the **Members** button.

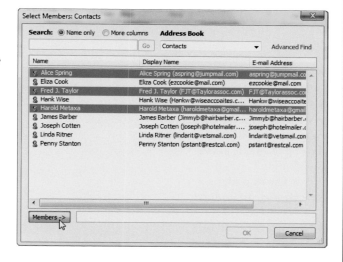

● The names now appear in the Members panel.
● To finish creating the list, click the **OK** button.

● We can now type in a name for the list in the space provided–in this example it's **Recreational Help**–before clicking the **Save & Close** button.

● Returning to the Contacts module, we can now see that Outlook has added a new item to our list of contacts–in bold letters, we can see the **Recreational Help** list we just created.

MAILING A DISTRIBUTION LIST

● We can now use the list to send the same e-mail to everyone on it. Right mouse click on the name of the Distribution List and choose **Create** and then **New Message to Contact**.

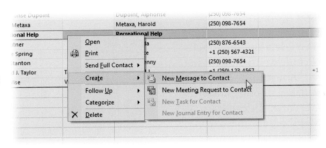

● Now we can go ahead and give the e-mail a subject and type the message into the main menu. When we click on **Send**, the same e-mail will go out to everyone on the list.

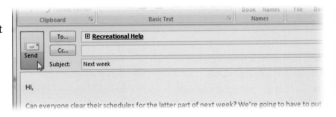

POSTPONING MAIL

● By default, Outlook sends e-mail messages to the Outbox as soon as you click the **Send** button, but sometimes it's useful to delay sending an e-mail.
● To do this, address and write the e-mail as usual and then click the **Options** tab at the top.

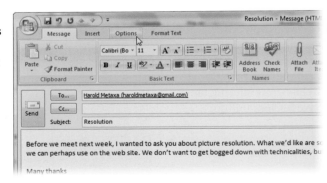

● When the toolbar changes to reflect your choice, click the **Delay Delivery** button as shown here.

● This opens the **Message Options** dialog box where you can specify a specific date and time to send the message, ensuring that it reaches the recipient exactly when–and not a moment before–you want it to.

● Once you've set the delivery options, click the **Close** button and then click **Send** to put the e-mail in a queue to be sent later.

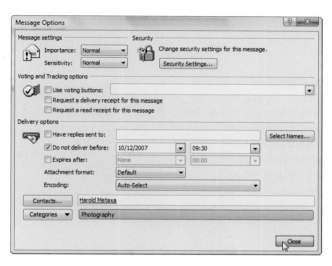

SENDING A BUSINESS CARD

● Once you've created a business card/contact, it's easy to e-mail it to someone else who uses Outlook.

● Switch to **Business Cards** view in the Contacts manager, right click on a card, and choose **Send as Business Card** from the pop-up menu.

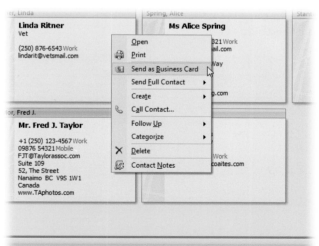

● When the Message window opens, you'll see the business card is already included. Click the **To** button to add an address.

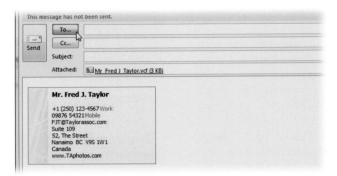

● When the Contacts window opens, select the person you want to send the business card to and double click on their name to add it to the **To** field. Then click the **OK** button.

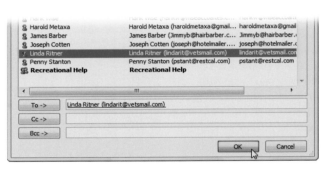

● You can then include an "as promised" message and send the e-mail by clicking the **Send** button.

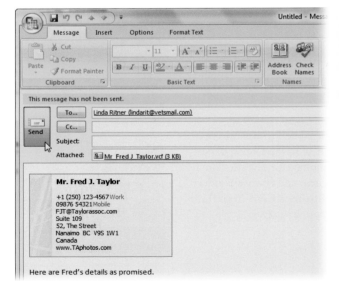

RECEIVING E-MAILS

In the normal course of events, once the program has been set up, e-mails will arrive in Outlook's inbox, where they can be read, stored, deleted, and so on. However, in the context of our Bed & Breakfast business, there are a couple of useful features we want to highlight so that you can take advantage of them.

RECEIVING A BUSINESS CARD

● When someone sends you their business card, it arrives along with the e-mail as an attachment. Outlook displays it next to the **Message** icon at the top of the e-mail.

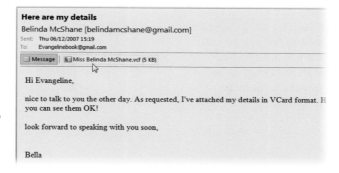

● Click once on the card name to open it in the e-mail window, as we are doing here.

● Once you've received a card like this, you can just right mouse click on the name and choose **Add to Contacts**.

● This opens the full contact in the Contact window where you can check over the details and then click the **Save & Close** button to add it to your list of contacts. It's much easier than typing all those details in yourself.

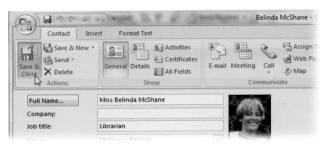

● Switch back to Contacts and you will see the card that you just received displayed alongside all your other contacts.

RECEIVING A PHOTOGRAPH

● Windows users can attach photos to e-mails by right clicking on them and choosing **Send To** and then **Mail Recipient** from the pop-up menu. When you receive a photo like this attached to an e-mail, it's listed next to the message icon, just like the business card. You can view the photo by clicking on its name once.

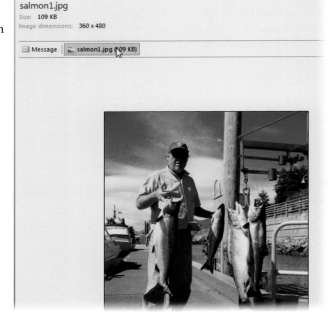

● To store the photo for later use, right click on the name and choose **Save As** from the menu. Then use Windows' file commands to give it a name and save it for later use.

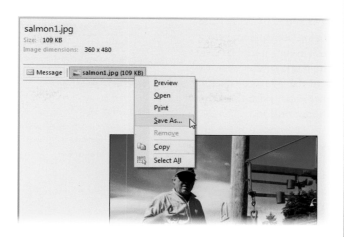

Organizing E-Mails

Outlook provides a number of ways to organize the e-mails that you receive. In this way, you'll be able to find individual e-mails more easily or integrate certain ones into a schedule. You can also remind yourself to reply to a message, mark individual e-mails for a follow up, get prompted when a message arrives from certain people, funnel messages into specific folders, and so on.

E-MAIL ALERTS

● One of the best ways to keep track of e-mails from individuals related to a particular project is to have Outlook notify you when they arrive, using the rules feature. Find an e-mail from the person in question and right click on it, then choose **Create Rule** from the pop-up menu .

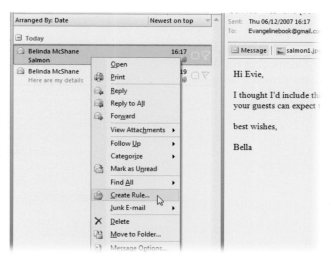

● When the **Create Rule** dialog box appears, put a tick in the check box next to the name of the person who sent the e-mail by clicking there once with the left mouse button.

● Next, put a tick in the check box next to the **Display in the New Item Alert window** and then click the **OK** button.

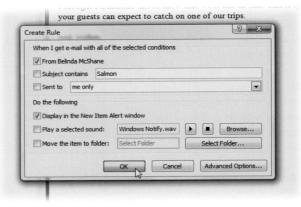

● Finally, click on **OK** to confirm your actions.

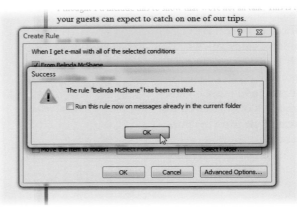

● The next time a message arrives from this person, Outlook will display an alert dialog box like the one shown here–even if you're using another Windows program. Click **Open Item** to open the message.

CATEGORIZING E-MAILS

● Another way to stay on top of a project is to assign categories to incoming e-mails in the same way you can to appointments and tasks. That way, you can organize messages by category–and it'll help later on should you need to track down all the information you've got that relates to a particular category. With the Message window still open, click the **Categorize** button and select an appropriate category.

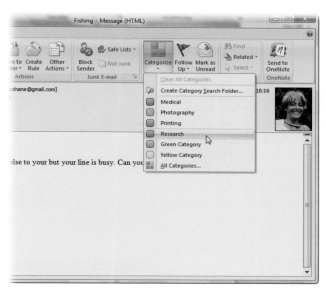

ADDING REPLY REMINDERS

● If an e-mail needs a reply but you have to wait until you have all the information that you need, simply add a reminder to it. With the Message window open, click the **Follow Up** button and choose a date from the menu for your reminder.

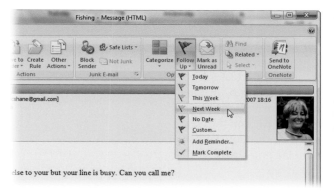

● Having added the category and the reminder (which can be seen beneath the Ribbon) to your e-mail, close the Message window by clicking on the "x" in the top right-hand corner. Outlook automatically saves your changes.

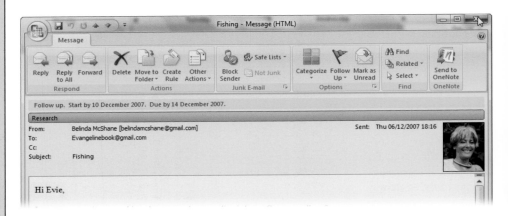

● Click on the **E-mail** button to display the **Inbox** and you'll see that the mail we just edited now has a category color and a reminder flag next to it.

STORING E-MAILS

● If you're working on a specific project alongside your day-to-day life, it makes sense to organize things so that all the e-mails associated with that project go into a particular folder. To do this, start by making sure you're in the **Mail** view, and then click on the **New** button and choose **Folder** from the pop-up menu that appears.

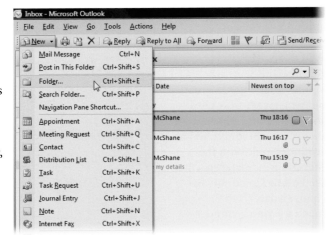

● When the dialog box opens, give the folder a name. In this example it's **Bed & Breakfast**. Click **OK** to create the folder.

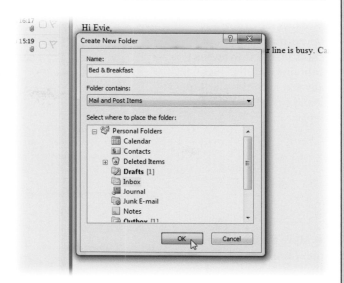

● Look over at the **Inbox** icon. If there's a little "+" sign next to it, click that to reveal the new Bed & Breakfast folder.

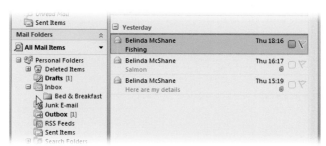

● Now let's create another rule so that all e-mails with B&B included in their subject lines will be stored automatically in this folder. We'll right click on an e-mail from someone involved with the project and choose **Create Rule** from the menu.

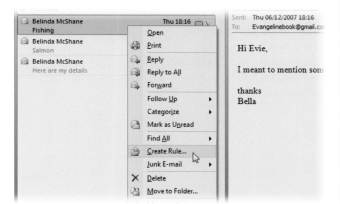

● When the dialog box opens, put a tick in the check box next to **Subject contains** and then highlight any text in the box next to it and type **B&B** there to replace it.

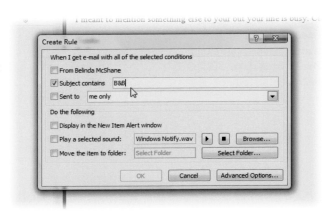

● Move the cursor down to the check box next to **Move the item to folder** and put a tick there. This opens the **Rules and Alerts** dialog box.

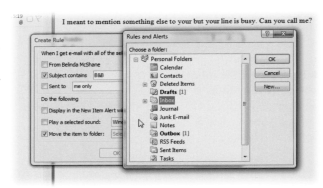

● Next, click the "+" sign next to **Inbox** to reveal the folder we just created (it's called **Bed & Breakfast**) click on that folder name and then click **OK** to close the dialog box.

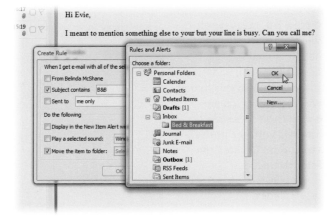

● Click **OK** to close the **Create Rule** dialog box and confirm your changes.

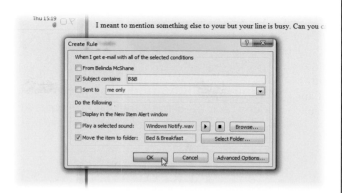

● Then click the **OK** button to finish creating the new rule. (You will need to tell everyone involved in the project to include B&B in the subject line!)

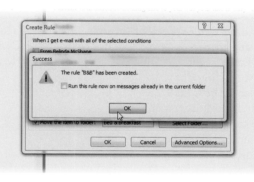

● Here a new e-mail has arrived, but instead of going to the Inbox, it's gone straight into the Bed & Breakfast folder.

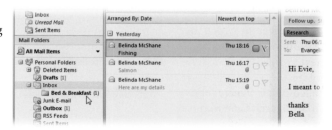

● Clicking on the new e-mail folder reveals that a message has arrived with B&B in the subject line, which is why it's been filed in this folder.

SEARCHING

Outlook incorporates powerful search features, which means that you can always find what you're looking for–whether it's a contact, an e-mail message, a task, or an appointment.

PERFORMING A SEARCH

Like Vista itself, Outlook's search feature is much improved over earlier versions. The main difference, which you'll notice right away, is the speed with which it begins to search. The moment you type in the first character of whatever it is you're looking for, Outlook is off trying to find it. Here's how to use this practical tool.

SIMPLE SEARCHES

● Search works the same in the calendar, contacts, tasks, or e-mail modules. To demonstrate a simple search, we'll use the calendar. Click on the button at the bottom left of the screen to switch to the Outlook Calendar.

● Now slide the cursor over to the **Search Calendar** box at the top right-hand corner and click in the text panel.

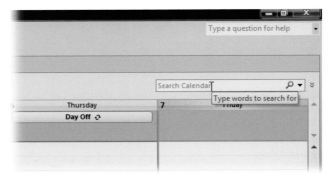

● Start typing in whatever you're looking for and Outlook will search backward and forward through the calendar to find it. Here we're searching for the appointment that relates to a visit to a place called Bamfield. As soon as we type the letter B, Outlook begins to search and displays the results window.

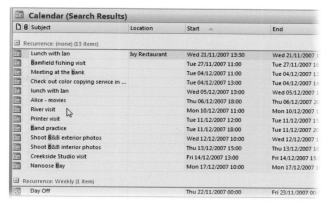

● By the time we've typed in "Ba," Outlook has reduced the number of possible matches to four, and it's easy to double click on the first one in the list to open the appointment and then check its details.

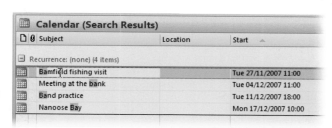

COMPLEX SEARCHES

● You can also perform more complex searches and find, for example, all the appointments or tasks or e-mails that are related to a particular category; this works the same way in all the Outlook modules.

● In this example, we're going to find all the tasks associated with the Photography category. Switch to **Tasks** and then click the double chevron to the right of the empty **Search To-Do List** box.

● The panel that opens along the top of the **To-Do List** allows you to search by a range of criteria, including the category, due date, and subject of the task.

● Click on the arrow next to the **Category** panel and select Photography.

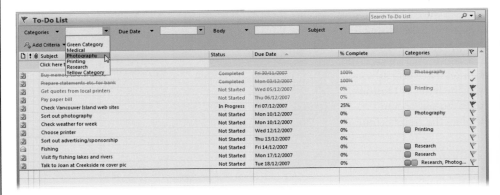

● This returns all of the tasks (including completed ones) associated with this particular category.

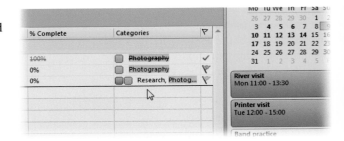

● There are lots of different criteria that you can use to perform complex searches.
● To see them all, open the value list next to the **Add Criteria** button.

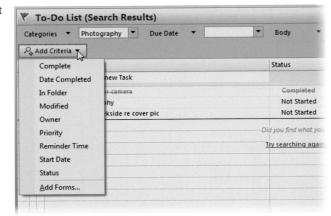

SEARCHING TASKS AND EMAILS

● From the Task list you can also look inside e-mails for what you're trying to find. Here, for example, we've performed the same search but in the meantime an e-mail has arrived that we've categorized as being to do with photography. When we search for that category again, the e-mail appears alongside the tasks in the results list.

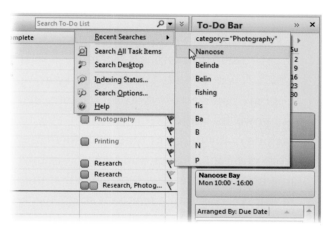

SEARCHING AGAIN

● Although you can't save searches in Outlook, it does keep recent searches handy in a list so you can use them again without having to type anything in.

● Click the arrow next to the magnifying glass in the search box to open the menu and then select **Recent Searches**. Choose the one you want to use again from the sub menu.

XP USERS

If you're using Windows Vista then "instant search"–the way results appear as soon as you start to type–is already installed. If you're using Windows XP, however, you'll have to do it yourself. When you load Outlook, you'll see a yellow bar along the top of the main window that says **Click here to enable Instant Search**. Make sure you're connected to the Internet and click there. When the dialog box appears asking if you want to proceed, click **Yes**. When the web site opens, follow the instructions to download and install the file.

ONENOTE®
2007

COMPARED WITH THE OTHER PROGRAMS that go to make up Microsoft Office, OneNote is a relative newcomer, so even if you're familiar with Word and Excel, you may not have come across it. As this chapter demonstrates, OneNote is a powerful and versatile program, able to create notes that include many different types of information, gathered together from different sources, and then to organize them using a clever notebook/sections/pages interface that manages to pack plenty of information into a relatively small space.

OneNote is only included in the *Home and Student* and *Ultimate* editions of Office 2007, so if you have a different edition, you'll need to buy OneNote separately. We think it's such a worthwhile product–and such a valuable part of Office–that we recommend you do just that.

ONENOTE ON SCREEN

In this section we'll introduce you to OneNote, Microsoft's über-note-taking program that's perfect for collating information from disparate sources and organizing them into notebooks.

WHAT IS ONENOTE?

OneNote is a free-form note-taking program that's organized into notebooks, sections, and pages. You can click anywhere on a page and start typing, and text can be formatted in various ways–bold, italic, underline, colors, bullet lists, tables, etc..

In addition you can grab "clips" from web pages, import pictures from your PC's hard disk, other programs, or from external devices such as scanners and digital cameras. OneNote also integrates with Outlook and other Office programs.

WHAT CAN I DO WITH IT?
- Make simple notes for a project, a homework assignment, a presentation, or a business plan.
- Gather information that you've imported from other sources, such as Office programs and web pages.
- Organize your notes into books, sections, and pages.
- Use OneNote's powerful search features to find information much more quickly than you ever could in a printed book.
- Integrate OneNote information with material from other Office programs, such as Outlook.

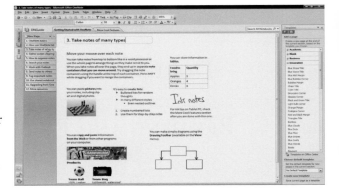

KEEPING NOTES SECURE

In order to store your notes more securely, OneNote allows you to protect specific sections in a notebook with a password.

Click on the section tab at the top of the page with the right mouse button and choose **Password Protect this Section** in the menu.

KEY ONENOTE FEATURES

● NOTE TAKING

Use OneNote to jot down anything from a phone number to a task list complete with tick boxes that you can use to check items off as they're completed. Use it for roughing out layouts—almost like a desktop publishing program—adding tables, diagrams, contents lists, noting down web addresses, and so on.

● IMPORTING INFORMATION

OneNote will import just about anything digital. Files can be placed directly onto a note as icons or displayed as printed images for quick reference. Pictures can be imported from almost any source, placed anywhere on the page, and re-sized, while the web clipping feature allows you to grab and add screen shots of web pages (or parts of pages). OneNote also integrates with Internet Explorer, adding a **Send to OneNote** button to the toolbar that allows you to capture and copy the web page you're looking at.

● ORGANIZING INFORMATION

The key to organizing information in OneNote is the way the program uses tabs down either side and along the top of the main editing window to divide the workspace into notebooks. Notebooks contain sections, which in turn contain pages. These levels are electronically stacked on top of each other, so you can gather and display an enormous amount of information in a very small space. You can navigate between them by clicking on their individual tabs. OneNote is extremely flexible, information can be moved around freely, and sections and pages can be re-arranged or moved between notebooks by clicking and dragging.

● SHARING INFORMATION

OneNote readily shares information with other Office programs and is particularly useful if you have Outlook installed, because of the way the two programs can swap information back and

forth. For example, it's easy to take a note and convert it into an Outlook task. However, OneNote is also able to import data from programs such as Internet Explorer, Word, and Excel, and it also supports standard formats for exchanging information with other people, for example, exporting information as an Adobe PDF or Microsoft XPS file.

● THE TABLET PC

Although it's a powerful and useful program to have on a desktop or notebook PC, OneNote has some features that are only available to users of so-called tablet PCs, who can "write" directly onto the screen using an electronic stylus. Tablet PC users can handwrite notes into pages, scratch them out, move information around by clicking and dragging with the stylus, and so on. Being able to enter and manipulate information one handed like this is convenient in certain out-of-the-office situations where a desk-and-chair setup isn't always available.

ONENOTE IN ACTION

OneNote shares the same look and feel as other Office programs, so you'll probably be familiar with many of the commands on the menu and the icons on the button bar before you start. However, OneNote uses a free-form approach when it comes to mixing and matching text, pictures, and other media, so you will find that there's a small learning curve. One good thing, though, is that it's easy to get started with OneNote, and you can just pick up the nuances and deeper features as you go.

FEATURES KEY

❶ Notebooks
Individual notebooks are represented as tabs down the side of the main working window.

❷ Button Bar
Access many of OneNote's commonly used features from here.

❸ Menu
Like other Office programs, OneNote uses menus to store most of its commands.

❹ Sections
These tabs along the top of the page indicate sections in a notebook.

❺ Formatting
Any text in a note can be formatted from here, for example, bold, italic, underline, and colors.

❻ Table
OneNote allows you to create simple tables, similar to those you'll find in Microsoft Word.

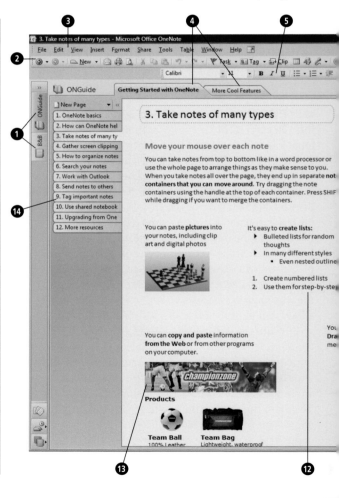

AUDIO AND VIDEO NOTES

With the appropriate equipment–which means just a microphone and a webcam–attached to your PC, you can record both audio and video notes and then drop them into a OneNote page. Gathering this kind of information is becoming increasingly useful, especially if the end product is something like a presentation using Microsoft PowerPoint.

FEATURES KEY

❼ Handwritten Text
If you have a tablet PC that supports handwriting recognition, you can write directly onto a OneNote page using a plastic stylus.
❽ Search
Find anything in your notebooks, sections, or pages from here.
❾ Task Pane
Click the drop-down arrow to select from a number of different tasks–this one shows OneNote templates.
❿ Template List
OneNote comes with a wide selection of visual templates to help make your notebooks more attractive and distinctive.
⓫ Flow chart
Use OneNote's simple drawing tools to make basic diagrams.
⓬ Bullet List
OneNote also supports bullet and number lists.
⓭ Pictures
Import photos or other graphics from your PC's hard disk or capture them from a web page with the clipping feature.
⓮ Pages
Inside every section there are pages, illustrated here by these tabs.

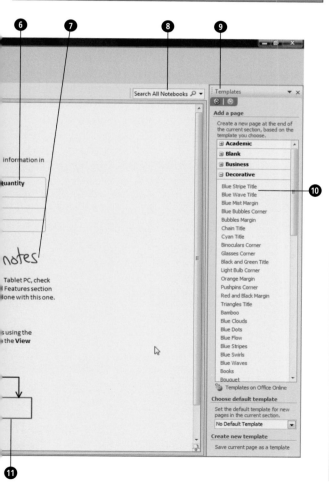

INTRODUCING ONENOTE

OneNote is a note-taking program par excellence.
Although it looks similar to Microsoft Word, OneNote is
organized rather differently, as this section explains.

GETTING STARTED

Despite the apparent similarities to a word processor, the OneNote working space has an innovative design. Instead of a single window that presents a working page, the program organizes content into notebooks, sections, and pages (you can have sub-pages as well). By arranging these around the central workspace, OneNote is able to cram a great deal of content into a relatively small area. Therefore, we'll start this chapter by getting to grips with the OneNote "space."

CREATING NEW NOTEBOOKS
● When OneNote first opens, you should see this demonstration notebook, which contains help on using the program.
● If the demonstration notebook doesn't appear, read our instructions on how to find it ⃞.
● To create a new notebook, right click anywhere on the plain blue bar on the left-hand side of the screen, below the existing notebook title (**ONGuide**).
● Choose **New Notebook** from the pop-up menu.

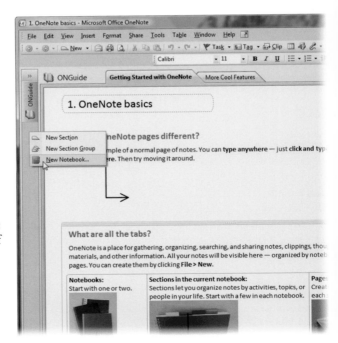

⃞ 125 | **Finding the Guide**

● When the dialog box opens, type in a new name for the notebook. In this example, we're going to call it **Test**.

● OneNote automatically selects a new color for the notebook and picks the Blank template. That's fine for now, so click on the **Next** button.

● OneNote allows you to share notebooks so they can be used on different computers, which is useful if you travel or work in different locations. However, we will leave the settings as they are, so just click on the **Next** button.

● Finally, OneNote tells you where it's going to store the new notebook–inside the Documents folder. This is the default location on your PC's hard disk. Click **Create** to finish.

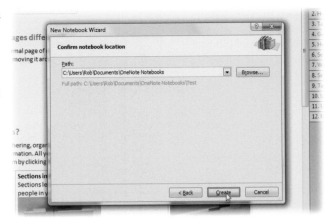

● Here's the new notebook positioned under the Guide that's included with the program.

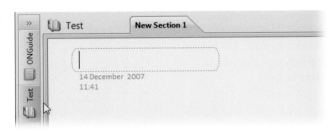

CREATING NEW SECTIONS

● New empty notebooks automatically include a **New Section 1** along the top. We'll now create a new section of our own by right clicking next to that and then choosing **New Section** from the pop-up menu.

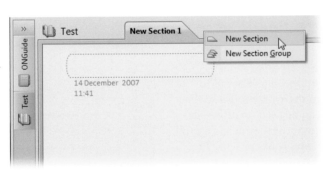

● OneNote calls this New Section 2, and handily highlights this so we can overtype it with our own name. Again, let's call it **Test**, so begin to type in the name.

● Here's the new section created next to the original.

FINDING THE GUIDE

If you've accidentally closed the Guide, load OneNote, go to the **File** menu and choose **Open** and then **Notebook**. OneNote will open the **Documents** folder.

Double click on **OneNote Notebooks** and then select **ONGuide** to open it. If you've accidentally deleted the Guide, then go to **File** and choose **Open**, then **Section**. Use Windows file commands to navigate to the **Program Files** folder, open **Microsoft Office**, then **Office12**, and finally **1033**. Double click on the ONGuide icon to open it again.

CREATING NEW PAGES

● As soon as you create a new section, OneNote creates a new untitled page to go with it.

● To add a new page of your own, click the **New Page** icon as shown here.

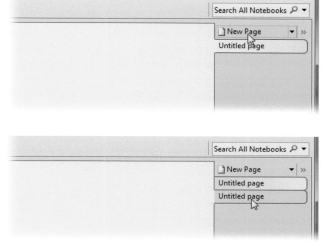

● OneNote creates the new page but doesn't give it a title and, unlike before, right clicking on the words **Untitled page** doesn't work.

● Instead, note that there's an empty slot on the page itself where the cursor is flashing, ready for us to type in a name for the page.

- Type in a name for the page. Again, we're going to call it **Test**. As you do, you'll see the name appear, not only where you're typing, but also on the tab at the right-hand side of the page.

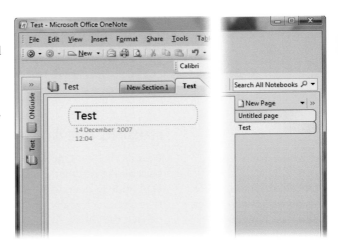

THE ONENOTE SPACE

Having created a Notebook, added a Section and some Pages, we are now going to look in more detail at the way in which OneNote uses the central window. We'll start with the Navigation Bar on the left, and then look at how you can edit the names of Sections and Pages. We'll also show you how to change their appearance to suit the content of the material that you're going to be adding.

THE NAVIGATION BAR

- By default, the Navigation Bar on the left-hand side of the main working window is "closed." Let's open it by moving the cursor over to the double arrow at the top and clicking there once.

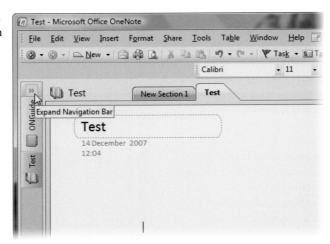

● This shows a different and more comprehensive view of the notebooks and sections currently opened. Here, for example, we can see the ONGuide notebook contains two sections, as does the Test notebook that we've just created.

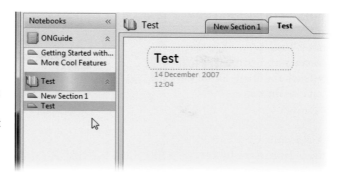

● Move the cursor over to **ONGuide** and click on it. The main window changes to reflect your choice and displays the contents of the **Getting Started with OneNote** section. Note that both the current notebook (ONGuide) and the current section (Getting Started) are highlighted in orange in the Navigation Bar.

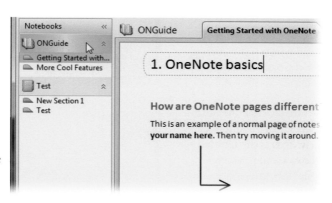

● Move the cursor down to the **More Cool Features** section and click on that. Note that the content of the main window changes to reflect your choice.
● You will also see that each notebook in the Navigation Bar has a double arrow next to it that can be clicked to expand or collapse the section underneath–this is useful if you have several notebooks all open at the same time.

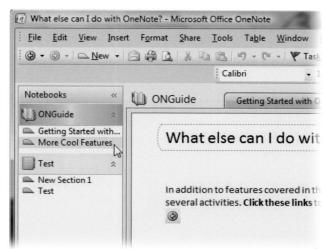

- It's also possible to look at the contents of your notebooks, even when the Navigation Bar is collapsed.
- Click the arrow at the top to close the bar.

- Now move the cursor to the button at the bottom of the Navigation Bar (it's called the **All Notebooks List**) and click it once. A little "drawer" slides out displaying all the current notebooks and their sections, as shown here.

- Finally, click the button above the All Notebooks List. This is the **Unfiled Notes** section, where OneNote puts material that hasn't yet been assigned to a specific notebook, section, or page. We'll be using this later in the chapter.

THE TASK PANE

OneNote has a handy Task Pane that focuses on the things you want to do. Switched off by default, it's a useful feature, especially if you have plenty of room on your screen. To display it, go to the **View** menu and click on **Task Pane**. When it appears on the right-hand side of the screen, it will initially display the **New** Task Pane, which allows you to create new pages, subpages, sections, notebooks, and so on. However, if you click the arrow in the top right corner and check out the drop-down list, you'll see that it's home to all sorts of helpful OneNote features, including tagging, lists, formatting, templates, research, and spelling. Each option is clearly explained when you select it, and you may find that always having the Task Pane open suits the way you work.

ONENOTE HEADINGS

The key to establishing a well organized Notebook or system of Notebooks is to get your headings right. As we've demonstrated in the previous sections, OneNote makes it easy to create headings, but it's also very straightforward to change your mind and re-name should you decide that it's necessary. This section explains how.

EDITING NOTEBOOK HEADINGS

● Now let's personalize our Notebook, Section, and Page headings. Start by right clicking on the Test notebook. Choose **Rename** from the pop-up menu.

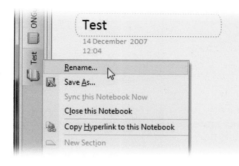

● When the dialog box opens, the Test heading is already highlighted, so we can just overtype a new heading. In this example, we've changed the name to **Photography**.

● You can change the color of the Notebook by opening the drop-down list and selecting a new color from the list. Here, we're choosing green.

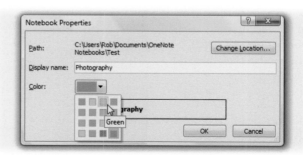

● Click the **OK** button to confirm the changes and close the dialog box.

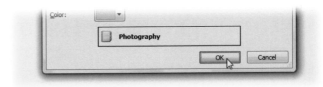

EDITING THE SECTION HEADING

● Double click on the **Test** section heading and OneNote will highlight it, ready for editing.

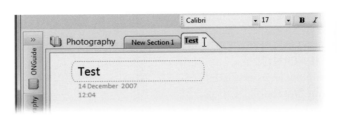

● Type in a new name for the Section. In this example, we're calling it **Wildlife**.

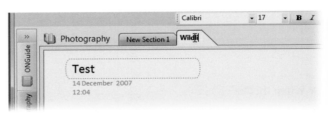

EDITING PAGE HEADINGS

● Finally, we'll edit the name of one of our pages.
● Click on **Test** page on the right of the main window as shown here.

● Next, move the cursor to the **Test** heading on the body of the page itself, and double click there to highlight it.

● Type in a new heading–in this example it's **Mammals**.

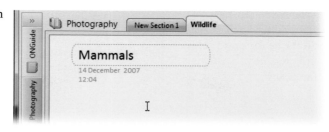

FORMATTING SECTIONS AND PAGES

We've seen how you can assign colors to Notebooks when you first create them, but it's also possible to change the colors and general appearance of both sections and pages. Although this may seem cosmetic at first, using colors and lined pages can create visual clues that help you to navigate around complex notebooks more easily.

SECTION COLORS

● Here you can see that the Wildlife Section has been assigned the color yellow by OneNote. Let's change that by clicking on the Section heading with the right mouse button.

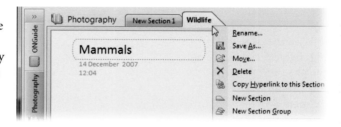

● Slide the cursor down the menu to the **Section Color** item and then select a new color by clicking on it once. We're going to turn the section **Green** to fit in with the overall color of the Notebook.

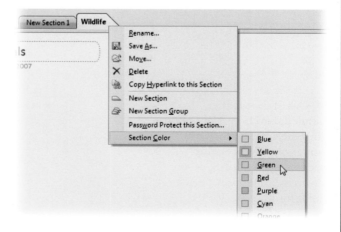

● Here's the result. The surround to the main page and the background color of the section tab itself is now green.

PAGE COLORS

● To change the color of an actual page, first click on the tab at the side with the page's name on it. When you do, you'll see that a solid blue line appears round the page. If you can't see this blue line, then the page isn't selected and you won't be able to change the color.

● With the page still highlighted, right click on the page and then choose **Page Setup** from the pop-up menu.

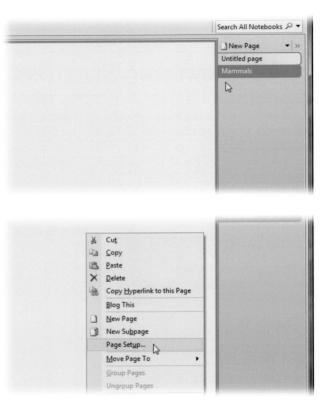

● This opens the Page Setup panel on the right of the OneNote window. For now, find the **Page color** section, open the drop-down list, and select a new color for the page. We're choosing **Green** again.

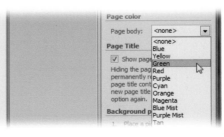

PAGE STYLES

● With the **Page Setup** panel still open, move the cursor up to the **Rule lines** section and then open the drop-down menu next to **Line style**. Choose **Standard Ruled** by clicking on it once.

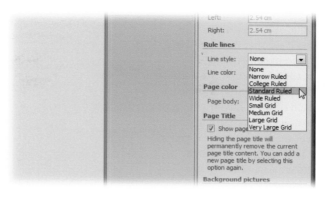

● Here's the result–a pale green page that gives the appearance of ruled paper.

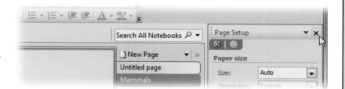

● Finally, close the **Page Setup** panel by clicking the little "**x**" in the top right-hand corner as shown here.

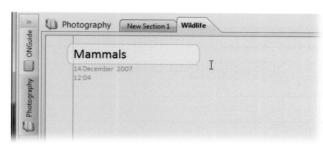

PAGE TEMPLATES

● OneNote also includes an excellent range of pre-designed templates that you can use. Some add practical value to a page, while others are simply fun. To start using templates, click the **Format** menu and choose **Templates**.

• When the Templates panel appears on the right, you'll see that there are five different categories–**Academic**, **Blank**, **Business**, **Decorative**, and **Planners**. Each of these has a "+" button next to it, indicating that there are items–i.e. the actual templates–hidden within. Click the "+" next to **Decorative**.

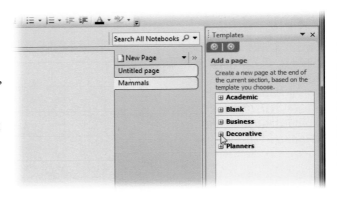

• Slide the cursor down the list that appears until you find a template that you find interesting–we've chosen **Blue Clouds**–and click on it once.
• OneNote creates a new page based on the template that you have selected.

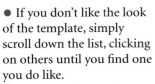

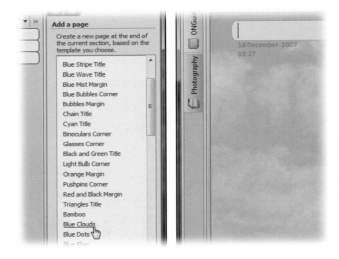

• If you don't like the look of the template, simply scroll down the list, clicking on others until you find one you do like.
• As you click on each one in turn, OneNote changes the main window design to reflect your choice.

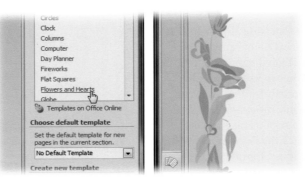

● To see a more practical set of templates that incorporate some other OneNote features that we'll be using later in this chapter, close the list of **Decorative** templates by scrolling back up to the heading and clicking the "-" sign next to it.

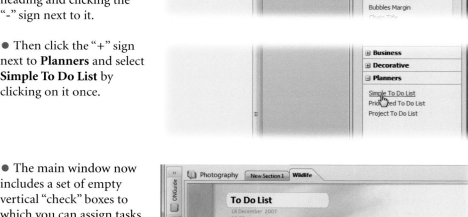

● Then click the "+" sign next to **Planners** and select **Simple To Do List** by clicking on it once.

● The main window now includes a set of empty vertical "check" boxes to which you can assign tasks.

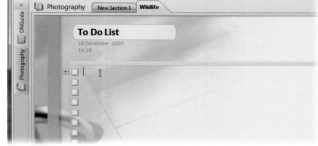

● For now, get rid of the To Do List page that you just created by right mouse clicking on the **Page** tab and choosing **Delete**.

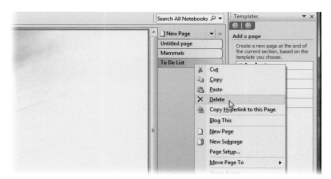

ONENOTE OPTIONS

Aside from changing OneNote's look and feel as described in the previous sections, there are also a number of important options that can be tweaked to suit your circumstances.

THE OPTIONS DIALOG BOX

Many of OneNote's options can be accessed from a single dialog box. The dialog box is slightly unusual in terms of the way that it's designed, however, in that it eschews the usual tabbed dialog box in favor of a split window that has headings down the left-hand side with options in the main window, as we'll see.

OPENING OPTIONS

● To access the dialog box where OneNote keeps many of its important settings, just go to the **Tools** menu and click **Options**.

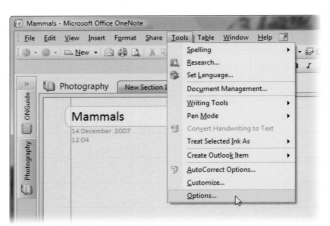

QUICK ACCESS

To get at OneNote's features quickly while you're working in another program, open the **Tools** menu and choose **Options**. In the dialog box, select **Other**, put a tick in the empty box next to **Place OneNote** **icon in the notification area of the taskbar,** and click OK. From now on, you'll be able to access OneNote by clicking on the icon at the bottom right of the Windows desktop screen.

● As you can see, what's displayed is quite different from the usual Windows tabbed style of dialog box.

● Here, the Categories are displayed down the left-hand side, while the options specific to them are shown on the right. In the example, shown here, we're looking at the **Display** options.

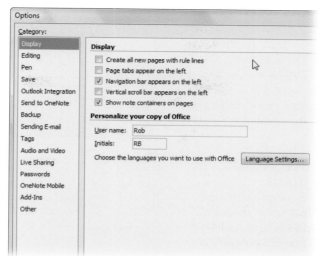

● Next, click on **Editing** and see what happens. The options in the right-hand window change to reflect our new choice of category.

● From here, for example, we could alter the default typeface used by OneNote, along with the size and the color of the font.

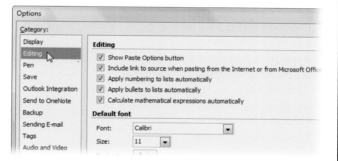

MOVING PAGE TABS

● We're going to make a change to the OneNote layout, so switch back to the **Display** category and put a tick in the checkbox next to the **Page tabs appear on the left** option.

● Click **OK** to confirm the
change and return to the
main OneNote window.
● The Notebooks, Sections,
and Pages are now over on
the same side of the screen,
making more efficient use
of the available screen space.

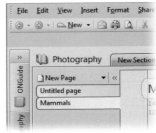
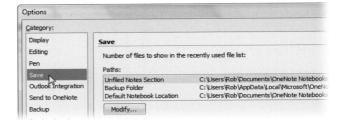

CUSTOMIZING BACKUP

● Next, go back to the
Tools menu, choose
Options again, and then
select the **Save** option in
the left-hand column.

● OneNote makes back-up
copies of your Notebooks,
Sections, and Pages, but for
some reason keeps them in
an obscure folder tucked
away where you might
never find them again.
● We can change that by
clicking on the **Backup
Folder** item in the **Save**
section of the main window.

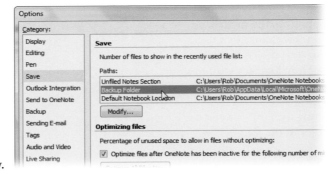

● With the item still
highlighted, click the
Modify button.

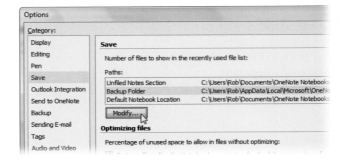

● When the window opens, click the **Documents** link in the left-hand column.

● Next, double click on the **OneNote Notebooks** folder to open it.

● When that folder opens, click the **New Folder** button on the button bar.

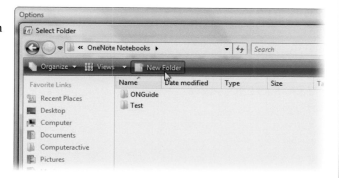

● When it appears in the window, type over the "New Folder" text that's used as a placeholder and replace it with **Backup**.

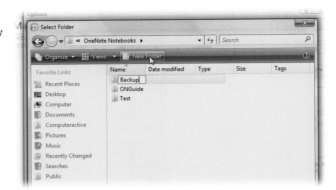

● Then, making sure that the newly created folder is still highlighted, click the **Select** button at the bottom of the window.

● Back at the Options dialog box, you can now see that the settings have been changed so that OneNote will back up everything into the new folder that you've just created.

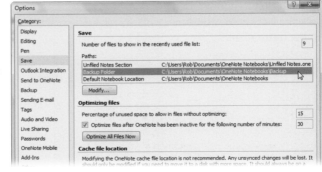

● Click **OK** to close the dialog box and confirm the changes.

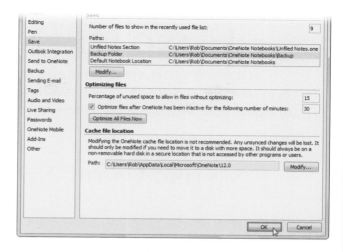

● OneNote will then display a dialog box telling you that you will need to restart the program for all the changes that you've made to take effect (this is because you have changed the location of the back-up folder). Click on **OK**, close OneNote, and then restart it again. Your changes will now have been saved.

ONENOTE TEMPLATES

We've seen how you can change the look of the pages in OneNote by altering the background color, adding ruled lines, or even picking one of the program's pre-installed templates, but the customization on offer doesn't stop there. Make sure you're connected to the Internet and then click on the **View** menu and choose **Task Pane**. In the open Task Pane, click the arrow at the top right to open the drop-down list and select New. Clicking on the **Templates on Office Online** link will load Internet Explorer and take you to a web site that has dozens of useful OneNote templates to download, install, and use for free. By default, the web site lists free templates for all Office products, but you can see just those available for OneNote by clicking on the arrow next to **All Products** and choosing **OneNote**. Here you'll find templates for calendars, agendas, plans, reports, time sheets, stationery, and much more.

USING ONENOTE

As its name suggests, OneNote is essentially a note-taking program, but as this section will demonstrate, it is also able to collate and organize many different types of information.

SETTING UP THE NOTEBOOK

If you'd like to follow this chapter step by step, then we'll need to take a minute or so to set up the OneNote space properly. Doing this will also demonstrate some of the other features of the program that you may find useful; if you don't want to do this, then you can skip forward and just start entering notes 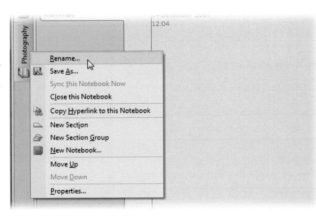.

RENAMING NOTEBOOKS

● We'll begin by right clicking on the Photography Notebook that we created in the previous section and choosing **Rename** from the pop-up menu.

● When the **Notebook Properties** dialog box opens, type in the new name– **B&B**–and then click **OK**.

CREATING NEW SECTIONS

● Next, create four new sections along the top by right clicking next to an existing section tab and choosing **New Section** from the pop-up menu. Name them **Accommodation**, **Attractions**, **Transport**, and **Photography**. You can also use the techniques described in the previous section to change the color and format of your sections.

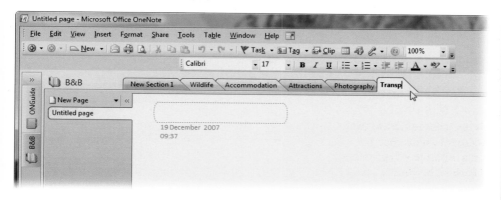

DELETE UNUSED SECTIONS

● Since we don't need the original **New Section 1** that was created automatically along with this Notebook, we can delete it by right clicking on the tab and choosing **Delete** from the pop-up menu.

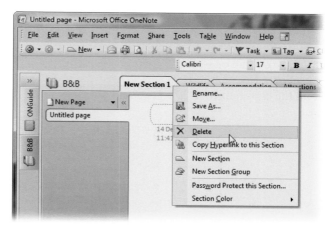

● When the dialog box asks if you're certain that you want to delete the section, just click **Yes** to continue.

● Follow the same procedure to delete the Wildlife section as well.

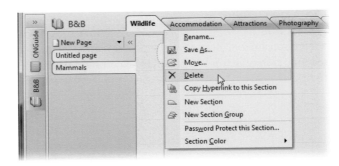

CREATING PAGES AND SUB PAGES

● Switch to the **Attractions** section by clicking on it once, and then change the name of the Untitled page there to **Wildlife** by typing the word into the empty heading slot.

● Next, right click on the Wildlife page tab on the left and choose **New Subpage** from the pop-up menu.

● Type in a title for the subpage–we're going to call it **Mammals**.

● Then right click on the **Wildlife** page tab again and create a second subpage, this time called **Birds**. Now we have two subpages under **Wildlife**.

● Finish adding pages to the various sections as follows: Accommodation has Tariffs and Facilities; Attractions has Wildlife (Mammals and Birds), Hiking, Riding, Hunting, Fishing; Transport has To and From B&B, Car Hire, Taxis; Photography has Interior, Exterior, Places of Interest, and Activities.

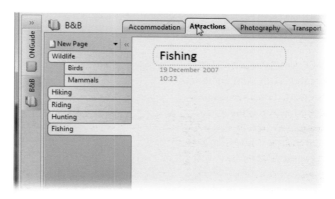

WORKING WITH TEXT

Most of the time, you'll be typing notes directly into OneNote. This section covers how to add, edit, and format text, as well as looking at some of the other note-taking features offered by the program. While it doesn't offer as many fancy features as a dedicated word processing program such as Microsoft Word, OneNote is still an excellent way to record all kinds of written information.

ADDING TEXT

● We'll start by making some rough notes in the **Accommodation** section. Switch to that by clicking on its tab and then click on the **Tariffs** page tab. Then click anywhere in the page with the left mouse button.

● Note that the cursor starts to blink wherever you click, indicating that you can start typing at that spot.
● OneNote differs from a word processor in that you can start typing anywhere on the page. Start by typing **Quick List Of Jobs**.

● As you type, OneNote creates a box that encloses the text. This box–usually called a container–can change in size, and, depending on how you drag its right-hand edges, will get wider or narrower. Here we've finished typing the heading for a list.

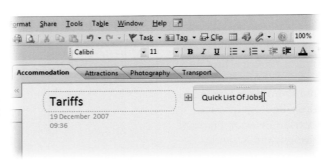

FORMATTING TEXT

● Text in a note can be emphasized in lots of different ways. Click and drag the cursor across to highlight the words you want to work with and then, for example, click the **Bold** button in the button bar.

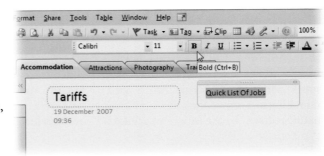

THE FORMAT MENU

As well as changing the way text appears in your notes by using the commands on the button bar, you can also access them by clicking on the text with the right mouse button. When the menu appears, you'll see options there for **Font**, **Bullets**, and **Numbering**. Choose one of these and the Task Pane will open, displaying the full range of numbers, bullets, and fonts that are available.

● You can jazz up your text in lots of different ways, but the process is always the same–highlight any text you want to change and then apply the required formatting using the buttons on the button bar. Here we've increased the size of the heading, changed its color, and underlined it.

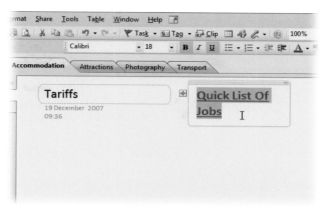

● Note how the heading now wraps onto the next line. Fix that by clicking and dragging the right margin of the note container until the heading fits on one line as shown here.

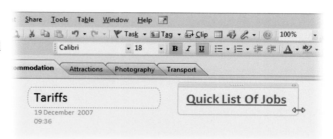

● Press ⏎Enter a couple of times to move down a few lines, and then remove any special formatting you've used by clicking the relevant buttons again (i.e. click the **B** to remove the bold emphasis, the **U** to remove underlines, and so on); if you don't, then when you start typing, the text will still be in the same format as the **Quick List Of Jobs** heading shown here.

● Then type in a rough list of things that need doing. Don't forget to drag the right-hand edge of the container out if you need to make things fit onto a single line.

● Next, highlight the text by clicking and dragging with the mouse.

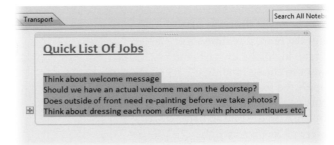

● Move the cursor up to the button bar and then click on the **Bullets** button.

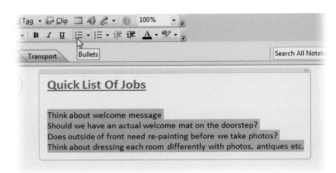

● The result is a neatly bulleted list of the kind you can produce in Microsoft Word. You can use different formatting styles like this with OneNote to help distinguish notes from each other.

MOVING TEXT

● Just as you can start typing text anywhere on a OneNote page, so you can move a text container wherever you like. Move the cursor over the top bar until it turns into a four-headed arrow as shown here.

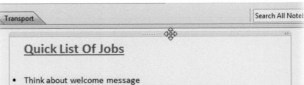

● Click and hold the left mouse button down, and drag the container into a new position. The original stays in place and a shadow version moves with the cursor. Let go of the mouse, and the text will appear in its new position.

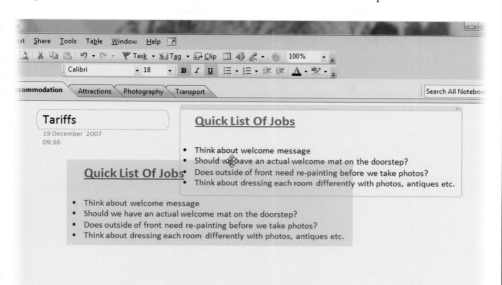

● Here's the container in its new position on the left-hand side of the page. OneNote maintains the highlighting on everything associated with the container in case you want to continue working with it.

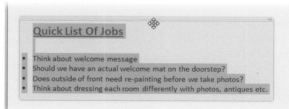

● You can also move text within a container. For example, click anywhere in the main OneNote window to remove the highlight, then click and drag across the bottom line so it's the only item highlighted.

● Next, move the cursor over to the left of the container until it turns into a four-pointed arrow like the one shown here.

Quick List Of Jobs

- Think about welcome message
- Should we have an actual welcome mat on the doorstep?
- Does outside of front need re-painting before we take photos?
- Think about dressing each room differently with photos, antiques etc.

● Click and hold down the left mouse button and then drag the highlighted text up through the list until it's in the correct, new position.

Quick List Of Jobs

- Think about welcome message
- Think about dressing each room differently with photos, antiques etc.
- Should we have an actual welcome mat on the doorstep?
- Does outside of front need re-painting before we take photos?

● Let go of the left mouse button to drop the text into the new position. You can drag and drop individual words, sentences, and paragraphs in the same way. Click anywhere on the page to remove the highlight.

Quick List Of Jobs

- Think about welcome message
- Think about dressing each room differently with photos, antiques etc.
- Should we have an actual welcome mat on the doorstep?
- Does outside of front need re-painting before we take photos?

DELETING TEXT
● Any highlighted text can also be deleted, though in this example we'll just show the menus in action, rather than actually deleting anything. Highlight the text, then click on it with the right mouse button and choose **Cut** from the pop-up menu.

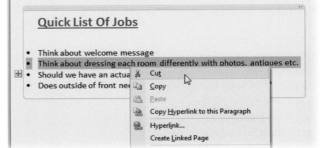

Quick List Of Jobs

- Think about welcome message
- Think about dressing each room differently with photos, antiques etc.
- Should we have an actua
- Does outside of front nee

- Cut
- Copy
- Paste
- Copy Hyperlink to this Paragraph
- Hyperlink...
- Create Linked Page

● Alternatively, you can delete an entire container from OneNote in a similar fashion. Move the cursor over the text so the outline of the text container appears as shown here.

Quick List Of Jobs

- Think about welcome message
- Think about dressing each room differently with photos, antiques etc.
- Should we have an actual welcome mat on the doorstep?
- Does outside of front need re-painting before we take photos?

● Slide the cursor up to the top edge of the container until it turns into a four-pointed arrow.

Quick List Of Jobs

- Think about welcome message
- Think about dressing each room differently with photos, antiques etc.
- Should we have an actual welcome mat on the doorstep?
- Does outside of front need re-painting before we take photos?

● To remove the entire container from the OneNote page, right mouse click and then choose **Cut** from the pop-up menu.

ist Of Jobs

t welcome message
t dressing each room differently w
have an actual welcome mat on th
de of front need re-painting before

✂	Cut
📋	Copy
📋	Paste
✕	Delete
📋	Copy Hyperlink to this Paragraph
	Blog This
	Hide Levels Below ▶
	Order ▶
	Move
	Resize
📝	Convert Handwriting to Text
	Select ▶

UNDO

Like other Office programs, OneNote has an Undo feature. Should you change your mind about deleting work, go to the **Edit** menu and choose **Undo** to reverse your last action. You can also use the Undo button to step back through lots of commands and correct a mistake you made 10 or 15 minutes ago!

ONENOTE TAGS

In the same way that Outlook uses Categories to help you identify different types of tasks, e-mails, and appointments, so OneNote uses visual "tags." There are 29 available to use right away and you can also create your own. By adding visual "clues" to different notes, it's possible to find your way around complex pages quickly and easily. This screen shot shows some of the most useful tags available and also considers some associated features and formatting styles. In every case, highlight the section of text you want to tag, go to the **Tag** button, and select the one you want to apply.

FEATURES KEY

❶ Tag Button
Access and apply OneNote's 29 different tags from here.

❷ Tags
Some tags are purely visual, while others add extra functionality, for example, tick boxes for a task list.

❸ Web Tag
Used to indicate that we'd like to visit this site at some point.

❹ Tables
Not a tag, but a good example of the Word-like formatting features included in OneNote.

❺ Tags Summary
This Task Pane neatly summarizes all of the tags across all of our Notebooks, grouped here by tag name. Use the scroll bar to see any that are currently out of sight.

❻ Search
This drop-down list allows you to specify which Notebooks to use when

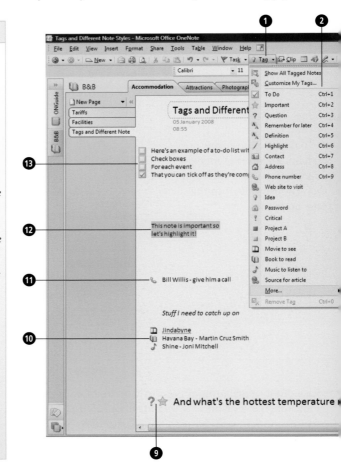

CREATE YOUR OWN TAGS

It's easy to create your own unique tags. Click the arrow beside the **Tag** button and then choose **Customize My Tags** from the menu. This will open the **Customize My Tags** Task Pane on the right of the screen. Click the **Add** button at the bottom of the list. When the dialog box opens, type in a name for your new tag. Pick an icon for it and then click **OK** to close the dialog box and add to the Tag list.

FEATURES KEY

displaying information in the Tags Summary box–currently it's set to show tagged notes in all Notebooks.

❼ Create Summary Page
Click here to generate a concise summary of all tagged notes across all Notebooks on a single page.

❽ Idea Tag
This shows that tags can also be attached to other items on a page, such as pictures.

❾ Multiple Tags
It's also possible to add more than one tag to a note item.

❿ Visual Tags
Here we've tagged three items in a text container as follows: Movie to see, Book to read, and Music to listen to.

⓫ Telephone Tag
Adding a simple visual tag such as this makes it easier to remember to carry out the task.

⓬ Highlight Tag
Familiar to users of Microsoft Word, the yellow highlight tag is a great way to make a note stand out from the rest of the page.

⓭ To Do Tag
*By highlighting this list and choosing the **To Do** tag, we can add a box to each item, which we can tick off as we complete the task in question.*

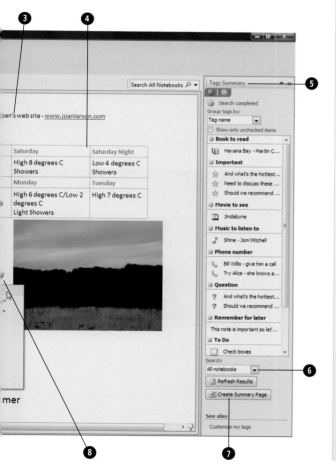

WEB INFORMATION

As well as allowing you to type in notes yourself, OneNote makes it easy to gather and organize information from elsewhere, especially from that great information resource, the Internet.

CAPTURING WEB INFORMATION

The Internet is such an incredible source of information that it's important for any note-taking program to make it easy to bring together potentially useful web material. Sometimes this will take the form of background information that you will simply want to gather for reference or to support a particular element in your project or presentation; at other times, there will be web sites that allow you to reproduce their content for free as part of what you're doing. While it's up to you to always make sure you have the right to use the material you include in your work, you can leave it to OneNote to look after the organization for you.

CAPTURING A PAGE
● Start by loading Internet Explorer as usual and navigating to a web page that includes information that interests you.
● If you want to follow this example exactly, type in **www.mountwashington.ca**, the site of Vancouver Island's alpine ski resort.

● Look at the buttons along the top on the right-hand side of the main Internet Explorer window and you'll see one with the OneNote icon on it.

● When you installed OneNote, the program automatically added this link to the Internet Explorer toolbar.

● If the OneNote icon is missing, go to the box on the following page .

● To copy this entire web page–even the information that's scrolled off the screen and out of sight–just click the **OneNote** button.

● Switch to OneNote and you will see that the Mount Washington web page has been copied into a new note in the special **Unfiled Notes** notebook, which is where OneNote stores anything that doesn't have a specific destination. We'll file it somewhere more appropriate later on, but for now leave it as it is.

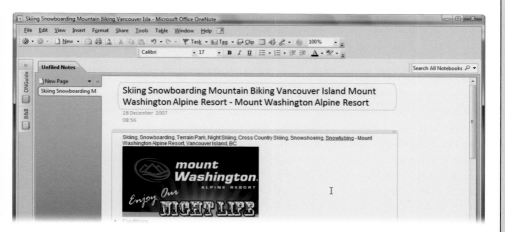

Where's the OneNote Button?

- Of course, OneNote can only approximate the web site on its pages.
- Here, the links that were ranged horizontally across the original page (**Conditions**, **Winter**, **Summer**, **Accommodations**, **Resort Information**) are represented vertically. The links all still work, however.
- Here, we're clicking on the **Conditions** link.

- In this screen, we've temporarily re-sized the OneNote window to show you the web page that we just clicked on—this one shows the resort's current conditions via a webcam.

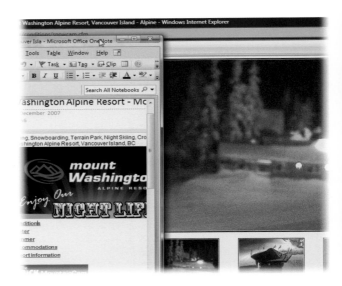

WHERE'S THE ONENOTE BUTTON?

If the OneNote button isn't on Internet Explorer's button bar, here's what to do. Right click anywhere on the button bar and remove the tick next to **Lock the Toolbars**. Now, you'll notice a small vertical line to the left of the **Home** button. Slowly click and drag that line to the left. As you do, new buttons will be revealed, including the OneNote button. To fix the buttons in their new position, right click and then click on **Lock the Toolbars** again.

CAPTURING A SECTION

- If you don't want to copy an entire web page, you can simply grab the part that you need.
- Navigate back to the front page of the resort web site.
- This time, click and drag with the left mouse button to highlight just the opening section as shown here.

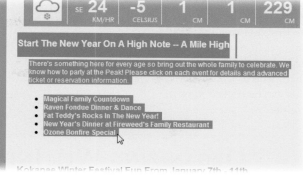

- With the section still highlighted, slide the mouse over to the **OneNote** button and click on it again.

- Switch back to OneNote again and you'll see that a new page has been created, as before. What is different this time, however, is that instead of copying the entire web page, you will only find the information that you just highlighted.

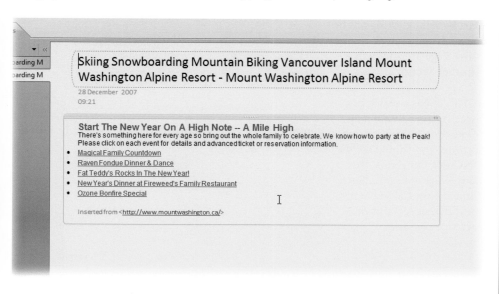

• Again, if you hover the cursor over one of the links on this note you'll see that it changes from an arrow to a pointing hand to indicate that this is a "live" hyperlink that can be clicked to open another web page.

Start The New Year On A High Note -- A Mile High
There's something here for every age so bring out the whole family to celebrate. We know how to
Please click on each event for details and advanced ticket or reservation information.
- Magical Family Countdown
- Raven Fondue Dinner & Dance
- Fat Teddy's Rocks In The New Year!
- New Year's Dinner at Fireweed's Family Restaurant
- Ozone Bonfire Special

Inserted from <http://www.mountwashington.ca/>

ORGANIZING WEB INFORMATION

By default, OneNote places anything that's not assigned by you to a particular page, section, or notebook into the Unfiled Notes Notebook. Although this is useful for odd bits of information that you may need to refer to but that don't warrant categorizing, most of the time it's useful to be able to integrate new items grabbed from the web into existing Notebooks. This next section explains how to do that.

MOVING THE PAGE

• We want to add the second page we've just grabbed from the web to our B&B Notebook, so we'll start by right clicking on the **Page** tab and then choosing **Move Page To**, and then **Another Section**.

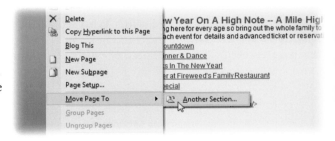

• This opens a dialog box that displays a visual map of our Notebooks and our sections. You should see the ONGuide Notebook, the B&B Notebook, and then Unfiled Notes, along with the different sections that each one contains.

CREATING A NEW SECTION

● We're going to put this page into a new section in the B&B Notebook, but first we'll have to create it. Start by clicking on the **B&B** Notebook to highlight it.

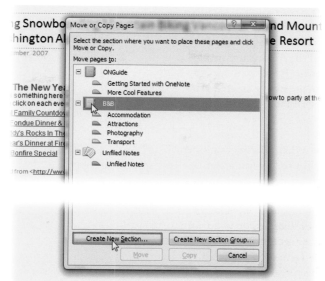

● Next, slide the cursor down to the **Create New Section** button and click on it once.

● When the dialog box opens, type in a name for the new section– in this example it's **Web Stuff**. Click **OK**.

● OneNote creates a new Section in the B&B Notebook called **Web Stuff** and then highlights it to indicate it's the destination for our new page. Click the **Move** button to continue.

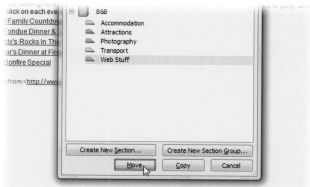

• Now switch to the B&B Notebook by clicking on its tab on the right-hand side of the main window, and then slide the cursor across to the newly created **Web Stuff** tab.

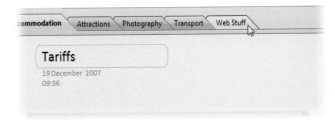

• When that section opens, click the tab underneath the **Untitled page** tab at the side (remember that OneNote always creates a new blank page to go with a new section).

• Here's the page that we just created and copied from the web.

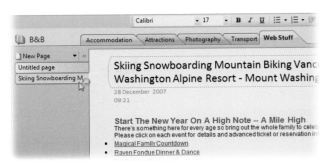

WEB CLIPS

As well as allowing you to copy entire pages or parts of pages from the Internet, OneNote has another interesting feature called Clipping. Instead of grabbing the actual information, the Clip feature lets you take a screen shot of something on a web site–it's as if you'd photographed it with a camera. This allows you to grab a quick visual reminder of what's on a page and drop it anywhere in a OneNote Notebook–for example, photographs and other images, travel itineraries, and so on.

GRABBING A CLIP

• With the Notebook page and web site still open, switch back to Internet Explorer and choose something to grab.

• In this example, we're going to clip the current weather conditions displayed at the top of this web page.

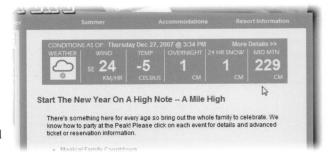

● Switch back to OneNote and then click on the **Clip** button on the button bar.

● When you do, Internet Explorer automatically appears, displaying your chosen web page, but with everything grayed out except for the cursor, which has changed from an arrow to a crosshair.

● Move the cursor to the top left corner of whatever it is you want to grab–in this example it's the weather report box–and then click and hold down the left mouse button.

● Next, drag down and to the right. As you do, you'll see your chosen area start to appear.

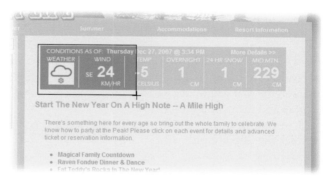

● When you've highlighted the area you want to grab, let go of the mouse button.

● After a second, you'll switch automatically back to OneNote, and you'll see the area you've just grabbed appear as a new container in the current note.

GRABBING A PHOTO

● You can grab a photo in the same way.

● Here, we've switched to the photo gallery on this same web site. This uses the kind of gallery that doesn't always make it easy to grab pictures, but with OneNote, it's very straightforward.

● Navigate to the photo on the web site that you want to grab and then switch back to OneNote.

● Click the **Clip** button.

● When Internet Explorer automatically appears, highlight the photo by clicking and dragging as we did a moment ago until it's selected. (You can just see the crosshair cursor at the bottom right of the photo.)

• Let go of the mouse button and you'll drop back automatically into OneNote, where you can see that the photo has been added to the current page.

RE-SIZING A PHOTO

• If you find that the photo is too large or too small, you can always re-size it.

• Hover the cursor over the photo's edge until it changes to a four-pointed arrow and then click once.

• Note that small boxes have appeared at each corner and halfway along each side.

• You can grab these with the cursor and then, by holding the left mouse button down, drag them in or out to alter the size or proportions of the image.

• Move the cursor over to the bottom right-hand corner and watch how it changes into a double-headed arrow.

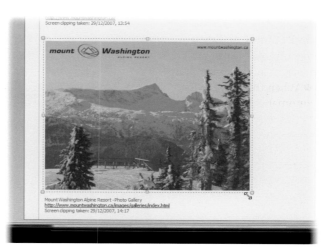

● Click and hold down the left mouse button and drag the photo in to make it smaller, or out to enlarge it.

COPY & PASTE

● You can also use Windows' copy and paste commands to grab web clips.

● Switch back to a web page that has some information you want to copy into OneNote. Here we've switched to **Alpine Facts** for the summer season.

● Position the cursor at the top left of the section that you want to copy.

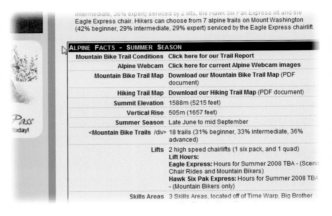

● Hold down the left mouse button and then carefully drag down and to the right to highlight all the text in the box.

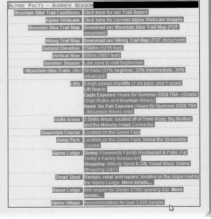

- Let go of the mouse button, move the cursor over the highlighted text, and right mouse click.
- Choose **Copy** from the drop-down menu.

- Flip back to OneNote and right click on an empty part of the current note.
- Choose **Paste** from the drop-down menu.

- Here's the table pasted into OneNote.
- Note that all the links in the table have been preserved, so it's easy to click on them and return to the original web site on the Internet.

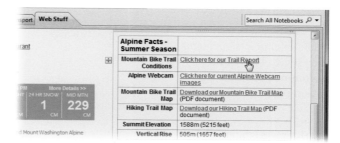

HYPERLINKS

OneNote will preserve hyperlinks when you copy and paste material from a web site or you use the **Send to OneNote** feature in Internet Explorer. However, there may be occasions when you'd rather the link wasn't live— for example if you're adapting information from a web site for something that's going to be printed. If that's the case, right click on the hyperlink and choose **Remove Hyperlink** from the pop-up menu and OneNote will convert it to ordinary text. You can also edit and copy hyperlinks from the same menu.

DOCUMENTS AND FILES

As well as getting information from a web site, OneNote can also import files from elsewhere on the PC, or from a device such as a scanner or digital camera.

INSERTING A DOCUMENT

On a project such as this, where there are so many different types of information, including visuals, text, financial calculations, facts and figures from the web, and so on, it's useful to be able to reference these from within OneNote.

That way, they become part of a single file, which you can then save or email to others who are involved in the project. Keeping everything in one place like this makes for better organization and prevents items from getting lost.

INSERTING A FILE
● If you want to follow this exactly, make sure the **B&B** Notebook is open and then switch back to the **Accommodation** tab by clicking on it.
● Click on an empty space on the page and then go to **Insert** and choose **Files** from the menu.

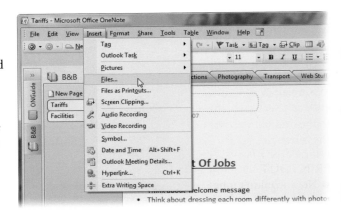

INSERTING SYMBOLS

As well as documents, files, and pictures, you can also add special characters to your notes. In the **Insert** menu, choose **Symbol** to open the dialog box. Here you'll discover hundreds of symbols for currencies, fractions, punctuation, and accents. To add one, click on it and then click the **Insert** button.

- Use Windows' file commands to navigate to the **Documents** folder and then choose a file to insert.
- In this example, we're going to add an invoice that's been created using Microsoft Word.
- Click once on the file and then click the **Insert** button.

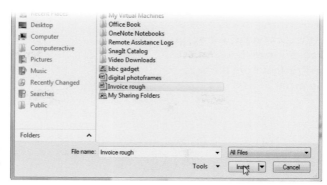

- OneNote adds the file to the current page and represents it with the appropriate icon–in this instance, the one for Microsoft Word.

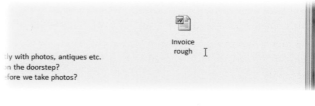

OPENING A FILE

- This document will now be attached to the OneNote file and, as a result, there are plenty of things that we can do with it.
- Right click on the icon and choose **Open** from the menu, and it opens.

INSERTING A PRINTOUT

- Now, wouldn't it be useful if we could see a smaller version of this for reference in OneNote, without having to load Word? Fortunately, we can.
- Close Word and the document by clicking the "**x**" at the top right corner.

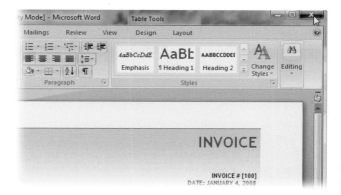

● Next, back at OneNote, right click on the icon again and this time choose **Insert as Printout** from the pop-up menu.

● Word briefly loads the document again, but this time copies it back into OneNote as a re-sizeable image that can be printed out. (It cannot, however, be edited like a normal Word document, because it is only an image of the original.)

● You can now re-size this, just as if it were a picture.
● Move the cursor to the outside edge and click once. Then grab one of the corner handles and drag it in to make the image smaller.

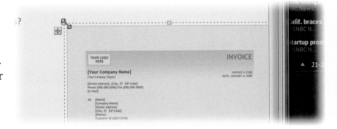

DO THE MATH

You can do basic math in OneNote. Just type in a mathematical equation (for example **56+78=**) and then press the [Enter ↵] key. OneNote will do the calculation for you and insert the answer after the "equals" sign. OneNote can handle multiplication, division, addition, and subtraction like this.

INSERTING A PICTURE

Given that you won't always be inserting photos that are either already stored on your PC (in which case they can be inserted as a file as we've described in the previous section) or grabbed from the Internet (always assuming you have permission to do this), you may need to use another OneNote facility–the ability to grab a photo from a digital camera or scanner that's plugged into the PC.

SCANNING A PHOTO

● Start by making sure the scanner is installed and working properly.
● Next, switch to the page where you want to place the photo, and then click on the **Insert** tool. Choose the **Pictures** option followed by **From Scanner or Camera**.

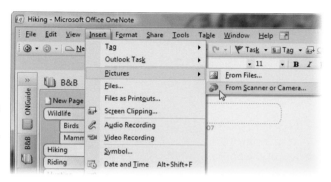

● When the dialog box opens, you should see any attached devices displayed in the drop-down list. As we only have a single Canon scanner attached via a USB connection, it's the only device in the list.

● Although it's tempting to try the **Insert** button, experience has taught us that it's better to click on **Custom Insert** as shown in this example.

● What happens next will vary slightly depending on the scanner you're using. In this example it's an inexpensive Canon LiDE 60. When the scanner software loads, look for an option to preview the image first– this will help to reduce the size. Here, there's a very obvious **Preview** button to click to see the image.

SIZING THE SCAN

● After a moment, a preview of the photo appears in the scanner software window.

● Although the software is clever enough to realize we don't want to include all of that empty space below, it's still intending to scan the blank space to the left of the photo.

● To remove the blank space, simply move the cursor over the dotted line on the left edge, then click and drag the frame to the right as shown here.

● Remove any other empty spaces round the photo in the same way until only the actual image is highlighted by a dotted line.

● At this stage you may wish to set the resolution of the scan and other details.

● Click the **Scan** button to start the process.

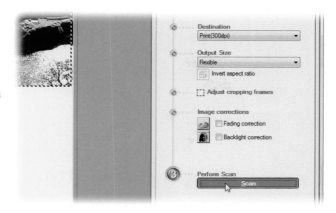

● Be careful not to nudge the scanner or open the lid while the image is being scanned. Most scanners display a progress bar while the scan is being made.

● Here's the finished scan, inserted into the current OneNote page.

● As before, if it's the wrong size, just click on the edge and then drag one of the handles in or out to make it larger or smaller.

PRINTING AND PUBLISHING

To share information with others who don't have OneNote, your best method is to print notes or publish them as pages that can be opened with Internet Explorer.

PRINTING

As OneNote doesn't create documents in the traditional sense (i.e., they're not designed as the kind of pages that go to make up a conventional portrait-style notebook), it's useful to spend a little time looking at some of the basic printing options that are available. This allows you to produce a printout that can be shared with others who don't have the OneNote program or it can be simply stuck to a pinboard where other people can refer to the hard copy version.

PREVIEWING
A PAGE

● Here we've added some more information to a OneNote page to make it more realistic.

● We'll begin by seeing what we'd get if we were to simply print a notebook page by clicking the **Print** button on the button bar.

● Go to the **File** menu and choose **Print Preview**.

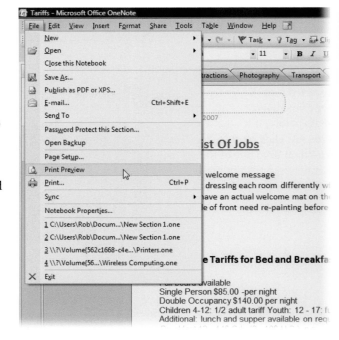

- When the dialog box opens you'll see a miniature preview of how the page will look when it prints out.
- As OneNote pages are more flexible than traditional notes, they may not fit neatly on the page. We'll change that in a moment, but for now, click the **Close** button.

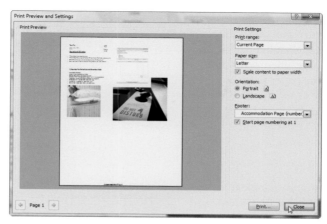

PAGE SETUP

- Go back to the **File** menu and this time select **Page Setup** by clicking on it.

- This opens the **Page Setup** Task Pane on the right of the main editing window. From here you can alter all of the settings that control the appearance of a printed OneNote page.

FANCY PRINTING

It's also possible to add a background color or ruled lines to your printouts, even if they're not part of the way it looks on the screen. These don't really serve any purpose, but they are visually pleasing. They are both available from the Page Setup Task Pane, and there is a wide variety of line styles and colors and background colors to choose from.

● Note that paper size is currently set to **Auto**. Let's see what happens to the page when we try to re-set the paper size.

● Open the drop-down list and choose **Letter**.

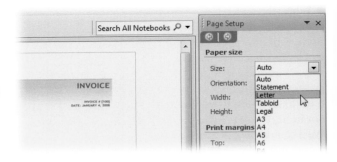

● Have a look at the page in the main window and you'll see that the right-hand edge now has a gray background–this indicates that anything over the gray area is outside of the page edge and will not print out.

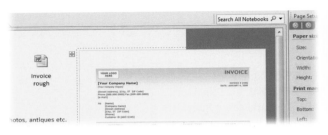

● We can fix this by returning to the Task Pane, opening the **Orientation** drop-down list and choosing **Landscape**.

● Now, if we go back to the **File** menu and choose **Print Preview** again we'll see that the page will print in landscape format on a single sheet of paper.

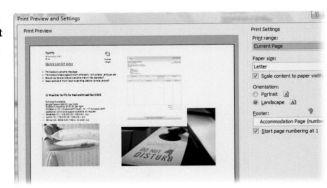

PUBLISHING

If you need to share one or more OneNote pages with someone else who doesn't have a copy of the program, one of the easiest ways is to "publish" those pages as a web page. You can then attach the resulting file to an email and send it to the person, or if you're able, post it to your own web site for him or her to visit. Due to the way that OneNote preserves important formatting– for example, web hyperlinks–publishing like this is an excellent way to let others see what you're planning.

PUBLISHING A PAGE
● Make sure the OneNote page that you want to publish is visible and then go to the **File** menu and chose **Save As**.

● When the dialog box opens, your file should have the same name as the page itself–in this example it's **Accommodation**. If the name's not suitable, highlight it and type in a new one.
● Then open the drop-down list next to **Save as type** and select **Single File Web Page**.

● Note that it's possible to save a Page or a Section of a Notebook as a web page, but you cannot save an entire Notebook.

● Here we've selected **Current Section**. Click the **Save** button to continue.

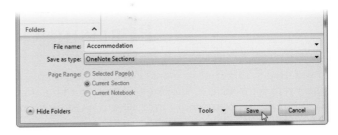

● Now navigate to the folder where you've just saved the web site (in this example it's in the default folder called Documents), and double click on it.

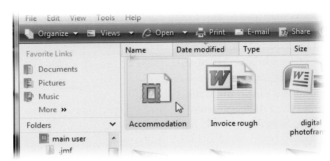

● After a moment, the section will load into Internet Explorer.

● Note that the formatting of your OneNote section has been preserved and that the hyperlink to **www.vancouverisland.com** is live and clickable. Here, we've clicked on it and Internet Explorer has opened the web site; we've then reduced the size of the window so you can see the OneNote "web page" behind it.

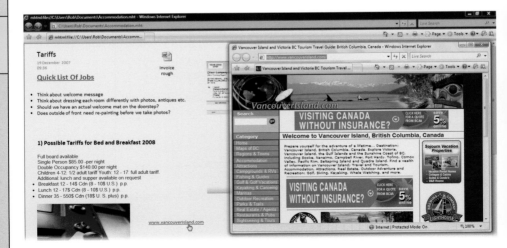

SHARING ONENOTE FILES

Microsoft offers a handy free download for Office 2007 users that makes it even easier to share OneNote Pages, Sections, and Notebooks with other people–even if they don't have OneNote themselves. By visiting the Microsoft Download Center at **www. microsoft.com/downloads** and then searching for "Save as PDF," you'll find a free file you can download called **2007 Microsoft Add-in: Microsoft Save as PDF or XPS**. Just follow the instructions to download this and install it on your

PC and you'll then see a new menu item in the File menu–**Publish as PDF or XPS**. Choose this option, give the Page or Section a name, choose which of the two formats (PDF or XPS) to save it in, and then click the **Save** button.

The PDF format is widely used as a way of sharing documents between different people who may not necessarily have access to the program that created the original. The XPS format is Microsoft's attempt to produce a similarly universal file

format for the same purpose. The screen shot here shows the Tariffs Page from the Accommodation Section of our B&B Notebook, which has been saved as a PDF file and can then be opened and read by the free Adobe Reader program (get it from **www. adobe.com**).

Having the facility to turn Office documents into files that can be displayed and read by anyone is a great feature, and we would advise every Office 2007 user to download this useful free program.

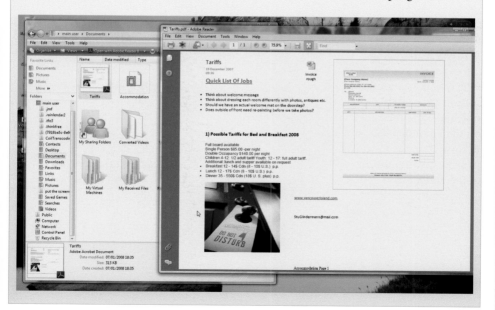

RESEARCH

One of the most useful and innovative ways to get information into OneNote is to use the Research tool. This section explains how to use this facility.

THE RESEARCH PANE

The Task Pane is an area of the Office workspace dedicated to helping you carry out specific tasks. As we've been using OneNote to assemble useful information that may help us to re-launch our Bed & Breakfast business, we're going to look at one of the most useful of these–the Research Pane. As this section shows, the Research Pane allows you to look for information using various Internet-based sources, such as dictionaries and encyclopedias. The way that it integrates seamlessly into OneNote (and other Office programs as required) makes it a very powerful tool. It can even translate simple sentences between different languages.

OPENING THE RESEARCH PANE

- If you're following our example exactly, then switch to the Attractions section of the B&B notebook and then click on the **Fishing** page.
- Now open the Research pane by moving the cursor to the **Tools** menu and choosing **Research**.

● This opens the **Research** pane on the right-hand side of the screen.

● As you can see from the screen shot, it includes a search panel and various other options.

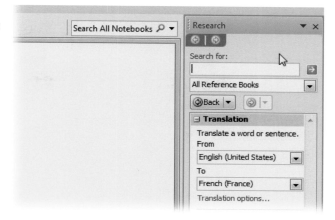

● Let's look for something that might be useful for our business–perhaps to include on the B&B web site or in the printed brochure, or to have handy as information for guests.

● Click in the empty search box and then type **Salmon**. Then click the green "go" arrow.

● In the Research Pane we now see a number of results, including dictionary definitions, which are useful, but not exactly the information we're after.

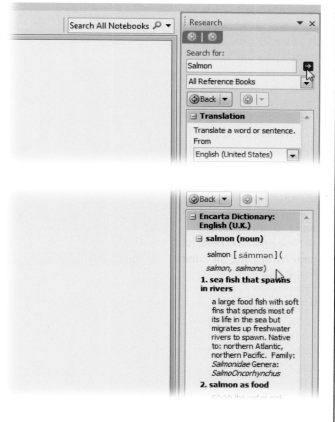

- What we need to do is to change the sources that the Research Pane is using to find the information that we require.
- So, click once to open the drop-down list next to **All Reference Books** and select **All Research Sites** by clicking on it once.

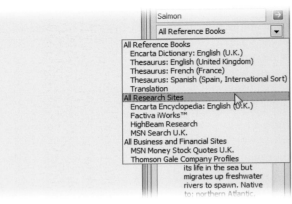

- OneNote returns a different set of results, including information from the Encarta online encyclopedia, which is listed at the top.
- Click on the **Article–Encarta Encyclopedia** link at the top.

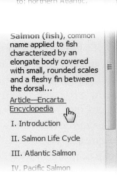

USING THE RESULTS

- After a moment, Internet Explorer loads the web-based Encarta encyclopedia and displays the section about Salmon (note the way that the Research pane is now integrated into the main browser window).
- Internet Explorer also opens a second, smaller window with your original query included in the Research pane.

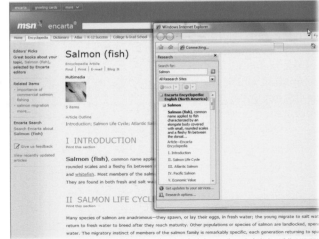

- Click on the window that has the "salmon" results in it to bring it to the top and scroll through it.
- You can now use the techniques described in the earlier section–Web Information 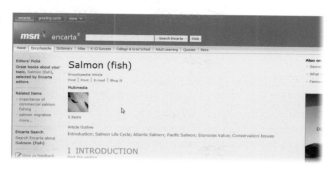–to grab what you need and include it in your OneNote pages.

- The second, smaller page has its uses, too. Switch to it and you'll see that it includes all of the results from the "Salmon" search in the **Research** pane.

- Use the links in the left-hand side to jump to other parts of the same Encarta site, or to visit other useful web sites if any others are included in the results.

- Here we've clicked on the words **Pacific Salmon** and Internet Explorer has opened a new tab in the main browser window with that section open.

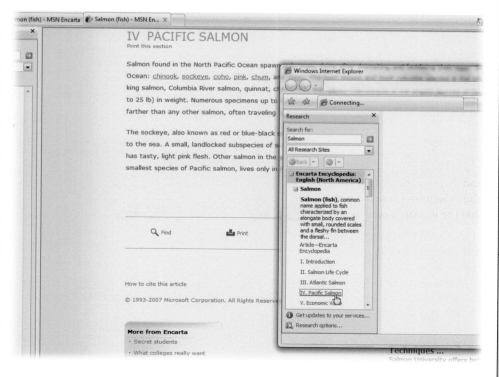

TRANSLATION SERVICES

Along with the kind of encyclopedia-style information we've described in the previous section, the Research pane can be useful in other ways. For example, as tourism becomes more international, so it's more likely that the visitors to our little B&B business may come from overseas and not use English as their first language. By making use of the simple translation features included in the OneNote Research pane, we can communicate with our visitors in their own language. In this section, we'll show you how to take an English sentence and translate it into French.

SWITCHING REFERENCE SOURCES

● Clear the screen by closing both browser windows by clicking on the "**x**" at the top right-hand corner of each and allowing OneNote to occupy the full screen again.

● Then, open the drop-down list next to **All Research Sites** and click on **Translation**.

CHOOSING LANGUAGES

● In the **Translation** part of the Research pane you can use the drop-down lists to select your translate "From" and "To" languages. Just click the arrows and choose from the list.

● In this example we're going to be translating English into French.

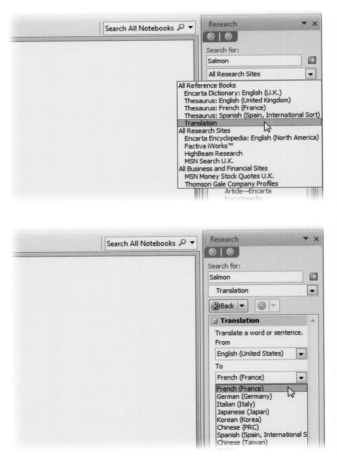

● If it's not still entered in the top search box, try typing the word **Salmon** again and clicking the green search button.

● The Bilingual Dictionary will display the French word for salmon, "**saumon.**"

TRANSLATING PHRASES

● Although that's a good start, the translation feature can do much more. Delete any words that are in the top search box and then type in a sentence. In this example, it's **The salmon fishing here is excellent**. Click the green "go" button.

● After a moment, the Research pane returns with the translation **La pêche saumonée ici est excellente**.

● Highlight the translated sentence with the mouse and then right click on it.

● Choose **Copy** from the pop-up menu.

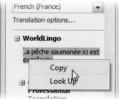

- Move the cursor over to a OneNote page and then right click.
- Select **Paste** from the pop-up menu.

- Here's the result, pasted into the page. It may not be perfect colloquial French, but your guests–and people in general–will understand and appreciate any efforts you make to provide them with information in their own language.

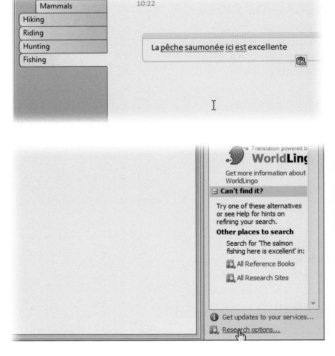

SETTING OPTIONS

- There are several settings in the Research pane, so we'll conclude by having a quick look at them.
- You can open the dialog by moving the cursor down to the **Research options** link at the bottom of the panel and clicking on it.

● When the dialog box opens you'll see the selection of available services.

● Simply use the scroll bar to move down through the list and put ticks next to the ones you want to use.

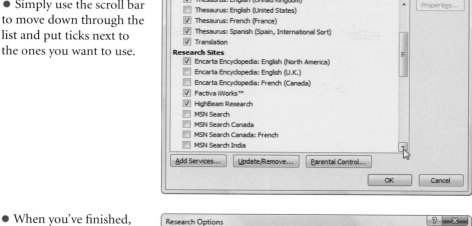

● When you've finished, click the **OK** button to close the dialog box and OneNote will change its settings accordingly.

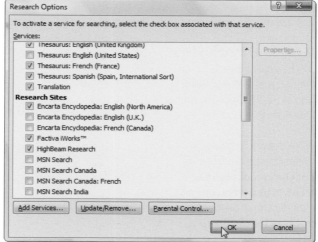

NAVIGATING THE RESULTS

You can use the two arrow buttons at the top of the Research pane to go back and forth between results, just as you can in Internet Explorer to move between web pages. To jump more than one set of results at a time, just click the little arrow next to each button and pick the result you want from the list.

SEARCHING ONENOTE

As we've seen elsewhere in this book, one of Office's key features is a superb Search facility that can help you find what you're looking for in double quick time.

SIMPLE SEARCH

At its most basic, you can use OneNote's search feature to scan the page in front of you to highlight all the instances of a particular word or phrase that you are trying to find. With short pages, or those that are mostly made up of photographs or pictures, this is merely a convenient feature. However, as your OneNote notebooks grow in size and you gather more–and more disparate–information about various subjects, the Search feature really begins to come into its own.

SEARCH PARAMETERS
● The Search box is precisely where you need it to be–at the top of every OneNote page.

● By default, it's set up to **Search All Notebooks**, but you can change the scope of searching by clicking the drop-down menu as shown here.
● In this example we're changing it to search the current section.

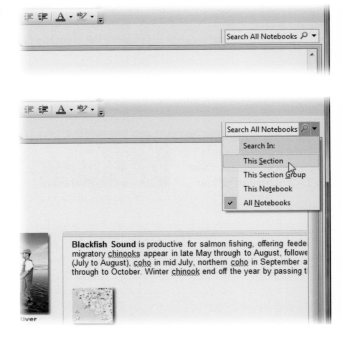

Blackfish Sound is productive for salmon fishing, offering feede migratory chinooks appear in late May through to August, followe (July to August), coho in mid July, northern coho in September a through to October. Winter chinook end off the year by passing t

SEARCHING A SECTION

● First we want to look for something we know is on the page, just to illustrate how OneNote carries out a typical simple search.

● We know, for example, that the word "salmon" appears in this section.

● To begin, we're going to click in the Search box and type in **salmon**.

● Then click on the **Search** icon to start the search.

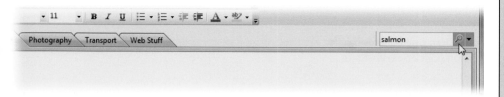

● OneNote goes off and scans the section, looking for the word that we typed into the Search box.

● Every time it finds an occurrence, the word is highlighted in yellow–like a marker pen–as shown in this screen shot.

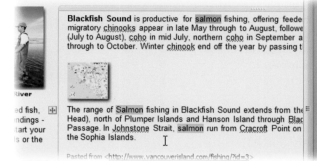

● Remember that we've also asked it to search the entire section, so OneNote also highlights the page tabs where the chosen search word appears. Again, these are highlighted in yellow.

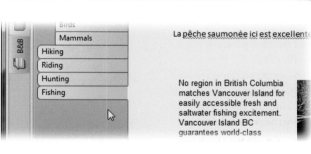

● Clear the existing search results from the box by clicking the little "**x**" as shown here.

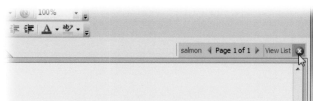

● To replace the word that you have just searched for, double click on the word to highlight it and then replace it with another word.

● In this example, we've deliberately chosen a word (August) that we know is on more than one page in this section. Click **Search** again.

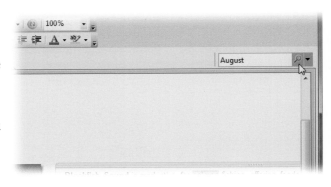

● This time, two of the Page tabs in the current section are highlighted in yellow to show that the chosen word occurs on each of them.

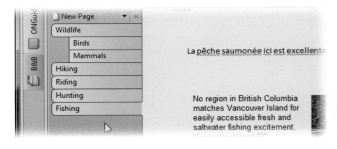

SEARCHING A NOTEBOOK

● Next, we're going to search all of the pages in our notebook and see what results that will bring.

● Start by clicking the "**x**" to remove the search results.

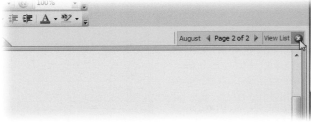

● Next, open the drop-down menu again and this time choose **This Notebook** by clicking on it once.

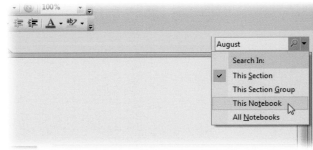

● Highlight whatever text is still in the search box and replace it with something you know appears on various pages and sections in the notebook, and then click **Search** again.

● Here, we're searching for "salmon" again.

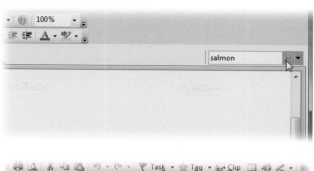

● Although OneNote doesn't light up the Section tabs at the top to indicate whether or not they contain what you're looking for, if you click on a tab then any pages inside it will be highlighted.

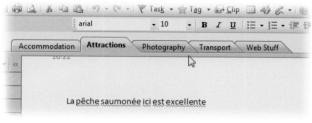

● Additionally, OneNote displays a small navigational tool over by the search box itself. This indicates what you've been searching for, the number of pages it's found in, and which page you're looking at relative to the others (here it's page 2 of 4), along with arrow keys to move you back and forth through the results list.

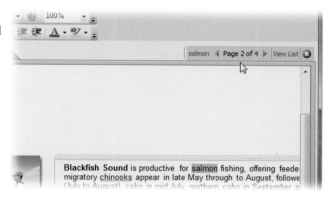

VIEWING THE RESULTS

● The arrow keys move you through the results one by one. In this example, there are four mentions of the search word, so clicking the arrow key will move from one to the next until we reach the last one.

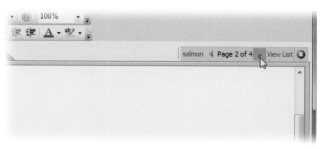

- You will not go to every page as you move between references, just the ones that contain the word. Here, we've moved to the next instance of **salmon** on an entirely new page in the next section by clicking the arrow button.

- You can continue to scroll through matches and pages in this way or click the **View List** link instead.
- Now you can look at the list that opens on the right-hand side of the main window in the Task Pane and jump straight to the instance you're searching for by clicking on its hyperlink.
- Here we're after the salmon pink wallpaper sample we researched for the inside of our B&B.

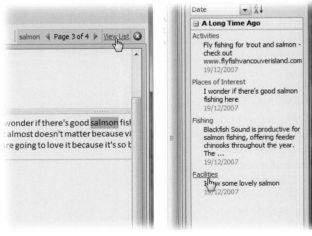

● Here's the match we were after—a wallpaper sample.

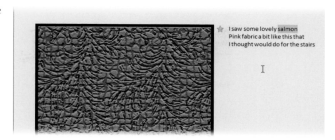

SORTING THE RESULTS

● By default, the results in the pane are sorted by date, but it's easy to change that.

● Move the mouse to the drop-down list at the top and click it once to open it.

● Then you can select to sort the results by **Section** or by **Title**.

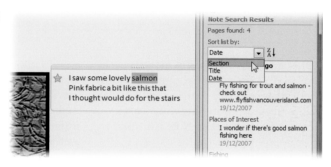

CHANGING THE SEARCH

● Finally, you can also alter the scope of your search by clicking on the drop-down list at the bottom of the results pane and choosing one of the other search destinations there.

● You can also find some further useful ways of using OneNote's search features by clicking on the **Search tips** link at the bottom of the Task Pane.

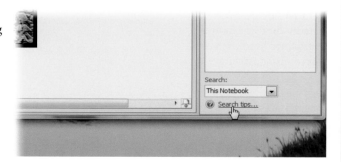

WORKING WITH OUTLOOK

One of OneNote's most useful and innovative features is the way in which it integrates with Outlook, allowing you to exchange information freely between the two programs.

SETTING UP

Although OneNote and Outlook are designed to work together out-of-the-box, there are several steps you can take so that things integrate more smoothly. That's because, by default, OneNote is set up to drop appointments, contact details, and e-mails into a new note in the Unfiled section, which is not necessarily where you want them to go. In this section, we'll explain how to set things up so that items from Outlook go into the correct OneNote sections and pages.

OPENING OPTIONS
● If the Task Pane is open, close it by clicking the "**x**" in its top right-hand corner to create more screen space.
● Then right click next to one of the existing section tabs at the top.
● Select **New Section** from the pop-up menu.

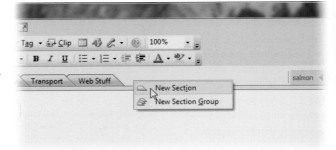

● Give the new section a name–in this example it's **Admin**–and then press
[Enter ←⏎] to create it.

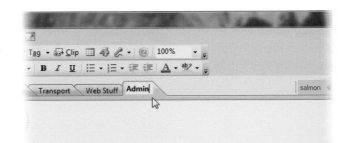

● Next, making sure you're still looking at your newly created section, click the **Tools** menu and choose **Options** from the menu.

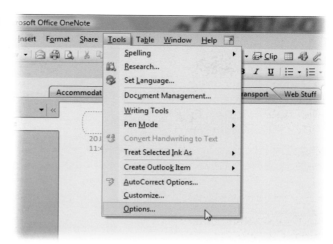

● When the **Options** dialog box opens, click the **Outlook Integration** heading in the **Category** column on the left.

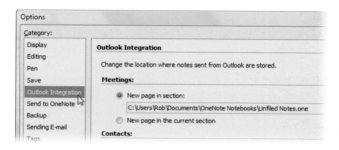

DEFINING A LOCATION

● The next step is to "tell" OneNote where to store items that you send to it from Outlook.

● Meetings, contacts, and e-mails are currently all going to go into the **Unfiled Notes** notebook. While this can be useful, it does mean manually moving all these items later on.

● Click the **Change** button in the **Meetings** section.

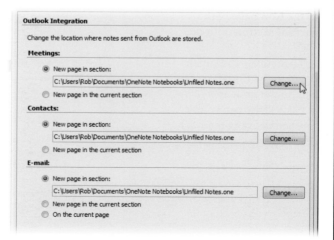

● OneNote opens the
Select a Section dialog box.
● To send information
about Meetings set up
in Outlook to your newly
created Admin section,
move the cursor down the
section list to **Admin** and
click on it once.

● Click the **Select** button
to continue.

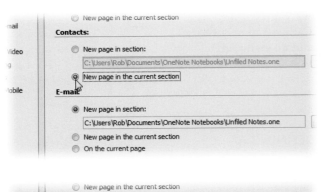

● Now we can use a
shortcut to achieve the same
effect with any Outlook
contacts or e-mails that we
want to include in OneNote.
● Move the cursor down to
the **Contacts** section and
click the radio button next
to the **New page in the
current section** option.

● Then, move the cursor
down to the **E-mail** section
and do the same there.
● Click **OK** when you've
finished defining the
destination locations.

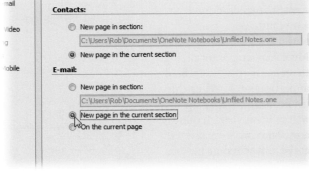

SENDING ITEMS TO ONENOTE

We're now in a position to send information about a meeting, or details of a contact, or any related e-mails that have been created (or perhaps received) using Outlook, so let's look more closely at how the process actually works. Although Outlook itself includes all the tools you need to manage quite sophisticated projects, it doesn't have the same free-form design as OneNote. OneNote has the advantage of a flexible layout that lets you mix and match different types of data, and this can really help to liberate and inform the creative or organizational process.

MEETINGS

- Now let's send some items to OneNote using the settings we just defined.
- Load Outlook and then open the Calendar.
- Click once in the main Calendar view and then create a simple appointment. Add an alarm or any other details you need to ⬐.
- Then, right click on the appointment and choose **Meeting Notes**.

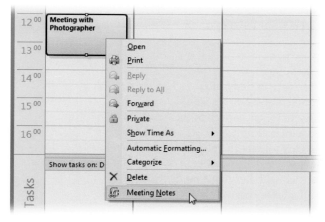

- You'll instantly switch back to OneNote, which now displays the new **Admin** section, along with a new page that's been automatically created called **Meeting with Photographer**, the name we gave to the appointment we set up in the previous step.
- Note, too, that it includes any notes that were created at the same time.

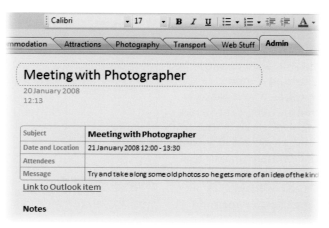

CONTACTS

● Next, let's add some name and address details in the same way.

● Leave OneNote set to display the same page and flip back to Outlook. Switch to the **Contacts** module by clicking the button in the left-hand column, select a contact from the main window and then right click on it. Choose **Contact Notes** from the menu.

● Earlier, when we defined a location , we set up OneNote so that both contacts and e-mails would be sent to a new page in the current section.

● This contact therefore now appears in a new page– labeled with her name–and with all her details intact.

E-MAILS

● Adding an e-mail works in much the same way.

● Flip back to Outlook and click the **Mail** button in the left-hand column.

● Click on your **Inbox** and find an e-mail there. We've chosen one with an attachment so that we can demonstrate what happens when we bring it into OneNote. Right click on your chosen e-mail and choose **Send to OneNote**.

● Again, remembering the settings we changed when we defined a location, OneNote creates a new page in the current section and drops the e-mail into it, noting the fact that there's a picture attachment by displaying a little icon.

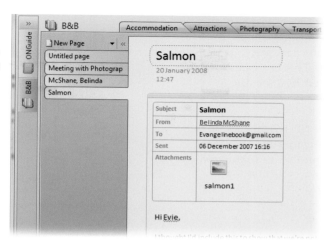

SENDING ITEMS TO OUTLOOK

Successful integration needs to go both ways, so having seen how you can send items from Outlook to OneNote, let's look at how it works the other way round. For example, if you're busily taking notes, it's convenient to create a task in OneNote and then have it appear in Outlook; similarly, if you're on the phone and someone gives you their address, it saves time if you can open a new address window directly in OneNote and then send it to Outlook, rather than having to load Outlook, switch programs, go to the Contacts area, create a new card and so on, while you're trying to have a conversation. This section explains how to do it all from OneNote.

CREATING TASKS

● To begin, click the **Task** button on OneNote's button bar.

● OneNote creates a text container complete with a little task flag.
● Type in a name for the task next the flag.

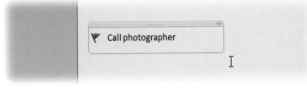

● Next, right click on the flag icon and change the due date to **Tomorrow**.

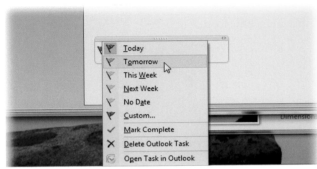

● Here we've re-arranged the OneNote and Outlook windows one in front of the other so you can see that although the new **Call photographer** task was created in OneNote, it now appears in Outlook as well.

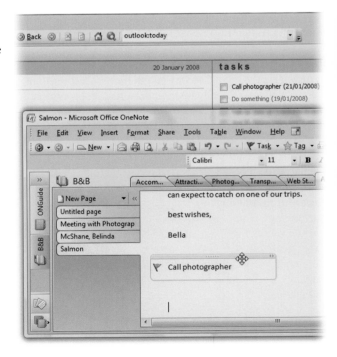

● Next, right click on the task in OneNote and then choose **Mark Complete**.

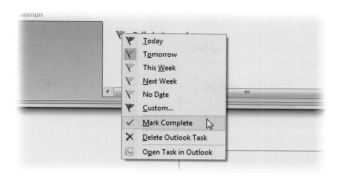

● The task is ticked in the OneNote window and marked as complete in Outlook as well.

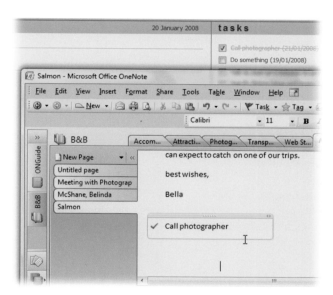

OUTLOOK INTEGRATION

You'll remember that we decided to send any contacts and emails into a new page in the current OneNote section because that suited the way we've put this notebook together. However, there's nothing to stop you from creating new pages, sections, or notebooks that are dedicated to specific types of information, such as contacts or e-mails, and keeping them separate. To do this, simply create the pages in OneNote and then use **Tools**, **Options**, and **Outlook Integration** to tell Outlook where to send the particular data.

CREATING CONTACTS

● To create a new contact in OneNote, imagine you're speaking to someone on the phone and they offer to give you their address.

● Go to the **Tools** menu and choose **Create Outlook Item** and then pick **Create Outlook Contact** from the sub menu.

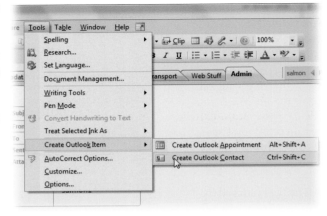

● OneNote opens up the **Contact** window, whether Outlook is loaded or not, where you can type in the details of your new contact and then click the **Save & Close** button.

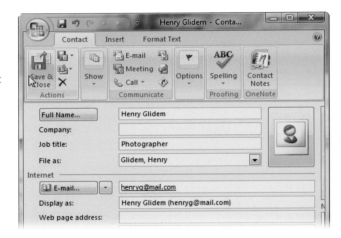

● Next time you open Outlook, the address will be in the **Contacts** section.

CREATING APPOINTMENTS

- You can create Outlook appointments in exactly the same way.
- In OneNote, click on **Tools** to open the menu, select **Create Outlook Item**, and then click on **Create Outlook Appointment**.

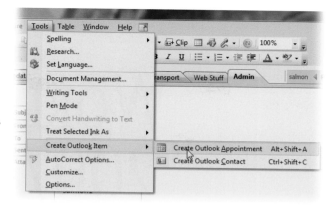

- The **Appointment** window opens. Here you can enter all the necessary details of your meeting.
- Then click **Save & Close**.

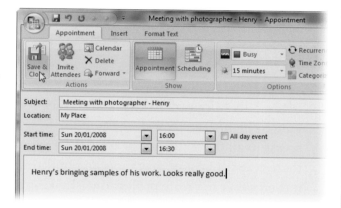

- Next time you load Outlook, switch to the Calendar view and navigate to the day the appointment is set for. Here you can see, in Outlook, the meeting with the photographer we just set up in OneNote.

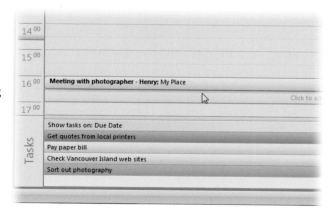

WORD 2007

UNDOUBTEDLY THE MOST POPULAR word processing program on the market, Word has been given a major make-over by Microsoft to create the Office 2007 version. The Office Fluent™ user interface lies at the heart of this, providing access to all the features that were there in earlier versions, but there is also a host of new tools and built-in elements that make it even easier to create professional-looking documents. In this chapter we look at the detail of the Word screen and ways of viewing the document, at formatting fonts and paragraphs, and using Word's ready-made Quick Parts. We then turn to the Styles and Themes that can transform the look of a document, and the templates that help in setting up a document in the way you want. The closing section shows how to create visual elements on the page or import them from other sources and programs.

WORD ON SCREEN

In this section we examine the layout of the Word screen, demonstrate methods for viewing and moving around within the document, and look at ways of personalizing the program settings.

WHAT IS WORD?

Word is one of the most powerful word processing programs now available. Although you can still key in and print out a simple letter, the real strengths of this program lie in its ability to style every aspect of the page layout and the text, check the spelling, add headers and footers, find and replace words and formatting, compile an index, create or import charts, tables, illustrations, and photos, and do a great deal more besides.

WHAT IS A WORD DOCUMENT?

● A Word document consists of pages whose content can be defined by the user. Pages can be given features such as borders, headers, and page numbers. Text can be keyed or pasted into the pages, and formatted accordingly. It can be edited, searched, checked for spelling or grammar, footnoted, and indexed. Charts, tables, graphics, and photos can be created or imported and then manipulated in a host of imaginative ways.

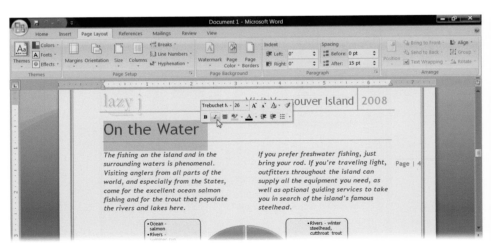

KEY WORD FEATURES

• IMPROVED INTERFACE

The Microsoft Office Fluent™ interface puts the tools you need within easy reach all the time by using the Ribbon along the top of the Word screen. Here you'll find tabs that open sets of commands related to the various aspects of creating a professional and well-designed document.

• FILE MANAGEMENT

The Office button at the top left of the Word screen opens all the tools you need to create new documents using a range of templates, open documents that you've been working on recently, search your computer for files, and save your document in a variety of formats. Here you can also send the document to print, prepare it for distribution, and send it by e-mail or fax.

• EASY CUSTOMIZING

The Word Options dialog box makes it easy to personalize your access to toolbars and tabs, control the way your documents are displayed on screen, and set the options for proofing, saving, editing, and printing. Keyboard shortcuts and the range of tools available in the Quick Access toolbar at the top of the screen can also be controlled from here.

• BUILDING BLOCKS

Word comes complete with an array of ready-made elements that can be inserted on the page, saving time and effort, and helping to establish a coherent design across your document. These include cover pages, text boxes and sidebars, headers and footers, and custom text blocks such as a company address, as well as items that you can create yourself and save to use whenever you need them.

• TEXT MANAGEMENT

The tools for formatting fonts and paragraphs are all arranged for easy access in the Home tab at the top of the screen and can generally be used without the need to open successive submenus. In addition, Word provides a text formatting mini toolbar that appears whenever you highlight text, and a text management menu that pops up when you right click, wherever you are in the document.

• QUICK STYLES AND THEMES

Word's range of Styles– formats that include font choices, colors, and styling– makes it quick and easy to give a distinctive character to each of the levels of text within a document. Styles can also be customized and added to the available options, or saved as Style Sets. Themes can be used to change the whole tone of a document by applying a consistent family of colors, fonts, and graphic effects throughout all the text and visual elements.

• LIVE PREVIEW

The effects of many of Word's formatting options, such as fonts, font colors, Styles and Themes, can be seen on the page as you roll the cursor over the options, enabling you try them out before you choose.

THE WORD WINDOW

At first glance, Word's document window may look dauntingly complex, but you'll soon discover that similar commands and actions are grouped together. This "like-with-like" layout helps you to understand quickly where you should be looking on the window for what you want. Have the window open, and experiment as you read through the details of the controls. The precise appearance of the window will vary depending on the resolution at which your monitor is set. In this particular screen shot, we have deliberately used a low resolution to maximize the size of the elements for clarity. At a higher resolution, the range of options is seen in more detail.

FEATURES KEY

❶ Office Button
Used to carry out actions such as opening, saving, or printing your document.

❷ Home Tab
Contains the most commonly used text formatting commands.

❸ Quick Access Toolbar
A handy set of tools that can be customized to suit.

❹ Other Tabs
Clicking on any of these brings up a specific ribbon of commands.

❺ Minimize Word

❻ Maximize/Restore

❼ Close Word

❽ Word Help
Click here for online help and advice from Microsoft.

❾ View Ruler
Clicking here brings a ruler into view along the top of the document.

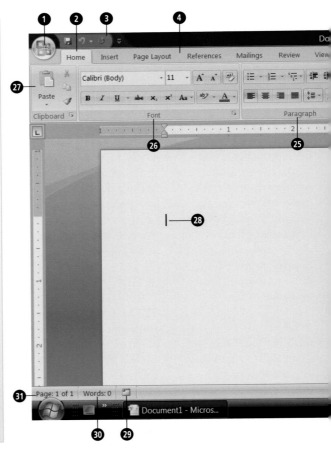

WORD'S RIBBON TOOLBAR

Word 2007 provides easy access to all the tools and controls needed to produce professional documents. This is achieved by using the Ribbon toolbar located along the top of the document window. The Ribbon consists of several tabs that relate to different aspects of the Word document, and within each tab the commands are grouped in a logical fashion. The Home tab, selected here, contains most of the common text formatting tools and commands.

FEATURES KEY

❿ Scroll-up Arrow
Moves up the document.
⓫ Scroll Bar Box
Moves text up or down.
⓬ Scroll-down Arrow
Moves down the document.
⓭ Page-up Button
Shows previous page.
⓮ Select Browse Object
Opens up the browse options menu.
⓯ Page-down Button
Displays next page of text.
⓰ Zoom Slider
Alters the magnification of the page.
⓱ Zoom Button
Opens the Zoom dialog box.
⓲ Draft View
⓳ Outline View
⓴ Web Layout View
㉑ Full Screen Reading
㉒ Print Layout
㉓ Editing Group
of Commands
㉔ Styles Group
of Commands
㉕ Paragraph Group
of Commands
㉖ Font Group
of Commands
㉗ Clipboard Group
of Commands
㉘ Insertion Point
Typed text appears here.
㉙ Record Macro Button
㉚ Word Count
㉛ Page Indicator

VIEWING THE DOCUMENT

Word offers you several ways of viewing your document on the screen to show you what you need to see in order to carry out the particular task. You can also view two parts of the same document, or the same part of two different documents, at the same time, and zoom in or out to see the fine detail or gain an overview of the pages. To demonstrate, we are starting here with a page that already has text on it.

VIEWING OPTIONS

● Word offers a choice of five different ways of viewing the pages of a document, and the five buttons that control the views are to be found in two places. The first set is the **Document Views** command group at the left-hand end of the **View** tab in the Ribbon.

● The second set, and the one that is always available, is at the bottom right of the screen, to the left of the Zoom slider. The icon for the current view is always highlighted. We're going to work our way along the tools from left to right.

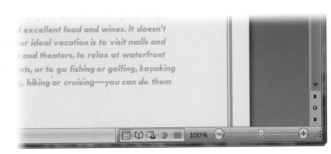

RULERS AND UNITS

In the Print Layout, Web Layout, and Draft views, there is an optional ruler along the top of the screen and down the left-hand side of the page. To turn it on or off, click on the **View Ruler** button at the top right of the page screen. To change the units of measurement, go to **Word Options** 🗋, select the **Advanced** tab, scroll down to the **Display** section, and select your preferred units.

**Customizing
Word Options**
218

PRINT LAYOUT VIEW

- When you open Word or create a new document, this is the default view, and it's the one that most people work in most of the time.
- Here you can see all the elements in the page as they will appear if you print the document.
- Now click on the **Full Screen Reading** button.

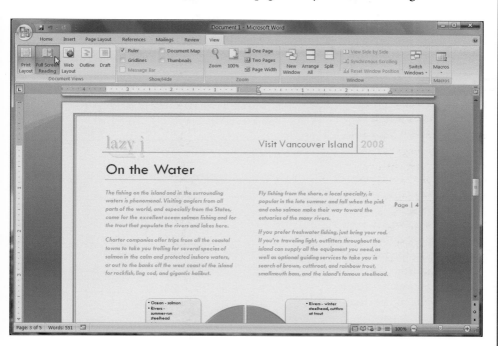

FULL SCREEN READING

- This is a good view in which to edit your document. The page itself now displays only text and graphics– borders, headers, page numbers, columns, etc. have all been removed.
- The Ribbon and ruler have both disappeared, leaving just two tiny toolbars at the top corners.

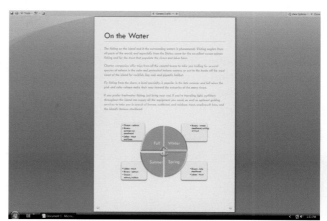

● On the left-hand toolbar you will find icons for saving and printing on the left, and for highlighting text and inserting a comment on the right.

● The **Tools** button in the center opens a menu that includes two particularly useful features–Research and Translation.

● Click on **Research** to open a pane on the screen.

● This is the same Research pane that we have already seen in OneNote 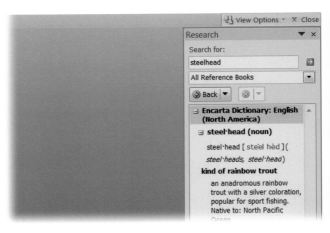.

● Click on a word in your text and, providing you are connected to the Internet, a definition from the online Encarta Dictionary should appear in the top portion of the Research pane.

● If the word isn't found, you can extend the search to other research sites.

● Back in the **Tools** menu, click on **Translation Screen Tip** and select a language from the drop-down menu.

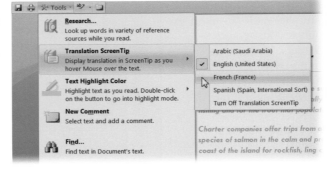

● Now move your cursor over a word in the text and a translation tip appears.
● Not all words are in the dictionary, but some tips are quite informative.

water
['wɔ:tər]
1. *noun* eau *féminin*, ***waters** plurie*/NAUTICAL eaux
2. *transitive verb* plant, garden arroser
3. *intransitive verb of eyes* pleurer; ***my eyes were watering** j'a
pleuraient; ***my mouth is watering** j'ai l'eau à la bouche

n the water

...ishing on the island and in the surrounding waters is phenomenal. Visiting a...

● Now moving over to the right-hand top corner, there are two buttons.
● Clicking on the **Close** button returns us to the Page Layout View, while clicking on the **View Options** button opens an extensive menu.

● Most of the options here are self-explanatory, but we are highlighting one that is important if you want to edit the document.
● Unless you click on **Allow Typing**, you will not be able to make changes to the document in this view.

● The three options below this one control the tracking of editorial changes and what aspects of the markup are shown or hidden.
● These same commands are available in other views in the **Tracking** command group on the **Review** tab.

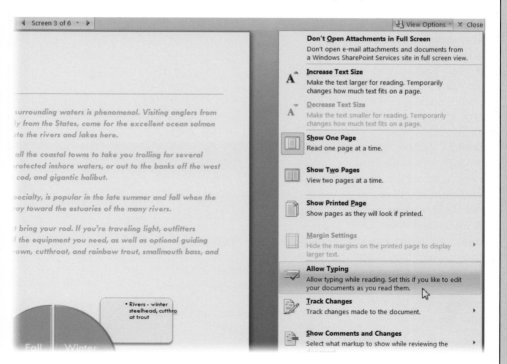

WEB LAYOUT VIEW

- In this view, we see the document as it would appear if it were saved as a web page and viewed in a web browser. The text is no longer set out in columns, and the text runs across a wider measure. The text can be edited in this view.

OUTLINE VIEW

- When you click the **Outline** button, the page opens with the Outlining tools available in the Ribbon.
- Using these, you can structure and organize a document in terms of the various levels of text.
- This view is useful for planning a new document from scratch.

DRAFT VIEW

- Lastly we see the **Draft** view, in which the Word document is reduced to just the bares bones.
- All boxes, borders, columns, images, headers, and graphics have been removed, leaving only the styled text. Section breaks are indicated, but not page breaks.

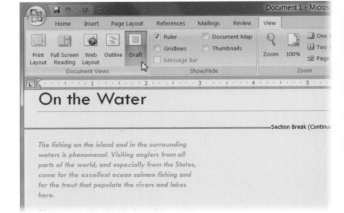

ZOOMING IN AND OUT

● In all views except Full Screen Reading, you can increase or decrease the size of the detail on the page by using the Zoom slider at the bottom right of the screen or by clicking on the "+" and "-" signs at each end of it.

THE ZOOM COMMANDS

● Still on the View tab in the Ribbon, the **Zoom** commands include options such as viewing two pages side by side.

● Clicking on the **Zoom** button at the left-hand end opens a dialog box in which you can choose to zoom to a specified percentage size or page/text width, or opt to view several pages on the screen at the same time.

THE WINDOW COMMANDS

● This group of commands controls the page view when you have more than one document open or you want to look at two parts of a document at the same time.

● Click on the **New Window** button to open another window on the same document.

● When you have two or more documents open on the desktop at the same time, clicking on the **Arrange** button will align them all edge to edge.

USING A SPLIT WINDOW

● Another way to look at two parts of a single document at the same time is to click on the **Split** button.

● Now click on the page, and the window becomes two windows, one above the other, each with a separate vertical scroll bar.
● You can now scroll through two separate parts of the same document.
● To return to the normal view of a single window, click on **Remove Split**.

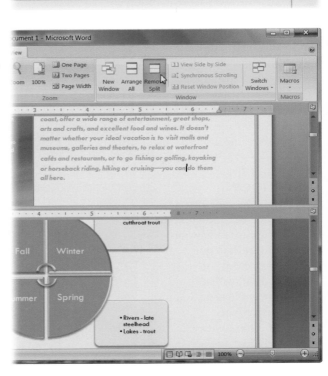

SIDE BY SIDE VIEWING

● When you have two documents open and you wish to compare them, Word offers a clever solution. Start by making sure that the part you want to compare is visible in each window and then click on **View Side by Side** to position them next to each other.

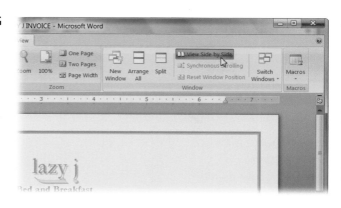

● Now click on the **Synchronous Scrolling** button in the **View** tab on both of the documents.
● You will now find that as you scroll through either document, they both scroll in parallel.

SWITCH WINDOWS

● If you have overlapping windows open on screen, you will be given the choice of switching between them if you click on **Switch Windows,** the final button in the Windows group.

Moving Around

In a short document, it's easy to find what you're looking for, but in a long typescript it's not so simple. Fortunately Word has several means of locating material within the document and of moving between pages, sections, and even headings.

BROWSING UP AND DOWN

● By default, the double up and down arrows at the bottom of the vertical scroll bar take you through the document a page at a time.

● This is a useful feature, but they can do much more than this. Click on the inconspicuous **Select Browse Object** button between them to discover the key.

● Roll your cursor over each of the icons in the pop-up panel to see what each one does.

● Clicking on one of these changes the function of the up and down arrows and allows you to go to the next section, footnote, heading, etc..

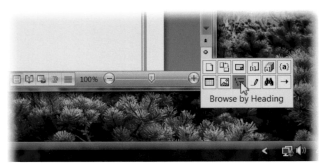

FIND (AND REPLACE)

● The binoculars icon is the same tool as the **Find** button at the right-hand end of the **Home** tab, and clicking on it opens the **Find and Replace** dialog box.

● Here, you can elect to find the next instance of a certain word or phrase in the text (and to replace it if you wish).

● Using the **Format** pop-up menu, you can also search for particular formatting (of a font, paragraph, etc.) within the document.

● The **Special** pop-up menu allows you to find a specified formatting mark or character.

● If the **Format** and **Special** options are not visible, click on the **More** button in the dialog box to reveal them. (This becomes the **Less** button when the dialog box is expanded.)

USING THE GO TO TAB

● The third tab in the **Find and Replace** dialog box, which opens automatically if you click on the arrow icon in the **Select Browse Object** menu, allows you to choose an element within the document and go to a specified instance of it, such as a particular page, section, or line.

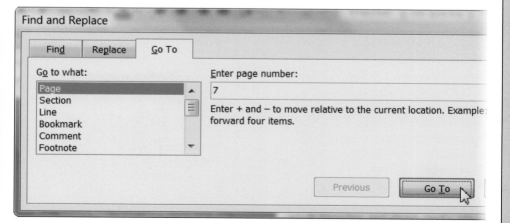

CUSTOMIZING WORD OPTIONS

In previous editions of Word, many of the options that control settings within the program were reached by clicking on **Tools** and then selecting **Options** from the drop-down menu. In Word 2007 these controls are accessed via the Office button at the top left of your screen. Here we will look at a few of the options as examples, but it is well worth spending some time opening the various "tabs" just to discover the wide range of useful choices that is available here.

OPENING THE DIALOG BOX

● Start by clicking on the Office button and selecting **Word Options** at the bottom of the panel.

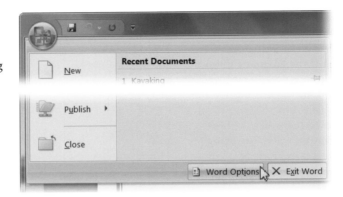

POPULAR OPTIONS

● The **Word Options** dialog box opens. The headings down the left-hand side are effectively tabs, and clicking on any of these will open the range of options contained in each heading.

● The **Popular** tab includes options to turn off features such as the mini toolbar, live preview, and screen tips, but you'll probably find these are best left on.

● The Word window color scheme can also be changed from here.

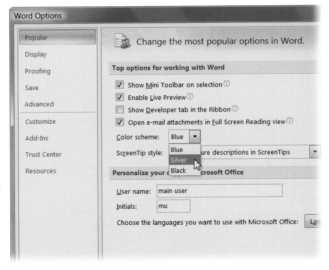

DISPLAY OPTIONS
● Under the **Display** tab, options exist to control the page display, to show selected formatting marks (which you may find useful), and to alter the printing options.

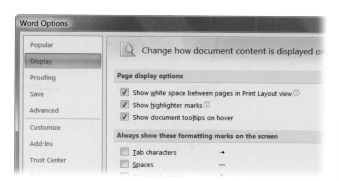

PROOFING OPTIONS
● The **Proofing** tab opens options that control Word's AutoCorrect feature, as well as spelling and grammar checking.
● Gray buttons within the box open further dialog boxes and an even greater range of choices.

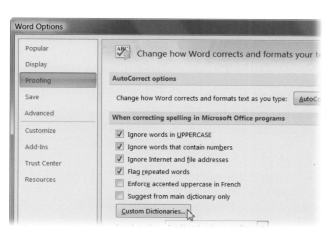

ADVANCED OPTIONS
● Skipping the **Save** tab, which controls the formats and locations in which files are saved, we come to the **Advanced** tab. This covers an extensive range of important areas and is well worth investigating, as it includes the editing and clipboard options as well as which elements are displayed on the screen.

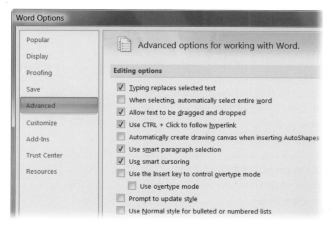

FORMATTING TEXT

The Home tab on the Ribbon toolbar is for manipulating and formatting text. Many of the commands are the same as in earlier versions of Word, but there are some exciting differences.

THE FORMATTING TOOLBAR

When you key text into a new Word document, it has the default formatting of Normal style, which is plain, black, 11 point Calibri. All of these qualities, and many others, can be changed individually using the Font group of commands.

THE FONT GROUP

● Each of the commands in the Font group will affect all of the text that has been selected, whether this is a single letter or the whole document.

● Several of the commands have downward pointing arrows next to them, and clicking on these opens drop-down lists from which to choose, for example, the font, font size, underlining style, change of case, font color, or text highlight color.

● The Clear Formatting button at the top right of the font group is particularly useful if you make several changes to a paragraph and then want to start over.

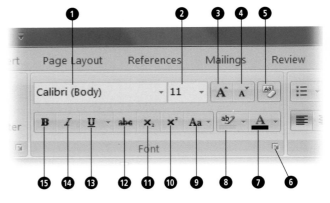

FEATURES KEY

❶ Font
❷ Font Size
❸ Grow Font
❹ Shrink Font
❺ Clear Formatting
❻ Clicking here opens the Font dialog box
❼ Font Color
❽ Text Highlight Color
❾ Change Case
❿ Superscript
⓫ Subscript
⓬ Strikethrough
⓭ Underline
⓮ Italic
⓯ Bold

OPENING THE FONT DIALOG BOX

● Most of the options in the Font group, as well as an interesting range of font effects, can be accessed by clicking on the small arrow at the bottom right of the panel and opening the Font dialog box.

● Here, you can change several aspects of the text at once, and the text **Preview** panel allows you to see the result of your choices. If you don't like what you see, you can keep on experimenting or click on **Cancel** to leave the text as it was.

● Only if you click on **OK** will the changes be made.

CHARACTER SPACING

● A second tab in this dialog box opens options that allow you to expand and condense the individual letters and to alter the spacing between them. Again, the **Preview** panel lets you see the effect.

● Here, we've removed the small caps formatting and expanded the text by 1 point to spread it out.

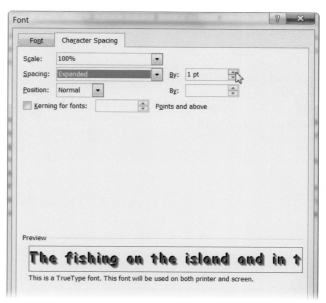

THE MINI TOOLBAR...

● Word assumes that if you have highlighted a word or paragraph you intend to do something to it, so a mini toolbar containing a selection of Home text tools is displayed when you hover your cursor over any highlighted text.

● Move your cursor over the toolbar and click on a button to make the change.

● Here, we're italicizing the highlighted paragraph.

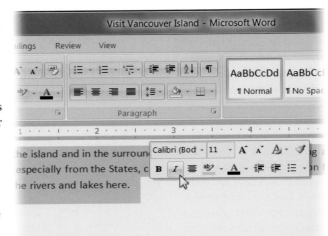

...AND MORE BESIDES

For an even broader range of Ribbon tools, right click anywhere in the document. The mini toolbar appears, along with a pop-up menu that includes the Clipboard tools and access to the **Font** and **Paragraph** ⬜ dialog boxes, as well as tools from the **Insert** ⬜ and **Review** Ribbon tabs.

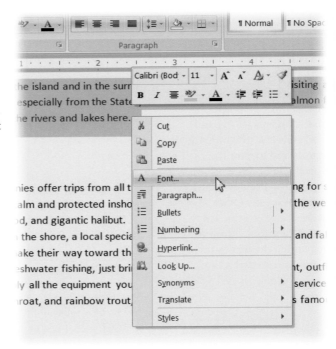

Paragraph Formatting

The formatting of a paragraph determines where and how the lines of text appear on the page. The standard formatting that Word gives the text automatically is designed to make it clear and legible, but you will often want to make text stand out by creating a list or having it indented or centered on the page. In this section, we are going to look at the tools for doing just this.

THE PARAGRAPH COMMANDS GROUP

● This group controls the organization of text entries into bulleted or numbered lists, the horizontal position of text, and the space between lines and between paragraphs. You can also sort text into numerical or alphabetical order, place colored shading behind the text, and add a border.

FEATURES KEY

● **Alignment**
These buttons are used to align the selected text with the left-hand margin, to center it on the page, range it right, or justify it with both margins.

● **Lists**
Click on one of these to create a bulleted list, numbered list, or multilevel list.

● **Decrease/Increase Indent**
To indent a selected paragraph or series of lines, click on the right-hand button. Successive clicks will steadily increase the indent. The left-hand button decreases the indent.

● **Sort Text**
With lines of text selected, clicking here brings up a dialog box allowing you to sort the lines into alphabetical order.

● **Show/Hide**
Click here to make formatting marks, such as paragraph marks and letter spaces, visible throughout the document. Click again to hide them.

● **Borders**
Click on the arrow to the right of this button to place a border around selected text.

● **Shading**
Click on the arrow to the right of this button to select a color and create shading.

● **Line spacing**
Click this button to change the spacing between selected lines of text, and to add or remove space before or after a paragraph of text.

ALIGNMENT OF TEXT

● The standard alignment of normal text in Word is ranged left, which means that the left-hand ends of the lines align vertically while the right-hand ends remain "ragged."

● With the text highlighted, simply click on one of the alignment buttons to change the text to centered (shown here), ranged right, or justified (with all the text except the last line aligned vertically at both ends).

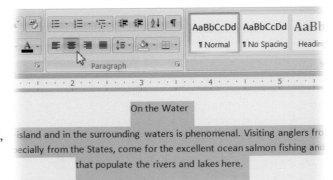

On the Water

island and in the surrounding waters is phenomenal. Visiting anglers fro
ecially from the States, come for the excellent ocean salmon fishing and
that populate the rivers and lakes here.

offer trips from all the coastal towns to take you trolling for several spe
and protected inshore waters, or out to the banks off the west coast of

LINE SPACING

● The space between the lines of text is proportional to the size of the font with an additional 1.15 points of space added in Normal text, but you can change this if you wish.

With the paragraph selected, click on the **Line** spacing button and select the amount of space you want to add.

● In the panel at the bottom of the menu you can opt to add space before

the paragraph or remove the space that Word automatically inserts after every Normal paragraph.

● If you click on **Line Spacing Options**, the Paragraph dialog box will open.

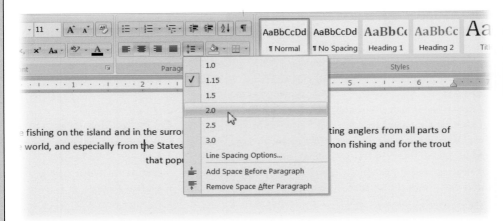

The Paragraph
230 Dialog Box

ADDING SHADING

● To place the selected text in a colored panel, click on the **Shading** button to open the color palette.
● Here you can choose from the Theme Colors and a range of standard colors, or create your own.
● As you hover the cursor over each color, a panel of that color appears behind the text.

ADDING A BORDER

● Click on the arrow to the right of the Borders button to open the drop-down menu. Here we are selecting **Outside Borders** to put a frame around the tint panel. Word treats each paragraph as a cell, and places lines between highlighted paragraphs if **Inside Borders** is selected.

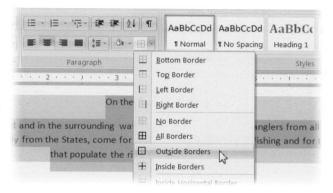

WHAT IS A PARAGRAPH?

In Word, a paragraph is any piece of text–be it a single word or several pages of text–that ends with a "hard" return, created by pressing [Enter ←] on the keyboard. The end of a paragraph is indicated in the text by a paragraph mark, which can be seen if you make the hidden formatting symbols visible by clicking on the Show/Hide button. Whereas most font commands affect only text that has been highlighted, paragraph commands affect the whole of the paragraph in which the insertion point has been positioned. If you want all the paragraphs in a sequence to be altered when a change is made to one of them, either highlight them all or create the breaks and line spaces between them using "soft" returns by holding the [⇧ Shift] key down when you hit the [Enter ←] key. They will then behave like a single paragraph.

269 Using Themes

223 Features Key

● Here we see the result–
a framed and tinted text
panel that stands out from
the page.

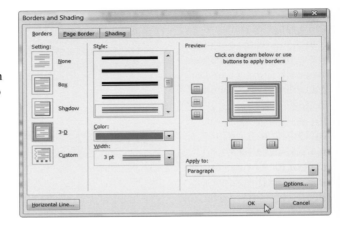

BORDERS AND SHADING

● For a wider sets of
choices, click on **Borders
and Shading** at the bottom
of the drop-down menu to
open this dialog box.

● Here you can choose
the style and color of the
border, as well as using
the other tabs to give the
page a border of its own
or pattern the shading of
the text box.

BULLETED LISTS

● Here we have keyed in the
names of the Southern Gulf
Islands off Vancouver, and
we want to make this into
a clear, bulleted list.

● We begin by highlighting
the names and then clicking
on the arrow next to the
Bullets button.

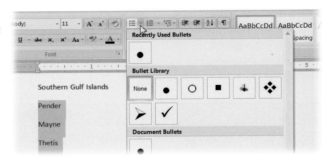

● As the cursor rolls over
each option in the **Bullet
Library**, the list adopts that
particular style of bullet.

● Click on an option to
finalize the choice.

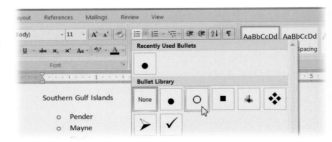

NUMBERED LISTS

- The next tool, which is **Numbering**, has a similar effect but places a number or letter before each entry.

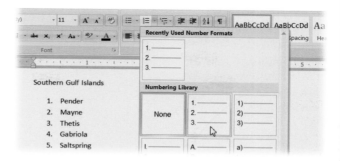

MULTILEVEL LISTS

- In this example, the list has a heading and two sub-headings, and we want to distinguish between the levels.
- With the text highlighted, click on the arrow to the right of the Multilevel List button.
- Here we have selected the first option in the second row of the **List Library**, and all entries have instantly been assigned a bullet and the first level of indent. To change the level of the sub-heading, select it and click on the **Multilevel List** button again.
- Now click on **Change List Level** and select the next level by clicking on it.

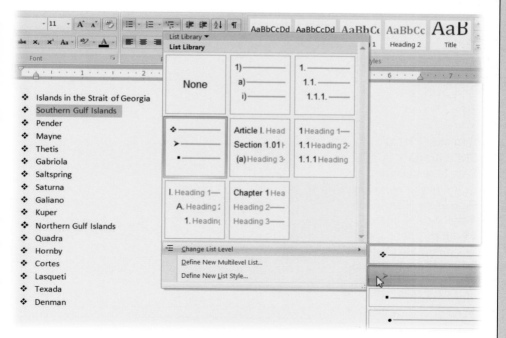

● We're now going to change the level of the island names, but we'll do this another way.

● Select the text and then click twice on the **Increase Indent** button.

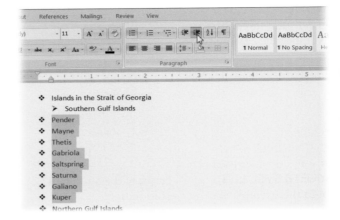

● With each click, the list is indented to the next level and the style of the bullet changes accordingly.

ALPHABETICAL ORDERING

● We have now formatted the list, but it would look neater if the islands were in alphabetical order.

● With the list selected, click on the **Sort** button to open the **Sort Text** dialog box. This is a simple list, so none of the options needs changing and we can just click **OK**…

● …and the islands are now in alphabetical order.

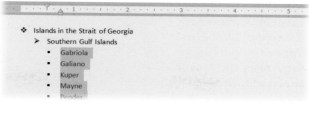

NUMERICAL ORDERING

● A list in which each line starts with a number can be put in order using the same tool, but select **Number** from the drop-down list in the **Sort by Type** panel before clicking **OK**. Paragraphs can be ordered by date in the same way.

INDENTING TEXT

● Paragraphs can be made to stand out from the rest of the text by using various forms of indent. These are controlled by using the indent markers on the ruler at the top of the page.

● The small rectangle at the left-hand end of the ruler and the upward-pointing triangle at the right-hand end are the left and right indent markers.

● Moving these in toward the center of the page will indent selected paragraphs on the left and the right.

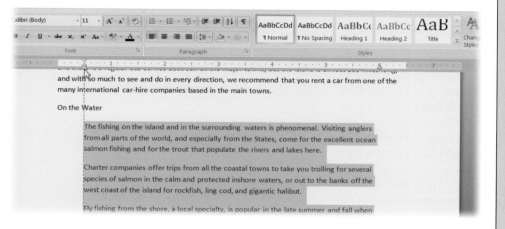

- The downward-pointing triangle at the top left is the first line indent marker.
- Move it away from the margin to indent the first line of a selected paragraph.

- The upward-pointing triangle at the left-hand end is the hanging indent marker. Moving this away from the margin will indent all the lines except the first in each selected paragraph.

THE PARAGRAPH DIALOG BOX

- As in the case of the Font group, many of the commands we have been looking at can be found in a dialog box.
- Click on the arrow at the bottom right of the **Paragraph** group to open the **Paragraph** dialog box.
- Here you can control alignment and indents, as well as line and paragraph spacing. If you are working on a document with lots of running text and you don't want a gap after every paragraph, you may want to put a tick in the check box next to **Don't add space between paragraphs of the same style**.

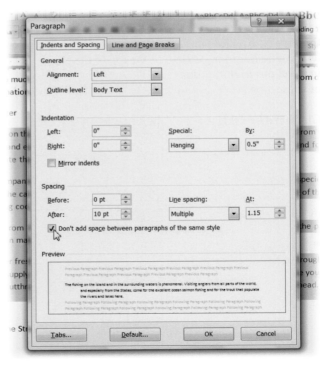

Cut, Copy, and Paste

The tools for cutting, copying, and pasting text, and for copying the formatting of text using the Format Painter, will be familiar to users of previous versions of Word and they work in the same way. However, the Clipboard is now much more accessible and you will undoubtedly find it much easier to use.

THE CLIPBOARD GROUP

● Located at the left-hand end of the **Home** tab, the **Clipboard** group of commands consist of **Cut**, Copy, **Paste**, and **Format Painter**. Unless some text has been highlighted, the **Cut** and **Copy** commands will be grayed out, as will the **Paste** command unless text has already been placed in the clipboard by cutting or copying it.

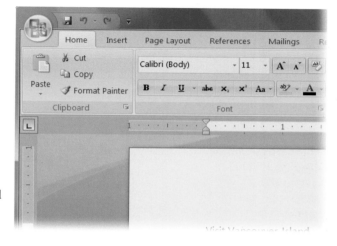

CUTTING AND COPYING TEXT

● Highlight the text to be copied by dragging the cursor through the text.
● Clicking on **Cut** removes the highlighted text from the document.
● Clicking on **Copy** leaves the text in place, but whether the text has been cut or copied, it will be placed on the Clipboard.

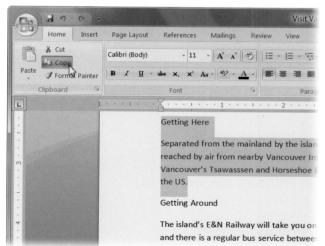

• Text can also be cut or copied by right clicking on the highlighted paragraph and selecting the appropriate command from the pop-up menu that appears.

• Alternatively, use the keyboard shortcuts Ctrl X to cut or Ctrl C to copy.

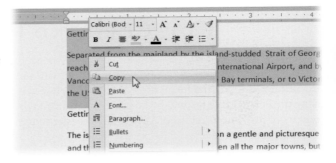

VIEWING THE CLIPBOARD

• To view all the text elements that have been saved to the clipboard, click on the arrow at the bottom right of the Clipboard group.

• Here we can see the paragraph that has just been copied, together with text that has previously been cut or copied.

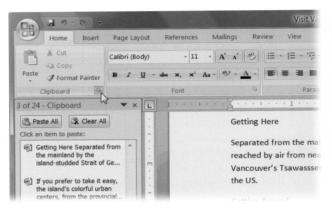

PASTING TEXT

• To paste cut or copied text into a document, left click to position the insertion point where you want the text to be pasted. In this case we have opened a new document.

• Clicking on the **Paste** button or using the keyboard shortcut Ctrl V will paste the last text that we cut or copied.

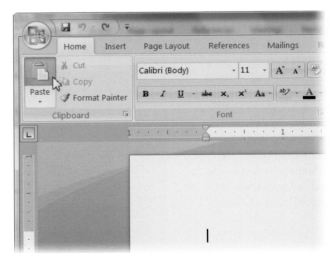

• However, the Clipboard offers a much wider range of choices, as it contains all the text elements that we have cut or copied.

• With the Clipboard open, any one of these paragraphs can be pasted simply by clicking on it.

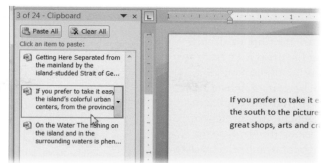

PASTE OPTIONS

• When the text appears in the new position, you will see a small Clipboard icon at the end of the paragraph.

island's colorful urban centers, from the provincial capital, Vict
hing towns of the northern coast, offer a wide range of entertai
excellent food and wines.

• Click on this icon to reveal the Paste Options. By default, the text will retain the formatting it had in its original position.

• You can click on **Set Default Paste** to change the default setting, or use this drop-down menu to change the option in a particular instance, as we are doing in this example.

island's colorful urban centers, from the provincial capital, Vict
hing towns of the northern coast, offer a wide range of entertai
excellent food and wines.

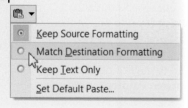

• The text now has the formatting (font, size, color, style, and line spacing) of the document into which it has been pasted.

URBAN CENTERS, FROM THE PROVINCIAL CAPITAL,
OWNS OF THE NORTHERN COAST, OFFER A WIDE RANGE OF
EXCELLENT FOOD AND WINES.

The Font Group

CLEARING ITEMS

● To clear all the items from the Clipboard, click on the **Clear All** button at the top of the panel.
● To clear an individual item from the Clipboard, right click on the item or click on the arrow to the right of it, and select **Delete** from the menu that appears.

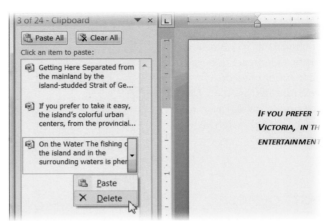

FORMAT PAINTER

● This is a very useful tool if you have formatted the individual aspects of a paragraph and want to use all the same formatting for other paragraphs.
● Here we wish to take the formatting of a paragraph in our second document and apply it to one in the first one we looked at.
● Highlight the paragraph, and then click on the **Format Painter** button.

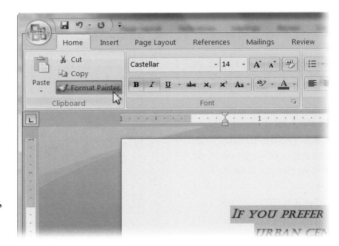

● When we go to the other document we find that the Format Painter button is still highlighted, showing that the tool is active, and when we move the cursor over a paragraph it turns into a paintbrush icon. Click and drag to highlight the whole paragraph.

● When you release the mouse button, the paragraph adopts the new formatting. When you click off the paragraph, you can see clearly that the font, size, and color of the text have all changed, and the line is now centered on the page.

VISIT VANCOUVER ISLAND

Vancouver Island, in British Columbia, is the largest island on the west coas
mountains and forests, rivers and lakes, and its fabulous coastline of sandy
inlets, Vancouver Island is the perfect location for every conceivable kind o
prefer to take it easy, the island's colorful urban centers, from the provincia
south to the picturesque fishing towns of the northern coast, offer a wide
shops, arts and crafts, and excellent food and wines. It doesn't matter whe
visit malls and museums, galleries and theaters, to relax at waterfront café
fishing or golfing, kayaking or horseback riding, hiking or cruising—you can

EASY ACCESS

● The Format Painter tool is also available in the mini toolbar that appears when you hover the cursor over highlighted text .
● If you move your cursor away from the highlighted paragraph several times, you may find that the mini toolbar stops appearing.
● If so, either highlight the text again or right click on it to bring the toolbar back.

MORE ABOUT FORMAT PAINTER

If you wish to copy the formatting of just the text and not the paragraph formatting, highlight just a few words before clicking on the **Format Painter** button. To "paint" the formatting to part of a paragraph, highlight only that part before releasing the mouse button. Clicking on a single word will apply the formatting to just that word. To apply formatting to separate paragraphs, double click on the **Format Painter** button when you select it. When you finish "painting," hit the [Esc] key to close the tool and return the cursor to normal.

BUILDING BLOCKS

To save you creating every aspect of your document from scratch, Word comes complete with a battery of ready-made elements from which to choose.

INSERTING STANDARD ELEMENTS

Whether you are writing letters, business reports, or school projects, you will frequently find yourself putting the same elements into your documents. These might include page numbers, headers and footers, or a cover page. Word has all of these ready for you to use in a wide range of styles, and also enables you to make your own custom elements. Most can be accessed from the **Insert** tab of the Ribbon toolbar.

INSERTING PAGES

● Starting at the left-hand end of the **Insert** tab, we have the Pages group.

● Click on **Cover Page** to display a palette of built-in cover page designs to give your document a truly professional look from the word "Go."

● Use the scroll bar on the right to look through them, and click on one to select it.

● Here, we are selecting the **Annual** style.

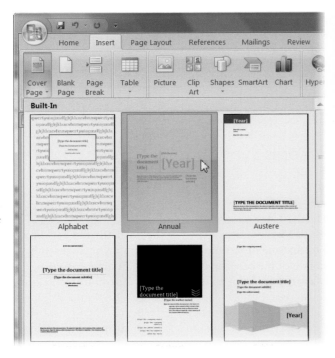

● The cover page, which automatically becomes the first page of your document, contains cells into which you can key your own text.

● If you change your mind, click again on **Cover Page** and select **Remove Current Cover Page.**

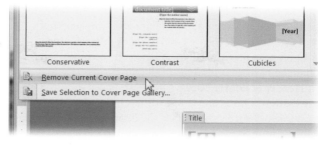

● The next button inserts a blank page, which you might want, for example, between the cover page and a list of contents.

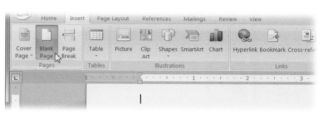

● Clicking on the **Page Break** button inserts a break at the insertion point and restarts the text on the following page, for example for the start of a new chapter or for a new topic.

HEADERS AND FOOTERS

● The next Building Blocks are to be found in the Header & Footer group.

● Click on the **Header** button to reveal a drop-down selection of built-in header styles from which to choose.

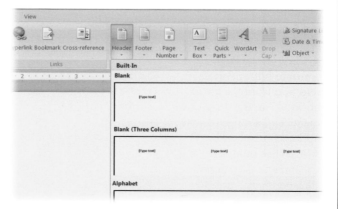

- Like cover pages, headers contain text to overtype.
- As you can see, the Ribbon has automatically changed to display a range of **Header & Footer Tools** for **Design**. This is an example of Word's context-specific tools.

- Here you can insert the date and time or other building blocks, move between sections of the document, specify that certain pages should have different headers, and adjust the depth of the header and the footer.

- **Table Tools** tabs for **Design** and **Layout** are also displayed, as the header is formatted as a table .
- To return to the document, double click in the text area or click on the **Close Header and Footer** button at the top right.

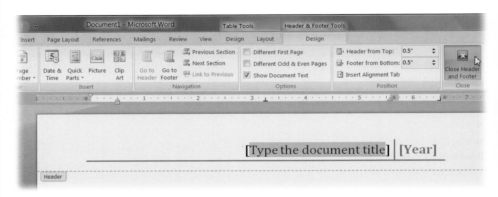

- The **Footer** button works in the same way for footers, offering the same range of styles as the **Header** button.

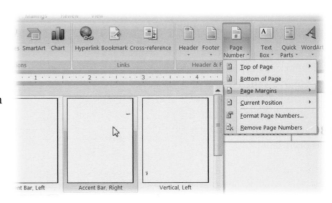

INSERTING PAGE NUMBERS

- Click on the **Page Number** button, make a selection from the list of positions on the drop-down menu, and a range of style options is displayed.
- Just click on one to select it and then double click on the text area to return to the document.

INSERTING A TEXT BOX

In anything but a simple letter or typescript, there will be times when text needs to be made to stand out from the flow of the main text. For example, you may need to create a side note, a quote, or a caption to a picture. Word makes this easy with the Text Box tool, in the Text group on the Insert tab.

SELECTING A TEXT BOX

- Clicking on the **Text Box** button brings up a selection of ready-made boxes and sidebars, as well as the option to draw your own text box.
- Here we're choosing a sidebar that matches the header we chose earlier.

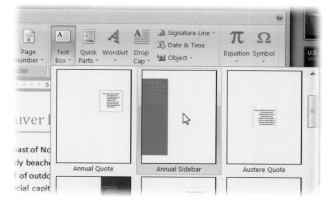

CHOOSING A POSITION

- The sidebar appears on the right-hand side of the page. We want it to be on the left, but that's not a problem. Together with the sidebar, a set of **Text Box Tools** has also appeared, and we can use this to adjust almost every aspect of the chosen text box.
- Begin by clicking on the **Position** button to see a range of options.

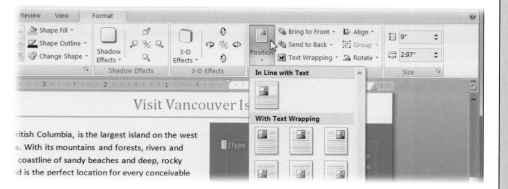

● As you hover the cursor over each of the **Position** options, the sidebar moves to a new position.

● We're choosing to place it on the left of the page, centered vertically, so we're clicking on that option.

The sidebar moves to the left side of the page

MOVING THE TEXT BOX

● To adjust the position of the box, move the cursor over an empty part of the box until it turns into a four-pointed arrow.

● Now click and drag the box in any direction.

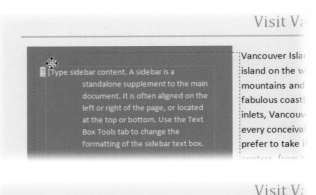

CHANGING PROPORTIONS

● The size and proportions of the box can be adjusted by using the handles at the corners and the midpoint of each side.

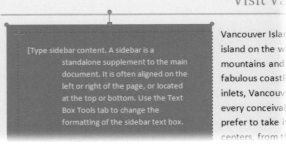

ROTATING THE TEXT BOX

● To change the angle of the tinted panel, move the cursor over the green rotation handle at the top of the box.

● Click, and then drag the box round.

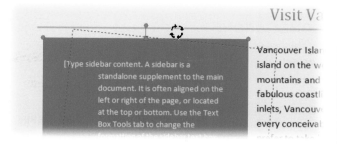

CUSTOMIZING THE BOX STYLE

● In the **Text Box Styles** group we can choose to change the box to one of a ready-made selection. These have a range of different colors, color gradients, borders, and shadow effects.

● Alternatively, we can adjust these elements separately using the **Shape Fill**, **Shape Outline**, and **Change Shape** buttons.

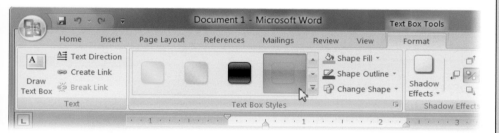

FILLING WITH A PICTURE

● Some interesting effects can be achieved by filling a text box with a picture.

● Simply click on the **Picture** option in the **Shape Fill** menu, navigate to a saved image on your computer, and click **Insert**.

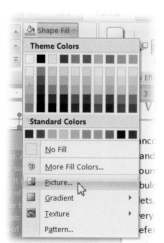

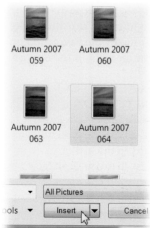

ENDLESS COMBINATIONS

● The rest of the Text Box **Format** tab contains tools to add a huge range of shadow and 3-D effects to the text box, and to alter its relation to the main text.

● You will see that at the top of the Ribbon, Word has now given us an additional set of **Picture Tools** for formatting the background image that we inserted–clever stuff.

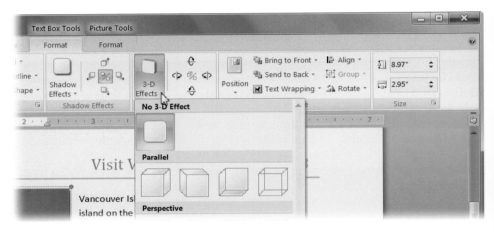

FORMAT AUTOSHAPE

● Many of these same options can be found in the **Format AutoShape** dialog box that opens if you click on the arrow at the bottom right of the Text Box Styles group or the Size group on the far right of the Ribbon.

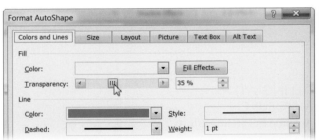

PLACING TEXT IN THE BOX

● To insert text, either overtype the placeholder text in the box or paste in text that you've already keyed in elsewhere.

● You can use the tools in the **Home** tab to reformat the text in the box .

QUICK PARTS AND BUILDING BLOCKS

The innocuous-looking **Quick Parts** button is actually at the heart of much of what we've been looking at in this section. Quick Parts and Building Blocks are the same things, and all the cover pages, headers, footers, page numbers, and text boxes that we have seen can all be reached from here. So, too, can additional useful building blocks such as watermarks, calendars, and equations.

QUICK PARTS BUTTON

- Click on the **Quick Parts** button and this drop-down menu appears.
- We're going to click on the **Building Blocks Organizer**.

BUILDING BLOCKS ORGANIZER

- Here we can select any of the building blocks that we have already seen, including the cover page that we chose earlier.
- A single click will give a preview of the particular item. Click on the **Insert** button to insert it in the document. In this view, the items are arranged in groups according the gallery in which they can be found, so, for example, all the cover pages are together.

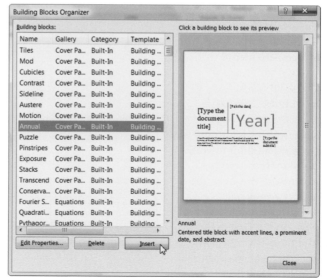

- If you want to choose elements that belong to the same design family, click on the **Name** column head at the top left of the list to arrange them by name.
- Now we can choose an Annual quote box that matches the Annual cover page and the sidebar that we selected previously.

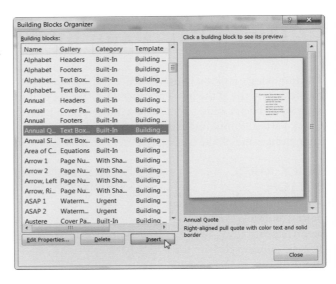

AN EASY SHORTCUT

- You can go straight to the Building Blocks Organizer from any of the galleries (such as a Cover Page or Header) by right clicking on any entry and choosing **Organize and Delete** from the pop-up menu.

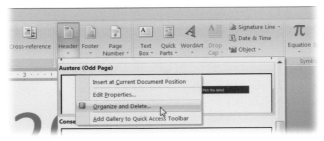

DELETING A BUILDING BLOCK

- As the menu option suggests, this is also the way to delete a building block– not just from your document, but from the gallery completely.
- With the item selected, click on the **Delete** button, and then–if you're sure– click **Yes** when asked to confirm your decision.

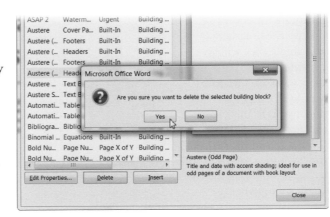

MAKE YOUR OWN QUICK PARTS

● One of the most vital features of Word's Quick Parts–and one that will save you hours of work if you regularly produce documents for business purposes–is the facility to add your own custom-made building blocks. You'll find it's all very easy.

● You remember the text box that we selected  and changed to make it the way we wanted it? Well, now we want to add our handiwork to the building blocks.

● First, select it by clicking on it on the page and then, on the **Insert** tab, select **Quick Parts** and then click on **Save Selection to Quick Part Gallery**.

● The **Create New Building Block** dialog box opens.

● Give it a name (the first line of text in the box is used as the default name, but we're calling it **Photo sidebar**), choose which gallery to save it in (**Text Boxes**, in this case) and give it a brief description.

● In the **Options** panel you can choose to insert it in its own page or paragraph (options that suit a cover page or block of text), but we're selecting **Insert content only**.

● Click on **OK** to complete the process.

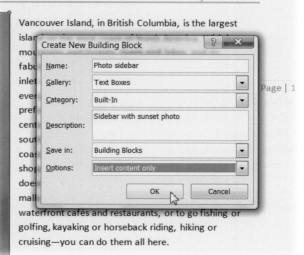

239 **Selecting a Text Box**

● Now, in any document, we can go to the Text Box gallery or the Building Blocks Organizer, find our Photo sidebar and insert it.
● In the Text Box gallery, its title and description appear next to the cursor if we hover over the item.

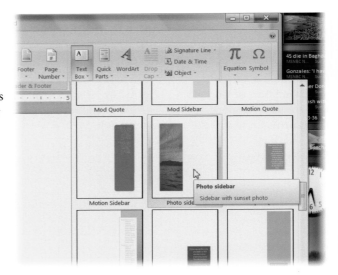

● In the Building Blocks Organizer, these details appear below the preview when the item is selected.

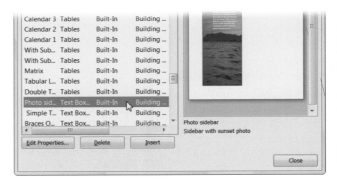

SAVING BUILDING BLOCK CHANGES

● When we go to close our document after amending or creating anything that is stored in the Building Blocks gallery, Word pops up a warning box.
● Before clicking **Yes** or **No**, consider for a moment whether or not you want to save those specific changes.
● If you've just been experimenting, you may not want the changes saved.

DOCUMENT PROPERTIES

Saving a selection to the Quick Part gallery can be used to turn any part of a document–be it a customized footer, your company logo, or a disclaimer paragraph– into a re-usable building block, but if you were thinking this would be a good way to insert your address every time you need it, Microsoft is one step ahead of you.

OPENING DOCUMENT PROPERTY

● To follow the steps in this section, start by opening a new document in Word.

● Now click on the **Insert** tab, and then on the **Quick Parts** button.

● Move your cursor over the top option, **Document Property**, and a list of "property controls" appears.

● To follow this example, click on **Title** at the bottom of the list.

KEYING IN THE PROPERTY DETAILS

● This **Title** box, or property control, appears at the insertion point, with placeholder text already highlighted ready for you to overtype it.

● Key in a sample title for your document.

USING THE PROPERTY CONTROL
● Now click on the **Cover Page** button and select the **Annual** cover page by clicking on it once.

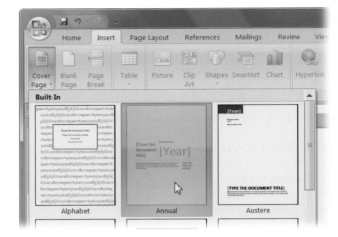

● When the cover page appears in your document, you will see, in the top left panel, the text you just typed in.
● This is because the panel contains the Title document property that we just completed in the Quick Parts Document Property list. Any building block that contains the Title property control will automatically display these words.

THE PROCESS IN REVERSE
● Now click in the **Abstract** box below the title and key in some text to replace the placeholder text that is already there.

Title

Visit Vancouver Island

[Pick the

[Type the abstract of the document here. The abstract is typ summary of the contents of the document. Type the abstra document here. The abstract is typically a short summary o of the document.]

Island

Abstract

Your guide to all that Vancouver Island has to offer, includin on travel to and around the island, accommodation, towns a national and provincial parks, hiking trails, and a wide range activities, with recommended charter companies and outfitt

● Scroll down to the top of the next page and double click below the Title text to position the insertion point.
● Click the **Quick Parts** button, select **Document Property**, and click on **Abstract**.

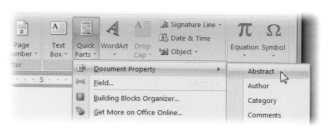

● The text that we just keyed into the Abstract property control panel on the cover page has now been pasted in here.

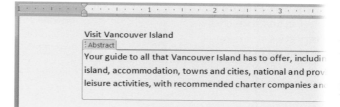

CHANGE ONE, CHANGE ALL

● To make things even more interesting, let's make a change to this text.
● Here, we've changed **Vancouver** to **Coney**.
● Now click in the text area outside the text box.

● Now scroll back up to your cover page and you will find that the Abstract text here has changed, too.
● Here we see the value of Document Properties. When a change is made to the property control in one place, that same change is made throughout the document wherever that property control appears.

DOCUMENT INFORMATION

- Some of the document properties can be input or updated in the Document Information Panel.
- To open this, click on the **Office** button at the top left of the screen, move your cursor over **Prepare** to select it, and then click on **Properties** at the top of the pop-up menu.

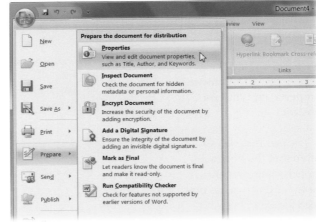

- The Document Information Panel opens between the Ribbon and the page top.

- Any changes you make to the document properties here will be made to those same properties throughout the document, and any changes made elsewhere will, in turn, be reflected here.

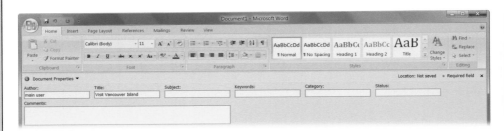

DATE & TIME

Although it isn't technically a Building Block or a Document Property, Word's "date and time" feature is a useful add-in. To place the current date and/or time in a Word document, go to the right-hand end of the **Insert** toolbar and click on the **Date & Time** button. In the dialog box that appears, choose from a selection of different formats in which the date, time, or both can be inserted on the page. If you place a tick in the check box next to **Update Automatically**, the date/time will be updated whenever you open the document. To update these manually, click on the date and then on **Update**.

Using WordArt

The WordArt button opens a gallery of decorative text styles to enliven and brighten your documents, but at first glance you may feel there's no style that matches precisely what you want. No problem. Like text boxes or any other ready-made element in Word, a WordArt item can be customized in any way you wish, and it can then be saved as a Building Block for you to use again.

OPENING WORDART
● Click on the **WordArt** button to open the gallery of styles.
● Here you will find 25 styles for horizontal text, and five styles for vertical.
● Click on one. It doesn't matter which one you choose for this example.

EDITING THE WORDART TEXT
● When this dialog box appears, simply overtype the placeholder text with the text that you want. This can be changed later, and you will be returning to this dialog box if you want to change the font or font size, or to embolden or italicize the text.

● With your text keyed in, click on **OK**.

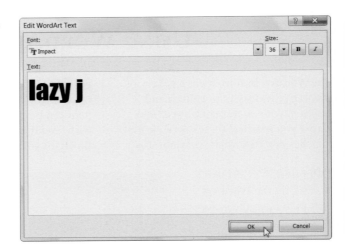

● Your text in the chosen WordArt style will appear in its own frame on the page at the insertion point.

UNLIMITED CHOICES

● As in the case of the text box , a new set of tools has appeared in the Ribbon. With these, you can do virtually anything to your decorative text.

● To begin with, as you roll your cursor over the WordArt styles on the Ribbon, you can see what your text would look like in that style.

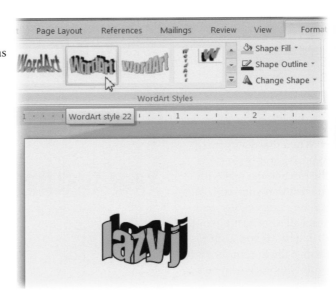

CHANGING SIZE AND PROPORTIONS

● Hover your cursor over any of the handles to drag the WordArt to the size and proportions you want.

FILL, OUTLINE, AND SHAPE TOOLS

● Use the **Shape Fill**, **Shape Outline**, and **Change Shape** tools to change the colors and overall shape of the lettering, but be aware that it's very easy to mangle the text so much that it's illegible.

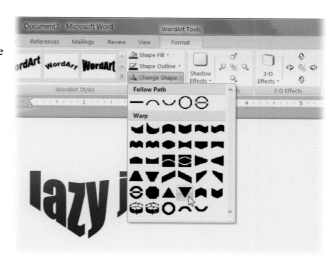

SHADOW AND 3-D EFFECTS

● With these tools, you can not only add shadows and perspective but also alter the direction from which the light appears to be falling and the tilt of the text itself.

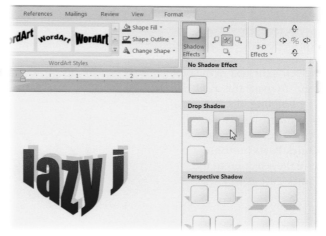

FORMATTING THE TEXT

● After a bit more tweaking, you may decide that you want to change the font.

● To return to the Edit dialog box, click on **Edit Text** at the left-hand end of the Ribbon, or right click on the **WordArt** and then click on **Edit Text** in the pop-up menu that appears.

● When the **Edit WordArt Text** dialog box opens, use the scroll bar to locate the font you want, and then click to select it.

● Click on **OK** to implement the change.

● Here's the text in the new font. To make this available as a Building Block to use as a company logo, we need only select it, click on the **Quick Parts** button, and save the selection to the Quick Part gallery 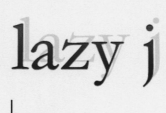.

Make Your Own Quick Parts

MOVING THE WORDART ITEM

● By default, the text wrapping–the way the item is located in relation to any text on the page–is set to be **In Line with Text**.

● As a result, you cannot move the item. To change this, begin by highlighting the WordArt, click on the **Page Layout** tab on the Ribbon, and then click on the **Text Wrapping** button on the right-hand side of the Page Layout toolbar.

● Now select any of the other text wrapping settings from the drop-down menu. We're selecting **Square**.

● The WordArt now has handles similar to those we saw on the text box .
● As the cursor rolls over it, a four-pointed arrow appears and you can drag it to a new position.

● You can also click and drag on the green rotation handle, and turn the WordArt to any angle.

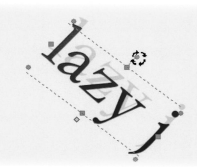

Styles and Themes

When it comes to making your documents look good, quickly and simply, two of the most useful features of Word 2007 are Quick Styles and Themes. This section shows you how to use them.

Using Quick Styles

We've seen how to format text to give it the font, size, color, and spacing that we want, but wouldn't it be great if combinations of these qualities came as ready-made packages? Well, that's what Quick Styles are. With names like Heading 1, Emphasis, and Quote, each style can be applied to selected text, and all the styles in a single Quick Style set work together to give your document a smart and coherent look.

SELECTING THE TEXT

● As when formatting text, the text must be highlighted in order to apply a new style. Here, we have begun by highlighting the heading on a page of our travel guide. We have clicked on the **Home** tab, and in the **Styles** group on the right-hand half of the Ribbon, we can see that the **Normal** style is selected. All text keyed into a blank Word document appears in this style by default. To see the full range of styles available in this set, click on the bottom arrow at the right-hand end of the **Styles** panel.

CHOOSING A STYLE

● Now move your cursor over any of the styles in the gallery that has opened.

● As you do so, you will see the selected text take on that particular style.

● In this case, the cursor is over the **Title** style, which is dark blue, underlined, 26-point Cambria with a 15-point space after it.

● All the styles in this gallery use either Cambria or Calibri in a range of sizes and colors.

● Click on your chosen style to apply it to the selected text.

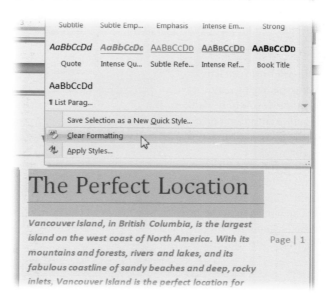

CONTINUING THE STYLING

● Body text, captions, boxed text, quotes, and various levels of heading can each be given their own style using this method.

● Here we have applied the **Intense Emphasis** style to the running text below the heading.

● If you wish to return text to **Normal** style, highlight the text, click again on the arrow to open the Styles gallery, and then click on **Clear Formatting**.

USING THE STYLES WINDOW

● The same styles can be seen, along with details of each one, in the **Styles** window, which opens when you click on the arrow at the extreme bottom right of the **Styles** group.

● A paragraph mark and an "a" after a style indicates that it includes paragraph, as well as font, formatting.

● If you hover your cursor over a style in the list, a pop-up box details the attributes of that style.

● If you click on it, that style will be applied to the highlighted text.

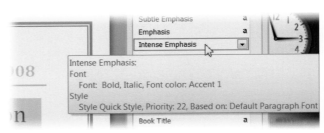

● If you find yourself using the **Styles** window frequently, you may want to pull it into the screen by dragging the top band of the window.

● Drag it back off the window to reposition it at the side again.

● The window can be closed by clicking on the "**x**" in the top right corner.

USING OTHER STYLE SETS

● As we have seen, this set of Quick Styles has a limited range of fonts and colors associated with it, but it doesn't end here. Click on the Change Styles button at the right-hand end of the Styles group.

● Move your cursor over **Style Set** in the drop-down menu to open this list.

● The tick next to **Word 2007** tells us that we are currently using this Quick Styles set.

● Now move your cursor over any of the Style Set names, and see how the text changes. The range of fonts remains the same but the styling of the text, including the header, changes to reflect the new style set.

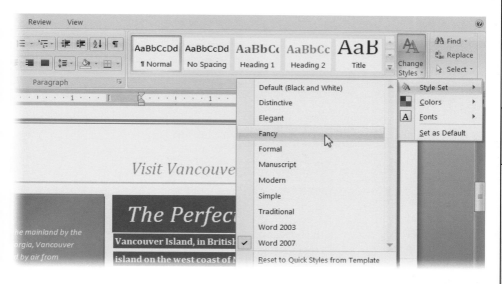

● Here, we've selected the Fancy style by clicking on it and then we've opened the Style gallery to display the new set of styles that is now available.

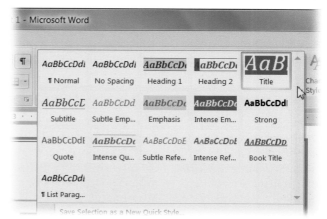

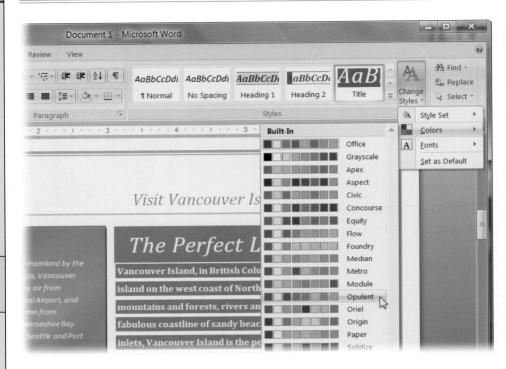

CHANGING THE COLORS

● To change the range of colors being used, click again on the **Change Styles** button and select **Colors**.

● A list of **Built-In** color schemes is displayed, and the border of the Office colors is highlighted, showing that this is the range of colors in use.

● Rolling the cursor over the various color themes changes the colors, not only of the fonts but also of the other color elements, including the page border and even the logo that we have inserted in the header.

● Click on a theme name to apply those colors to your text. In this example, we're selecting **Opulent**.

A QUESTION OF SIZE

While the first six styles in the gallery attribute a specific size and font to the text, the other styles leave the font and size as they find them and simply apply different formatting to them, e.g., bold or italic. For this reason, if you apply the **Intense Emphasis** style to **Normal** text, it remains in 11-point Calibri. On the other hand, if you apply this style to text that has already been styled as **Title,** it will appear as 26-point Cambria. Both, however, will be mid-blue bold italic.

CHANGING THE FONTS

● To change the pair of fonts that are used through the document, select **Fonts** from the **Change Styles** drop-down menu and then click on a new pair of fonts.

● You will see that these pairs have the same names as the color swatches that we've just seen, and the reason for this will become evident when we look at Themes a little later 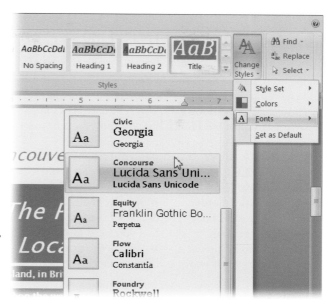. Here, we're choosing **Concourse**.

MAKING THIS THE DEFAULT SETTING

● If you feel that you'd like to use this combination of Style Set, Colors, and Fonts for all documents based on the Normal template, click again on the **Change Styles** button and then on **Set as Default**.

RESETTING THE DEFAULT

If you change your mind, you can reset the Style Set, Colors, and Fonts to Word 2007, Office, and Office respectively, and click on **Set as Default** again.

CREATING CUSTOM STYLES

So far we've looked at using Quick Styles and changing the look of the document by choosing from among a built-in range of style sets, colors, and fonts, but you can also use any of the font and paragraph formatting tools to create custom-made styles or to modify existing styles and style sets to meet your needs.

CREATING A NEW QUICK STYLE

● Let's suppose that you need a new style in order to make some aspect of your document, such as references to leisure activities in the body text, stand out whenever it appears. We can easily create a new style for this.

● Start by giving a piece of text all the formatting that you need in the style.

● Here, we're using the mini toolbar to embolden the font, italicize it, and change its color to purple. Note that we are choosing from **Standard Colors**. If we were to choose from **Theme Colors**, the color would change if we were to alter the Theme □.

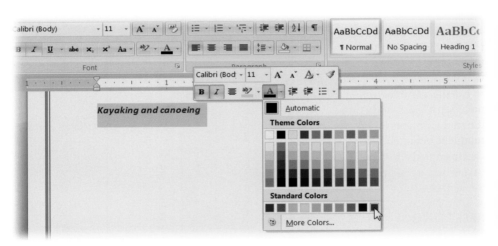

● Now right click on the text, go to **Styles** at the bottom of the pop-up menu and click on **Save Selection as a New Quick Style**.

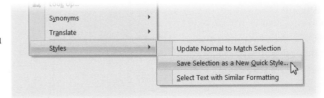

269 Applying a Built-In Theme

- In the **Create New Style from Formatting** dialog box, give the style a new name by overtyping the text in the **Name** panel, and click **OK**.

- The new style now appears in the Style gallery in the Ribbon.

- Now, when we highlight text and roll our cursor over the style, the text appears in that style. Click to select it.
- Note that this style has only been added to this document, and not to the template on which the document is based.

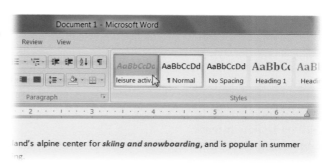

- To remove the new style from the document, open the **Styles** Window, right click on the style name, and then click on (in this case) **Delete leisure activity**.
- When asked to confirm, click on **Yes**.

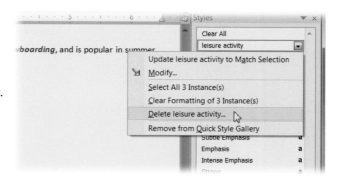

MODIFYING A STYLE IN USE

● When you are using a style in a document, you can easily modify it on the page and save these changes.
● Here, for example, we have highlighted a paragraph styled in **Intense Emphasis** and we're changing the color from blue to aqua.

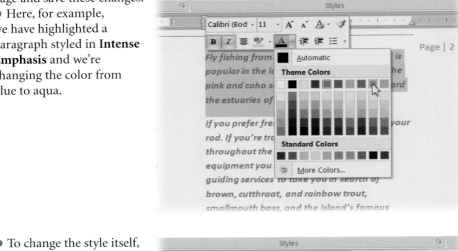

● To change the style itself, start by right clicking on the modified text.
● Now select **Styles** from the pop-up menu, and click on **Update Intense Emphasis** (or whatever the Style in question is called) **to Match Selection**.

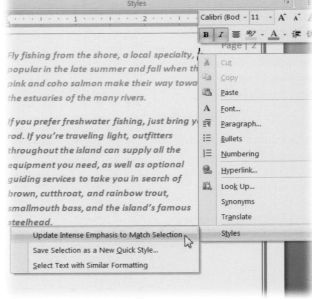

SEEING THE EFFECT

- We can immediately see the power of this tool.
- The color of this Quick Style displayed in the gallery has changed, and every instance of this style has been updated–not only on this page, but throughout the whole document.

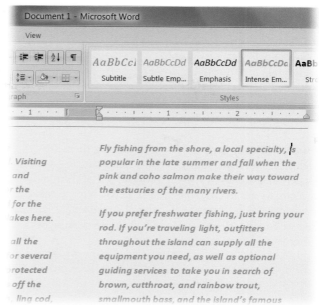

- If you change your mind, you can return to the default setting by clicking on **Change Styles**, selecting **Style Set**, and then clicking on **Reset Document Quick Styles**. This returns all the Quick Styles to their default setting and undoes any changes you have made to the Styles.

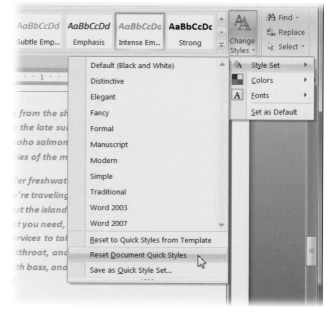

MODIFYING A STYLE DIRECTLY

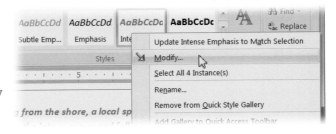

- Changes can be made to any Quick Style by right clicking on it in the Styles gallery or the Styles window and then selecting **Modify** in the pop-up menu.

- In the **Modify Style** dialog box you can change aspects of the chosen style.
- Here, we are making the same font color change that we made earlier.

- Note that there are two radio buttons at the bottom left of the dialog box. If you wish to make this changed style available in all future documents,

then you should click on the **New documents based on this template** radio button to select it.
- Click **OK** to confirm your selections.

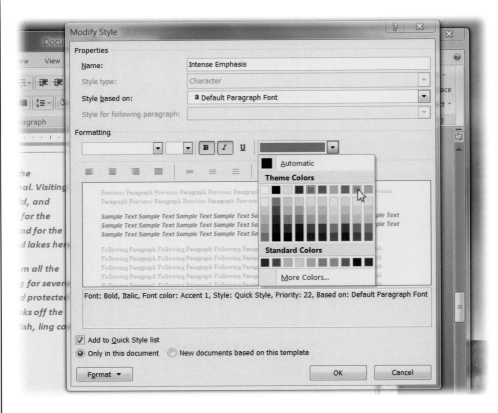

SAVING YOUR OWN QUICK STYLE SET

● To save all the changes you have made to the Quick Styles as a separate Style Set, click on **Change Styles**, select **Style Set**, and click on **Save as Quick Style Set**.

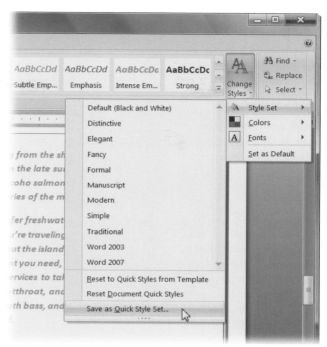

● In the **Save Quick Style Set** dialog box, give your style set a name by typing over the highlighted text in the **File name** panel (we're calling this one **B&B Literature**), and then click on **Save** at the bottom of the dialog box.

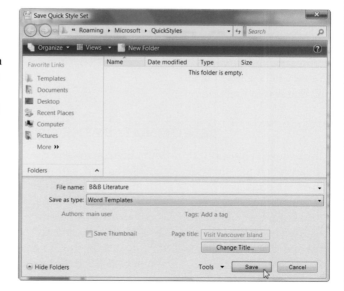

● If you now click on **Change Styles** and select **Style Set**, you will find your new Quick Styles set listed there, ready to use.

● Your custom style set is now part of the Normal template, and it will be available in all documents opened in this template.

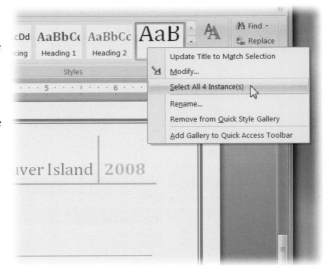

RESTYLING STYLED TEXT

● What happens if you have used a style throughout a document and then decide it's the wrong style?

● Fortunately, you can select all the text in one style and change it for another.

● In the Styles gallery, right click on the style you want to change, and then click on **Select All Instance(s)** in the pop-up menu.

● Any style that you now choose will be applied to all text that was in that style.

SELECTING TABS THE QUICK WAY

If you haven't already discovered it for yourself, there is a quick way of moving from tab to tab, for example when working with **Styles** in the **Home** tab and **Themes** in the **Page Layout** tab. Move your cursor anywhere over the Ribbon and, without clicking, roll your mouse wheel back and forth. As you do so, the tabs along the Ribbon will come to the fore one by one. When you have selected the tab you want, simply click on the tool you need. This is much more convenient than clicking one tab at a time, especially if you are looking for a particular command and you can't remember where to find it.

USING THEMES

We've seen how Quick Styles can be used to give a document a coherent feel by providing a palette of integrated styles, fonts, and colors. Well, Themes take this idea a good deal farther. Each Theme consists of a swatch of colors and a range of fonts, and they determine the range of available Quick Styles, but Themes also include a range of graphic effects. As well as affecting text, Themes also influence the look of every other element in the document, from headers and borders to charts and diagrams. Changing the Theme gives the whole document a complete makeover.

APPLYING A BUILT-IN THEME

● The Themes group of commands is located at the left-hand end of the **Page Layout** tab.

● Click on the **Themes** button to display the gallery of **Built-In** Themes and you will see that **Office** is highlighted, as this is the Normal template Theme.

● As you roll your cursor over the various themes, Word's live preview feature shows how your document would look if you were to apply each of them.

● Here, the cursor is hovering over the **Module** Theme, and we can see that the text fonts and colors have all changed, including the header, and so have the colors of the page border as well as the sidebar frame.

FINDING MORE THEMES ONLINE

- As if the 20 Themes in the gallery were not enough, clicking on **More Themes on Microsoft Office Online** opens the door to yet more.
- Providing you have an open Internet connection, Word goes online to Microsoft's Office web site.

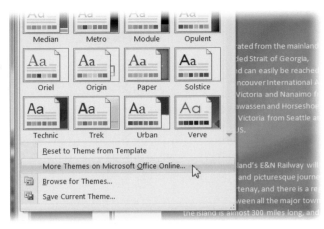

- In the Office Online **Office document themes** page, click on any of the theme titles to see the theme in more detail and then, if you wish, to download it to your computer.
- Before the download begins, Microsoft will automatically check your software to ensure that it is the genuine article.

CUSTOMIZING A THEME

● As in the case of the Quick Styles, we can select from the range of color palettes and font pairs (as well as the fill and line Effects) to create a custom Theme. Normally you would only amend one or two of these (or you might as well have chosen a different theme), but we'll look at changing all three.

● With the document set to the default Office theme, start by clicking on the **Colors** button in the Themes group, and then roll the cursor over the various options. Text, borders, and graphics all change color, but the fonts and styles, lines and fill effects remain unchanged.

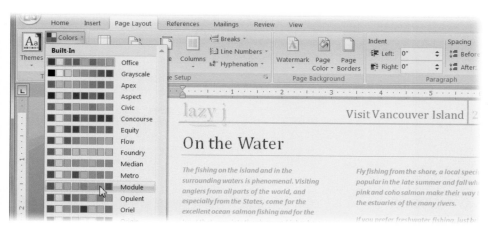

● Clicking on the **Fonts** button and scrolling through the different options, we can see just the font changing in the document.

● The colors and the graphic effects stay the same.

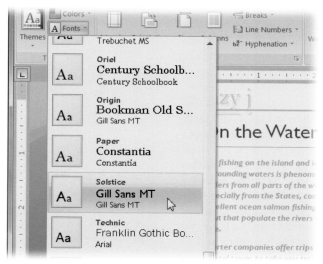

● The Effects are seen in action most clearly in charts and graphics. Click on the **Effects** button, and as your cursor rolls over the line and fill options you will see the changes reflected in any graphic illustrations in the document.

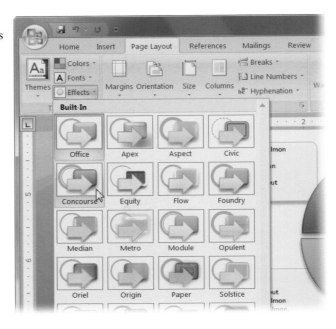

SAVING YOUR CUSTOM THEME

● We now have a Theme composed of the Module colors, the Solstice fonts, and the Concourse effects, and we feel we'd like to use this again in the future.

● To save the theme to the template, click on the **Themes** button and then on **Save Current Theme**.

● By the way, if you now click on the **Home** tab and check the **Styles** gallery, you will find that with your custom theme selected, all the Quick Styles now use Module colors and Solstice fonts.

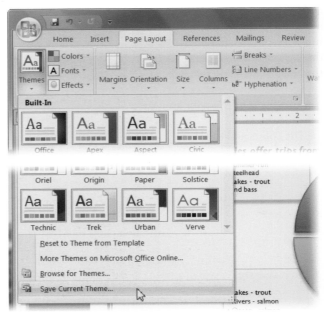

● In the **Save Current Theme** dialog box, type a name for your theme into the **File name** panel and click on **Save.**

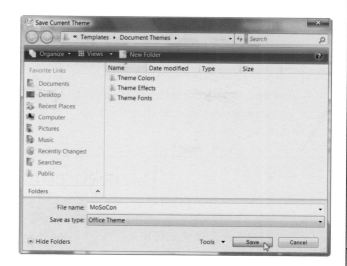

● Now, when we click on the **Themes** button, we see our new theme above the **Built-In** themes gallery in a newly-created **Custom** section. This theme will now be available in all documents created using the Normal template.

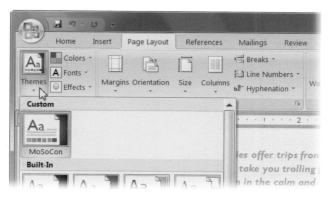

MICROSOFT HELP ONLINE

We have already seen that within Word we can go online to search for more Themes, but Microsoft's Office Online web site (**http://office.microsoft. com**) is well worth looking at for other reasons, too.

As well as details of all Microsoft products, you'll find free trials, training demos, hints and tips on using the various programs, downloadable software updates, Clip Art, and countless templates.

Office Online is also the site you'll be taken to if you click on the **Help** button within any of the Office programs. Here you'll be given a choice of topics from which to select in the **Help and How-to** panel.

LAYOUT AND TEMPLATES

In this section we look at how to change the setup of the document page itself, at choosing and using ready-made page templates, and at making your own custom templates.

PAGE SETUP

All the documents we've been working on so far have been based on Word's Blank document template, which is a plain US Letter (or A4) portrait page with one-inch (or 2.5-cm) margins and a single column of text. The Page Layout tab on the Ribbon contains the tools to change all these apects of the document, and we're going to start by looking at the Page Setup group of commands.

CHANGING THE MARGINS

● With your cursor on a page of your document that has some text on it (so you can see the changes that you make), click on the **Page Layout** tab and then on the **Margins** button.

● In the list of various options you will find the **Normal** option is already highlighted, as our page already has these margins.

● Move your cursor over the **Wide** option and click on it to select these margins.

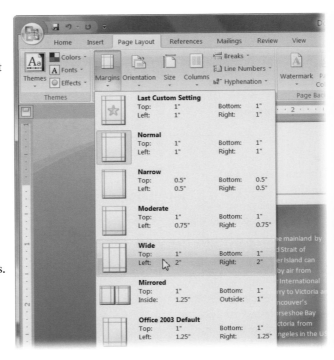

● This narrows the column in which text is running, and will cause text to flow onto successive pages, especially when there is a large text box on the page, as there is here.

● For this reason, margins are best set up before you start work on the document.

● If none of the available options suits your needs, click the **Custom Margins** option at the bottom of the Margins palette.

● In the **Page Setup** dialog box that opens, you have the option to adjust the top, bottom, left, and right margins independently.

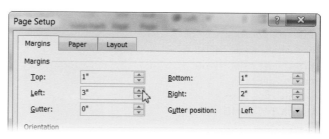

● The effect of altering the margins is displayed in the Preview panel.

● Here you can choose whether to apply the new margins to the whole document or from the insertion point forward.

● You can also choose to apply the new margins only to selected text. In order to do this, the text must already be highlighted.

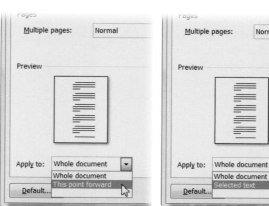

CHANGING PAGE ORIENTATION

● To change the orientation of your document pages from the standard portrait format to landscape, click on the **Orientation** button and select **Landscape** by clicking on it.

● All the pages in the document now have a landscape format.
● As you can see, the sidebar that we inserted earlier now runs over the header and will have to be adjusted–another reason for making these decisions before starting work on the document.

ALTERING THE PAGE SIZE

● To change the size of the page, click on the **Size** button. You are offered a list of more than 60 page sizes. Click on any one to select it.

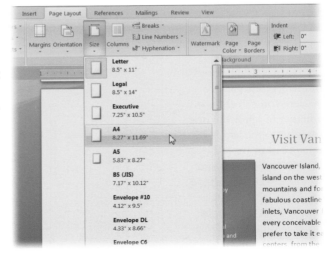

- To create a size that is not listed, click on **More Paper Sizes** at the bottom of the Size panel.
- The **Page Setup** dialog box opens with the **Paper** tab showing. Use the up and down arrows to define your custom size.

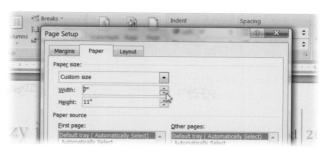

RUNNING TEXT IN COLUMNS

- To show the effect of the **Columns** command, we have clicked on the Show/Hide button in the Home tab, and highlighted several paragraphs of text.
- Now, still on the Page Layout tab, click on the **Columns** button and select **Two** by clicking on it.

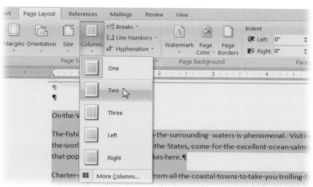

- The text is now in two columns, and we can see that above the highlighted text and to the right of the last line of it (above the cursor arrow) there are now "Continuous" section breaks. We can also see that the top of the second column aligns with the heading, rather than with the body text in the first column.

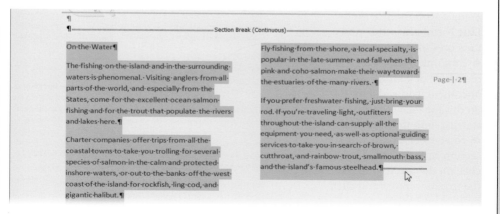

On-the-Water¶

The fishing on the island and in the surrounding waters is phenomenal. Visiting anglers from all parts of the world, and especially from the States, come for the excellent ocean salmon fishing and for the trout that populate the rivers and lakes here.¶

Charter companies offer trips from all the coastal towns to take you trolling for several species of salmon in the calm and protected inshore waters, or out to the banks off the west coast of the island for rockfish, ling cod, and gigantic halibut.¶

Fly-fishing from the shore, a local specialty, is popular in the late summer and fall when the pink and coho salmon make their way toward the estuaries of the many rivers.¶

If you prefer freshwater fishing, just bring your rod. If you're traveling light, outfitters throughout the island can supply all the equipment you need, as well as optional guiding services to take you in search of brown, cutthroat, and rainbow trout, smallmouth bass, and the island's famous steelhead.¶

223 **Features Key**

INSERTING BREAKS

- To balance the columns, click at the end of the first column, then click on the **Breaks** button, and then on the **Column** entry.
- This column break will push the paragraph mark onto the next column so that the text lines up.
- The Breaks panel also includes options for starting a new section on the following page, inserting a Continuous section break on the same page, and leaving a blank page before the start of a new section.

ADDING LINE NUMBERS

- The next command is for inserting line numbers beside the text–useful if you want to refer someone to a specific line in the document.
- To number all the lines in a document that consists of a single section, click on the **Line Numbers** button and then on **Continuous**.
- To number all the lines in the whole of a multi-section document, you will have to do this for each section, starting with the first.
- To number an individual section, as we're doing here, click on the text to position the insertion point and click on **Restart Each Section**.

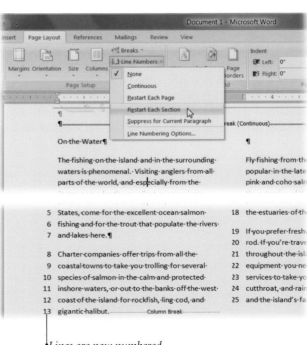

*Lines are now numbered

HYPHENATING THE TEXT

- This button needs to be used with caution. Unless the columns are narrow, you may be better off not hyphenating. Automatic hyphenation can break some words awkwardly.

- The **Manual Hyphenation** option gives you more control, as Word asks you to confirm each instance or leave it as it is.

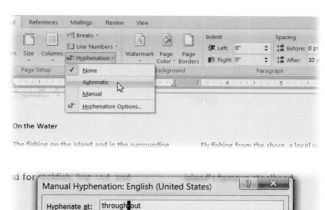

PAGE BACKGROUND

The Page Background group only contains three commands, but these can transform the look of your document. A watermark is useful and gives pages a professional look, while background and border colors, used wisely, can be extremely eye-catching.

ADDING A WATERMARK

- There may be times when you need to make it clear that a document is, for example, confidential or urgent. Adding a watermark is a good way to do this, and this can be found in the **Watermark** gallery.
- If the ready-made watermark is in the gallery, click on it to add it to all the pages in the document. To make your own, click on **Custom Watermark**.

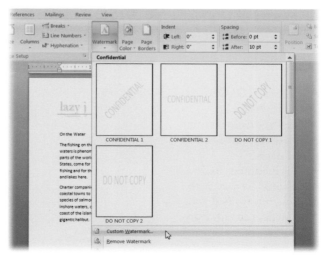

● When the **Printed Watermark** dialog box opens, click on the **Text watermark** radio button.

● Now type the text for your watermark into the **Text** panel, select a color from the Theme Colors  in the drop-down menu that can be accessed by clicking on the arrow at the right-hand end of the **Color** panel, and click **OK**.

● Your custom watermark now appears behind the text and graphics on all the pages of the document.

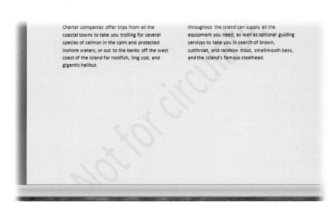

ADDING COLOR TO THE PAGE

● The **Page Color** button adds a background tint to all the pages.

● This is another tool that should be used with caution, especially if your document is already busy with other color elements.

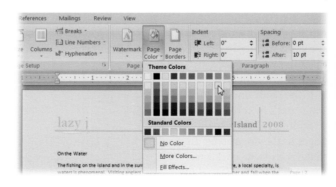

Using Themes

269

ADDING A PAGE BORDER

● A page border is a more subtle way of individualizing your document. Click on the **Page Borders** button to open the **Borders and** **Shading** dialog box. Here you can choose various aspects of the design of the page border, which edges of the page to apply it to, and whether to apply it to the whole document or only the current section.

● The options button lets you position the border in relation to the page edge.

● Click **OK** when you've made your choices. You can always click **Undo** if you don't like it, or return to the dialog box and select **None**.

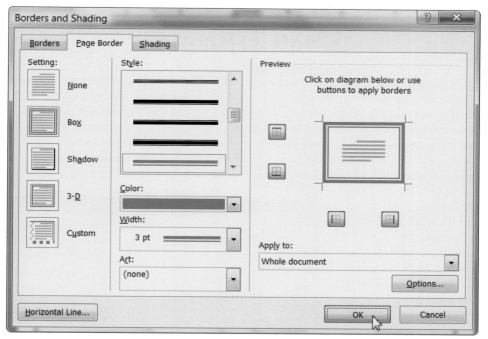

● The page border is now applied, in this case, on all the pages throughout the whole document.

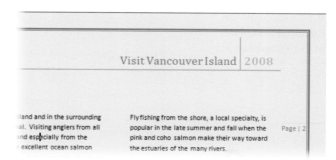

Visit Vancouver Island | 2008

land and in the surrounding
al. Visiting anglers from all
nd especially from the
excellent ocean salmon

Fly fishing from the shore, a local specialty, is
popular in the late summer and fall when the
pink and coho salmon make their way toward
the estuaries of the many rivers.

Page | 2

OTHER COMMAND GROUPS

The **Page Layout** tab also includes the **Paragraph** and **Arrange** groups. Using the **Paragraph Indent** scroll boxes has the same effect as moving the indent markers ⬜. The **Spacing** scroll boxes add space above and below the selected paragraph. These tools are the same ones that we saw in the Paragraph dialog box ⬜, which is just what opens if you click on the small arrow at the bottom right corner of this group.

USING TEMPLATES

Up to this point we've been looking at ways of tailoring your document, element by element, to make it look precisely the way you want it. However, wouldn't it be much easier if someone else had already done it for you? Happily, a whole host of page templates is available to you, all formatted, styled, and ready to go. When you use one of these, you open a copy of the template, so all the changes you make are kept in your document and the template itself remains unaltered. Word template files have the suffix **dotx** whereas Word documents have the suffix **docx**.

OPENING THE TEMPLATES LIST

● To create a document based on a template other than the Blank document, click on the Office button and select **New**.

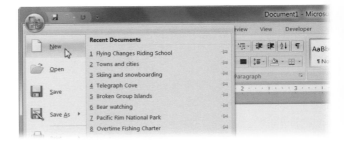

● Now click on the **Installed Templates** button in the **Templates** list.

● The **Installed Templates** gallery opens, containing more than 30 templates for letters, reports, fax cover sheets, and resumés.

● Using the scroll bar to the right of the gallery, look through the templates and then click on one. A preview of the page appears in the panel on the right. This one is the **Median Resumé**.

● To select a template on which to base your Word document, make sure that the **Document** radio button at the bottom left of the preview panel is "on" and then double click on the template or click on the **Create** button.

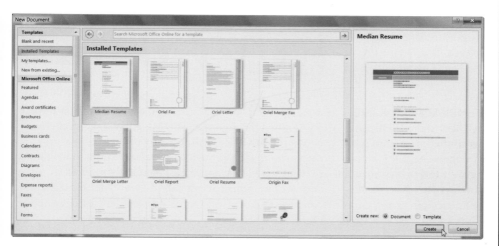

● The new document that opens is a copy of the Median Resumé template, and it contains placeholder text, in a range of styles, that you can overtype with your own details to complete the resumé. There's even a picture box into which you can import your own photo.

● As the upper part of the page is set out as a table, the **Table Tools** are available in the Ribbon, and when you click on the photo, the **Picture Tools Format** tab also appears.

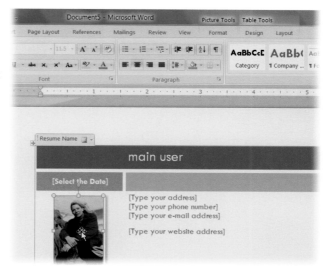

CHANGING THE THEME

● As the name of the template suggested, this document has the Median Theme, including the fonts, styles, colors, and effects of that theme. If this doesn't match your personal or corporate taste, simply select a new Theme on the **Page Layout** tab.

TEMPLATES ONLINE

● The Installed Templates are limited to certain types of document, but if you have an Internet connection you can go to Microsoft's online resources and choose from a truly vast selection.

● In the Templates list ⬛, scroll down through the list of **Microsoft Office Online** categories to gain some idea of what's available, and then click on one. Your computer connects to Microsoft Office Online and presents a gallery of templates in that category. A single click on any of these brings up a preview in the right-hand panel. If you think it's what you want, double click on the template or click on the **Download** button.

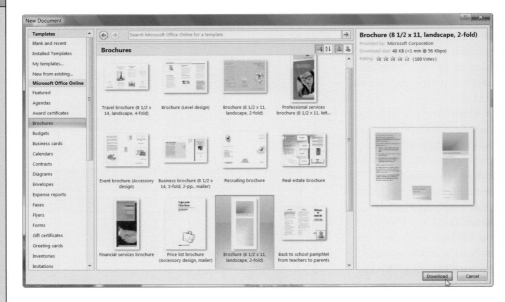

● Microsoft's site, not unreasonably, only makes these template available to "customers running genuine Microsoft Office," so if you want to continue, you must allow your software to be validated at this point.

● Assuming that your software is genuine, the new document now appears on your screen. This particular template is for a bi-fold brochure, something that could take you hours to lay out yourself. Complete with correctly positioned columns, headings, and placeholder paragraphs, it even includes instructions on how to personalize it and save it as your own template for future use.

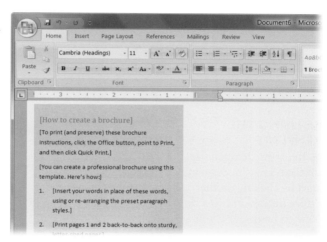

SAVING THE TEMPLATE

● When you have the document looking just the way you want it, it makes sense to save it not only as a document but also as a template that you can use time and time again.

● Save it as a document in the normal way first.

● Now click on the Office button, go to **Save As**, and click on **Word Template**.

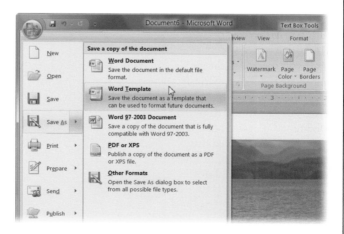

● In the **Save As** dialog box, give the file a name, choose to save it in the Templates folder, and click on **Save**.
● Here we've named it **lazy j brochure**.

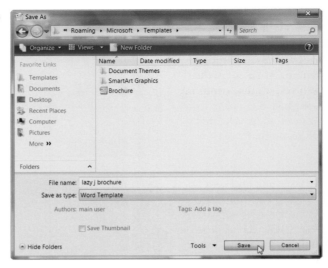

RE-USING THE TEMPLATE

● To use the template again to make a new document, start by clicking on the Office button and selecting **New**, as before. You will immediately see that the two templates we've been experimenting with are now listed in the **Recently Used Template** panel.
● If you then click on the template that we previously downloaded, you will be given the option to download it again, but we have already saved our personalized version of this, so click on **My templates**.

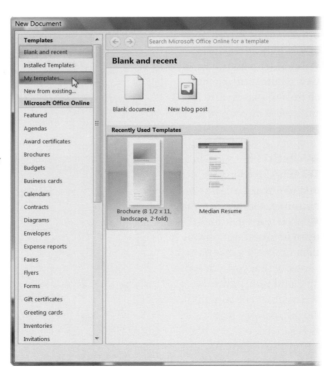

● The **New** dialog box opens, and we can see our template listed there. Select it and click **OK**, and a new document based on this revised template opens on your screen.

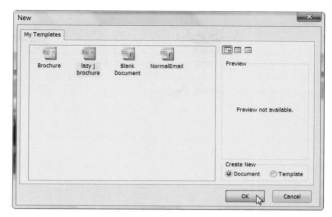

AMENDING A TEMPLATE

● If any of the details in your template become out of date, you will need to open the template directly, edit it, and save it again.
● Start by clicking on the Office button, and then click on **Open**.

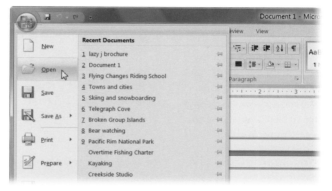

● Select the template in the **Templates** folder and click on the **Open** button at the bottom of the box.
● When the template opens, you can edit it and then save it in the usual way.

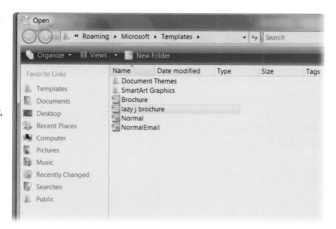

CREATING A NEW TEMPLATE

If, like many of us, you create invoices by opening the last one you sent, amending it, and then saving it with a new name, there is a better way. As we have seen, when a template is opened it makes a copy of itself, and the original doesn't change. Here we look at creating a document and saving it as a template for future documents. This way you won't accidentally send out an invoice with the wrong client's name on it!

CREATING THE DOCUMENT

- Begin by opening the document on which you wish to base your template, or open a blank document and start from scratch.
- Make sure that all the permanent elements, such as your logo, company address, and any headings, are correct and styled the way you want them.

OPENING THE DEVELOPER TAB

- We've already seen how to add property content controls to a document [ ], but you can also add text content controls containing placeholder text for you–or another user–to type over.
- To do so, you first need to make the **Developer** tab available on the Ribbon, so click on the Office button and then on **Word Options**.

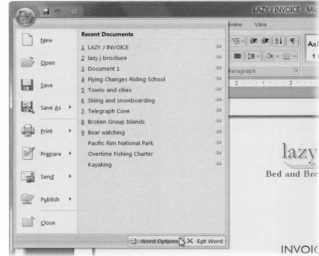

● Select the **Popular** tab if it is not already selected, and then click on the check box next to **Show Developer tab in the Ribbon** to put a tick in it.
● Then click on **OK**.

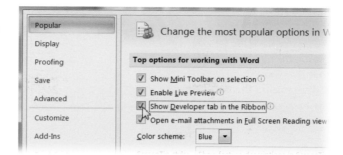

INSERTING THE PLACEHOLDER TEXT

● The new tab is now at the right-hand end of the Ribbon. Click in your document to position the insertion point where you would like to have the placeholder text, and then click on the **Developer** tab.
● In the **Controls** group of commands, click on the **Design Mode** button to switch this mode on.
● Now click on the top left button in the **Controls** group to insert a "rich text content control."

● This text box now appears at the insertion point. While you are in Design Mode, you can edit the text within it, so start by highlighting the text.

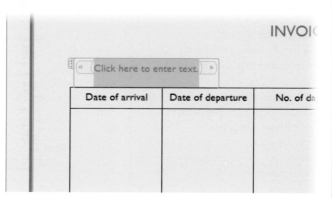

EDITING THE INSTRUCTIONS

● Now replace the text by typing in the instructions that you want to have here.
● We're using this box as the location for the guest's name and address.

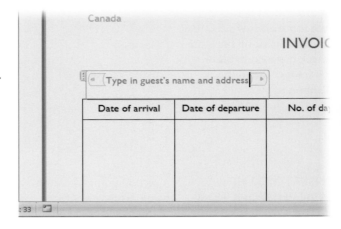

● Click on the **Design Mode** button again to turn it off, and then click outside the text box to see the results.

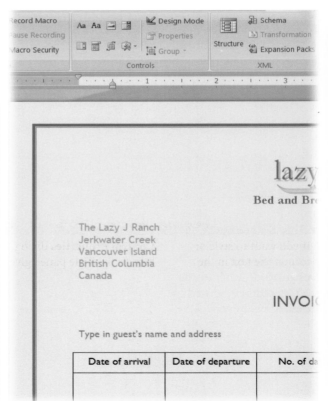

FILE SUFFIXES

In order to identify a template by its dotx suffix, file extensions must be visible. If they are not, click on the Vista **Start** button and then on **Computer**. Click on the **Organize** button and select **Folder and Search Options** from the drop-down menu. Under the **View** tab, remove the tick from the **Hide extensions for know file types** checkbox, and click on **OK**. The file extensions will now be visible.

● Now when you click on the instruction text, you will find that it is all highlighted and can be overtyped.

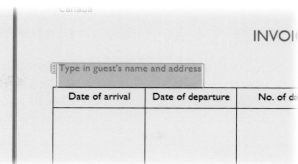

● When you start typing, the highlighted text all disappears, and the typed text appears in the style you have set up (see box below).

● You can add text boxes like these wherever the form or document needs to have information typed in.

● When the document is complete, save it as a Word template 🗋, and the new template will be available under **My Templates** 🗋.

FORMATTING PLACEHOLDER TEXT

If you want to style or format the text in the placeholder text box, turn off Design Mode and then click on the handle at the left-hand end of the text box to highlight it. Now click on the **Properties** button in the **Control** group to open the **Content** **Control Properties** dialog box. In the **Title** panel, give the box a name (such as Guest Address), and then click on the **Use a style to format contents** checkbox to put a tick in it. In the **Style** drop-down menu, select a Quick Style for the text that will be typed into the box. For a slick finish, put a tick in the **Remove content control when contents are edited** checkbox, and click on OK. Now when you click on the placeholder text, the title appears, the text you type is formatted, and the text box title disappears.

285 Saving the Template

286 Re-using the Template

TABLES AND ILLUSTRATIONS

**Whether you want to display information clearly, illustrate
a document with photos or clip art, use a flow chart or diagram,
or put a graph on the page, Word makes it simple to do.**

CREATING A TABLE

Text and numerical information is often most clearly presented in the form of a table, and Word's ability to do this has always been prodigious. In the 2007 version, the process is easier than ever. Here we look at using simple grids and ready-made Quick Part tables, drawing a table from scratch, and converting text into a tabular form.

INSERTING A STANDARD TABLE

● Click on the **Insert** tab, then on **Table**.
● Roll your cursor across the grid in the **Insert Table** menu. Rows and columns become highlighted as you move down and right, and you will see a table with the corresponding dimensions appear on your page at the insertion point.
● Click on the bottom right square of your chosen size to create a table.

● Alternatively, select **Insert Table** from the menu.

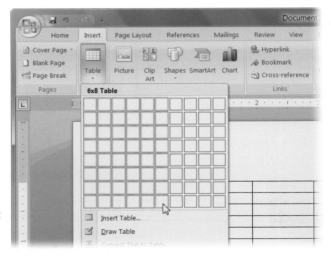

- The **Insert Table** dialog box appears. Here you can specify the number of columns and rows, set the width of the columns, or allow the columns to fit to the text that you type into them or to the width of the window. You can also tell Word to keep the settings for use in the future.
- When you've finished, click **OK** to create the table.

STYLING THE TABLE

- The table grid appears on your document at the original insertion point, and the insertion point is now in the top left cell of the table.

- As you can see, **Design** and **Layout** tabs for **Table Tools** have appeared in the Ribbon, and the **Design** tab is selected. At the left-hand end of the Ribbon you will find checkboxes for **Table Style Options**, and you will find that these are well worth exerimenting with, but for now let's simply select a Table Style.

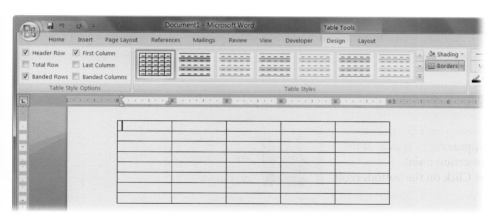

TABLE TERMS

A table consists of gridlines that create horizontal rows and vertical columns.

Together, these divide the table into cells, rectangular boxes into which text and numbers can be placed. Cells can also contain images and graphic elements.

- As you roll your cursor over each of the options in the **Table Styles** group, the table takes on that design.
- Clicking on any of them will select the style.

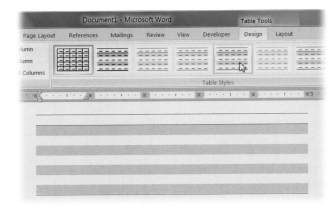

A WIDER SELECTION

- To see the more of the Built-In Table Styles gallery, scroll through them by clicking on the up and down arrows on the right of the **Table Styles** panel or click on the downward pointing arrow at the bottom right to see all of them.

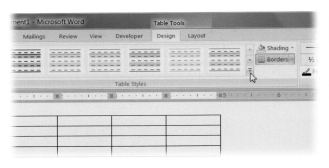

- The full drop-down gallery opens, and, again, rolling the cursor over these gives a live preview of the effects.
- Click on one to select it.

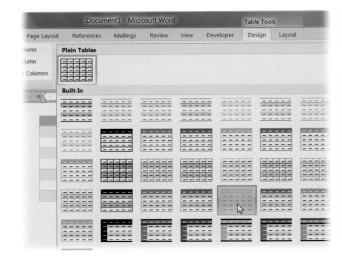

● Here we see the table, but the columns are no longer indicated. To make it easier to see where to insert text, got to the **Home** tab and click on the **Show/Hide** button, or use the keyboard shortcut Ctrl * (Ctrl Shift 8).
● Each cell now has a mark in it, indicating where your insertion point will appear if you click in the cell.

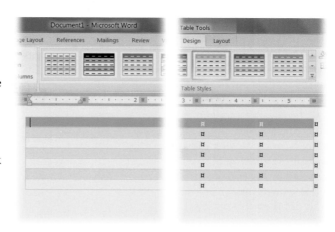

● At any time, you can alter the style of the box by clicking in the table to select it and then choosing again from the **Table Styles**, or by checking boxes in the Table Style Options tools on the left of the Ribbon.
● Here, we have turned the last row into a **Total Row**, and we're choosing another Table Style.

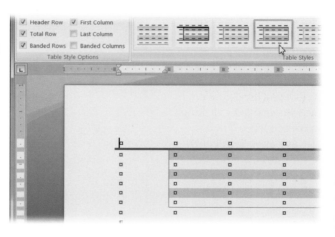

VIEWING THE GRIDLINES
● In this style, we can no longer see the outer edge of the table, or the divisions between some of the rows and columns. To make the layout of the table clearer to work on, select the **Layout** tab and click on **View Gridlines** in the Table tools.

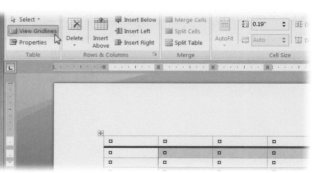

ADDING SHADING TO SPECIFIED CELLS

● To add shading, first select the cells you want to shade. This can be done by clicking in an individual cell, by clicking and then dragging across a range of cells, or by moving the cursor over the top of a column or the end of a row until it turns into an arrow. You can then click to select the column or row.

● Now click on the **Shading** button in the **Design** tab, and select from the drop-down color palette.

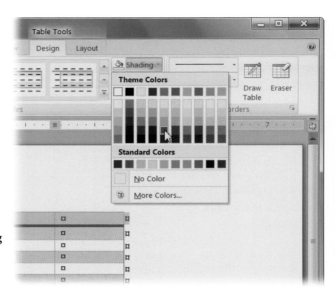

ADDING BORDERS

● To add a border, select the whole table by clicking in the top left cell and dragging across and down to the bottom right.

● Click on the **Borders** button and make your selection from the drop-down menu.

● All these options can also be opened by clicking on the **Borders and Shading** option at the bottom of the menu to open the **Borders and Shading** dialog box that we have already seen ◻.

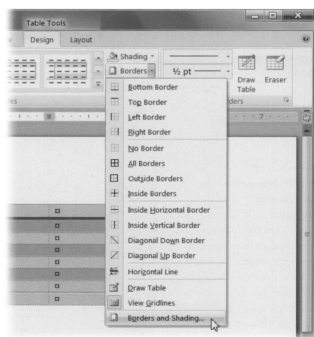

◻ **Adding a**
281 **Page Border**

USING QUICK TABLES

- Word contains a range of ready-made Quick Tables that includes calendars, styled lists, and headed tables. Check these out to see if there is one here that suits your need.
- Click on the **Table** button again 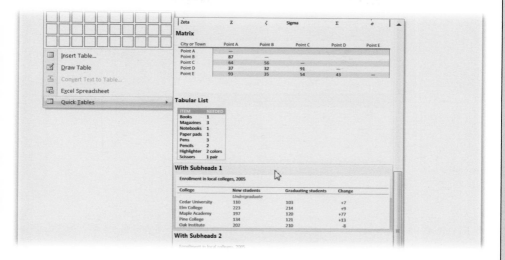, and then on **Quick Tables** at the bottom of the drop-down menu.
- Scroll down the panel to view the options, and click on one to select it.

DRAW YOUR OWN TABLE

- If you can see in advance that a regular grid won't meet your needs, then it may be better to draw your own table.
- Start by opening the Table menu , and then select **Draw Table**.

- Your cursor has now become a line-drawing pen.
- Click and drag to create the outer border of your table. Click again when you feel it's the right size. It can be adjusted later.

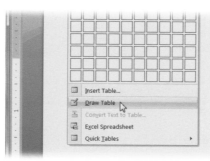

292 Inserting a Standard Table

- Now use the pen to draw the divisions between rows and columns within your table border. To return the cursor to normal when the table is complete, click on the **Draw Table** button at the right-hand end of the Design toolbar. All the styling options that we have just seen are available for this table.

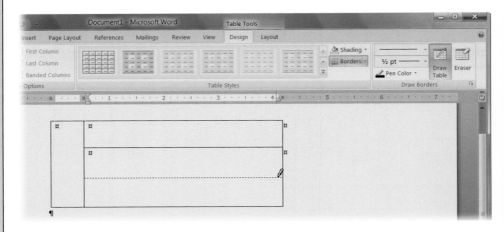

- To remove a gridline, click on the **Eraser** button at the right-hand end of the Design toolbar. Your cursor then appears as an eraser.
- Click on any gridline in the table to delete it.
- Click again on the **Eraser** button to return the cursor to normal.

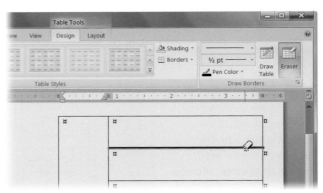

CHANGING THE PEN COLOR

On the left of the **Draw Table** tool you will find the **Pen Color** and line options. By selecting options from here, you can change the design, thickness, and color of the lines used in drawing your table. Once the pen has been set to your chosen specifications, you can change any existing gridlines to match by clicking on them with the pen cursor.

CONVERTING TEXT TO A TABLE

- If information is set out in the correct way, text and figures can be converted directly into a table.
- Here we have keyed in two simple columns with tabs between them.

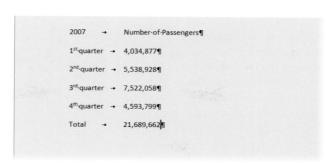

- To turn this into a table, start by highlighting both columns of text.
- Then click on the **Table** button in the **Insert** toolbar and select **Convert Text to Table** from the drop-down menu that appears.

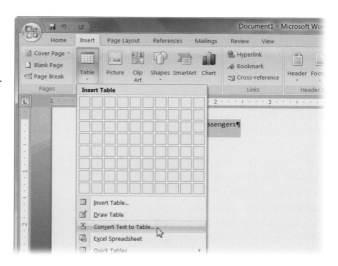

- The **Convert Text to Table** dialog box opens, with the correct number of columns and rows already displayed. Under **AutoFit behavior**, we have clicked on the **AutoFit to contents** radio button so that the column width adapts to the amount of text in it. Our text is separated at tabs, so we are leaving that option selected, and we're clicking **OK**.

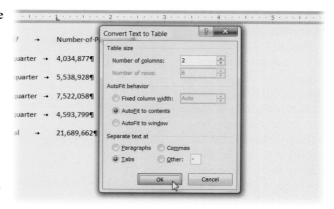

- The information is now in the form of a table, and we can apply styling to this by using the **Design** toolbar. We can also format any of the text in the table using the tools in the **Home** tab.

2007	Number of Passengers
1st quarter	4,034,877
2nd quarter	5,538,928
3rd quarter	7,522,058
4th quarter	4,593,799
Total	21,689,662

- Here we have selected the same style we used earlier, made some selections in the **Table Style** options, and emboldened the **Total** line.

2007	Number of Passengers
1st quarter	4,034,877
2nd quarter	5,538,928
3rd quarter	7,522,058
4th quarter	4,593,799
Total	**21,689,662**

SELECTING CELLS

In order to manipulate cells in a table, they must first be selected.

- Move the cursor over the top of the column until it turns into an arrow. Now click to select the chosen cells. To make things clearer, we've already clicked on **View Gridlines**.

MANIPULATING THE CELLS

- The **Layout** toolbar contains the commands for deleting, inserting, merging, and splitting cells, as well as specifying cell sizes.
- We're going to start by adding a column on the right of this table, so, with the right column selected, click on the **Insert Right**.

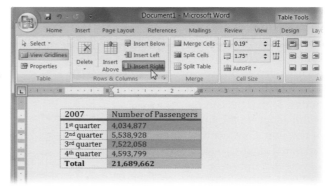

● The new column has been inserted and we can now type into each of the newly created cells.

● As we do so, because we selected **Autofit to contents** earlier, the column widens to fit the text.

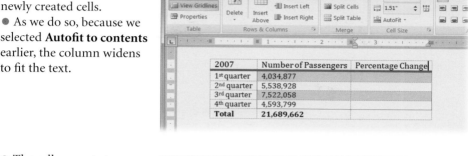

● The cells are set at the minimum depth to accommodate the text.

● As it looks slightly cramped, we're going to deepen all the cells apart from the heading row.

● Begin by highlighting them, and then click on the up arrow of the **Table Row Height** button.

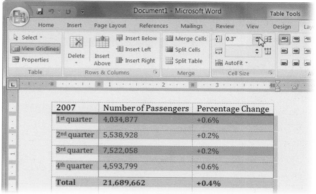

ALIGNING THE TEXT

● To center all the text vertically within the cells, select the whole table and click on **Align Center Left** button in the **Alignment** group.

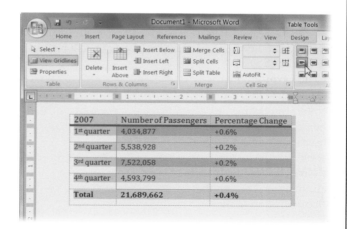

● The figures in the **Number of Passengers** column would look better ranged right, so highlight just those cells and click the **Align Center Right** button.

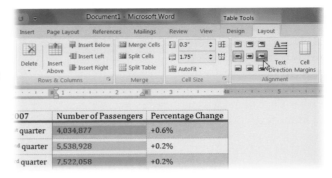

007	Number of Passengers	Percentage Change
quarter	4,034,877	+0.6%
quarter	5,538,928	+0.2%
quarter	7,522,058	+0.2%

● Now we've centered the right-hand figures, put a paragraph return in the two long headings to reduce the column widths, and turned off **View Gridlines**, and here's our finished table.

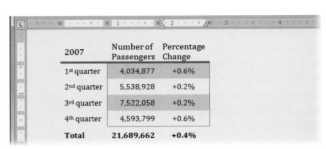

2007	Number of Passengers	Percentage Change
1st quarter	4,034,877	+0.6%
2nd quarter	5,538,928	+0.2%
3rd quarter	7,522,058	+0.2%
4th quarter	4,593,799	+0.6%
Total	**21,689,662**	**+0.4%**

INSERTING IMAGES

As well as making it easy to bring images into your pages, Word has all the tools you need to resize, adjust, frame, and position your pictures so they look their very best and add the most to your documents. Here, we're adding a photograph, previously saved on our hard disc, to a page of our vacation brochure.

IMPORTING THE PICTURE

● Start by clicking on the page to position the insertion point where you would like the image to be.

● Now click on the **Insert** tab, and then click on the **Picture** button in the **Illustrations** group.

- The **Insert Picture** dialog box opens.
- Navigate to the image you want to use, click on it to select it, and then click on **Insert**.

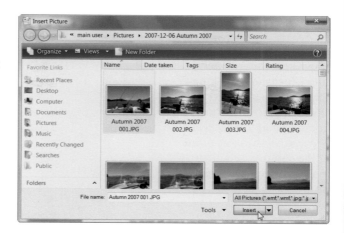

RESIZING THE IMAGE

- The picture is now on the page, but occupying the full width and pushing all the text down.

- To reduce the size, hover the cursor over one of the corners until it turns into a double-headed arrow. Now drag the corner in toward

the opposite corner. You will see a ghosted version of the image shrinking as you do so. Click when the picture is the right size.

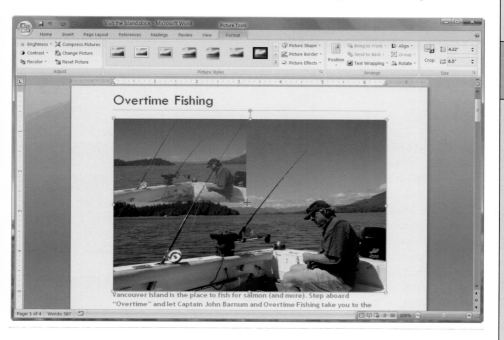

CHANGING THE TEXT WRAPPING

● That's better, but we want the text to run down the right-hand side of the image, so click on **Text Wrapping** in the Picture Tools Format toolbar, which appeared at the same time as the photo.

● Click on **Square** in the drop-down menu.

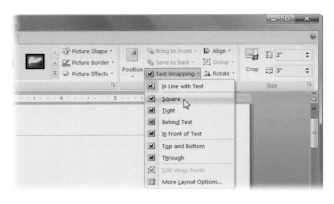

● To leave more space below the picture, return to the **Text Wrapping** menu and click on **More Layout Options** at the bottom.

● The **Advanced Layout** dialog box opens. Click on the **Text Wrapping** tab, and then type in or use the scroll arrows to increase **Distance from text** at the **Bottom** and on the **Right**.

● Click on **OK**.

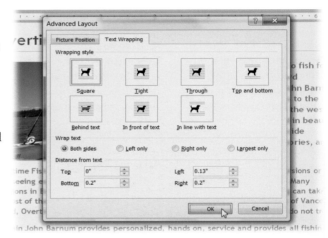

ADJUSTING THE IMAGE

● By using the **Adjust** group of tools at the left-hand end of the Ribbon, we can alter the brightness and contrast of the image, and even recolor it using a palette of options.

● If you regret any changes made since you inserted the image, click on **Reset Picture** to reverse them all.

STYLING THE PICTURE

● Moving to the right on the **Format** toolbar, open the **Picture Styles** gallery by clicking on the downward pointing arrow at the bottom right.

● This opens a range of preset formats for the photo.

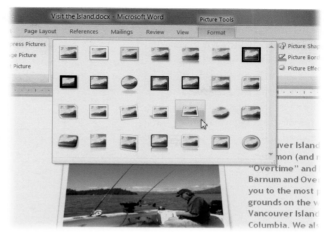

● The **Picture Shape, Border**, and **Effects** buttons open an almost infinite range of choices, offering every conceivable combination of shape, border, shadow, reflection, and 3-D effect.

● Bear in mind that many of these formats will change the overall size or shape of the image, and will affect the text. If you intend to use them, do so before fitting the text.

CROPPING THE IMAGE

● To crop an image, first select it by clicking on it, and then click on the **Crop** tool in the Format toolbar.

● Now drag the corners or the sides in to leave just the area of the image that you wish to select.

MOVING AND OVERLAPPING

● In order to move an image, you will need to change the **Text Wrapping** (in the **Arrange** group of commands) from **In Line with Text** 🗋, as this default setting holds the image to the left margin.

● Then simply click and drag to the new position.

● To rotate an image, use the green rotation handle on the top, or the **Rotate** button in this group.

● To overlap images in the right order, use the **Bring to Front** and **Send to Back** commands.

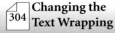
Changing the Text Wrapping
304

USING TEXT OVER AN IMAGE

- To run text on top of an image, select the image and then set the **Text Wrapping** to **Behind Text**.
- You can then type, or place a text box or table, over the top of it.

GRAPHIC ELEMENTS

Returning to the **Insert** tab, there are four more buttons in the **Illustrations** group. These are for calling up graphic elements from within Word, from other parts of Office, and from Office Online, to create the images and diagrams you need.

USING CLIP ART

- Microsoft offers a huge range of Clip Art images, and a powerful search tool to find them.
- Start by clicking on the **Clip Art** button in the **Illustrations** group. This opens the **Clip Art** pane at the side of the screen.
- Type a word into the **Search for** panel, and click on **Go**. A range of Clip Art answering that description will appear.
- Move your cursor over your chosen image and either double click or click on the arrow that appears and select an action from the drop-down menu. Here, we're choosing **Insert**.

- The Clip Art picture appears on the page, along with the **Picture**

Tools Format toolbar. All the tools that can be used to improve and

manipulate a photo 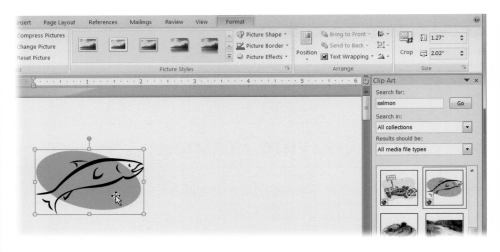 are available here to use on the Clip Art.

USING SHAPES

- Click on the **Shapes** button to display the extensive range of available shapes. These are grouped in categories, and once you've used one it will appear in the **Recently Used Shapes** group at the top of the panel.
- Click on any shape to select it.

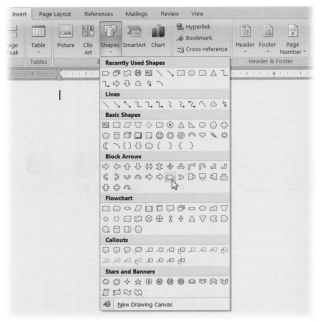

- When you select one, your cursor appears as crosshairs and you can click and drag to create the shape.
- Click again when it is the size you want. The shape appears on screen, complete with handles, as the picture did. On the Ribbon, the **Drawing Tools Format** toolbar appears with a range of tools, styles, and effects.
- To place text in the shape, click on the **Edit Text** button and a text box will appear over the shape.

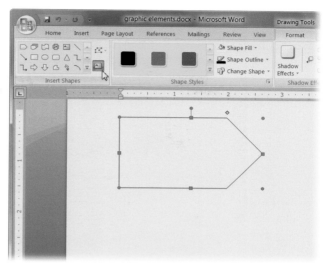

CHOOSING A SMARTART GRAPHIC

- If you need a flow chart or organizational diagram, SmartArt can probably offer you what you need.

- Click on the SmartArt button to open the **Choose a SmartArt Graphic** box.
- Here, the SmartArt diagrams are displayed under category tabs.

- Click on a tab to select the category, and then on a diagram to see a preview and description in the right-hand panel. Click **OK** to select the diagram.

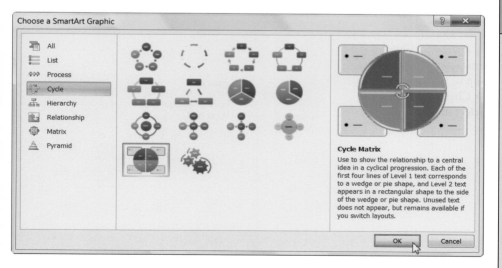

● When it appears on the page, along with the **SmartArt Tools Design** and **Format** tabs, you can style it and key in text in the Text Pane that appears at the side of the screen when the diagram text boxes are selected. Change the dimensions of the graphic by dragging the corners and the midpoint of each side.

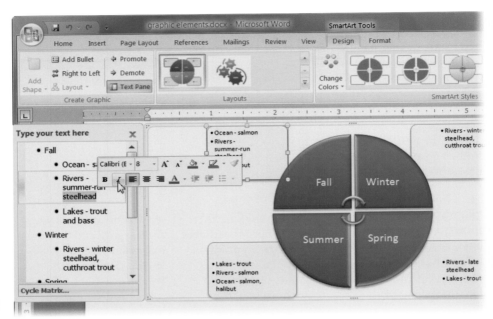

CREATING A CHART

● **Chart** is the last of the Illustration buttons.

● Click on this and the **Insert Chart** dialog box opens, containing a host of different charts and chart types.

● Select one and click **OK**.

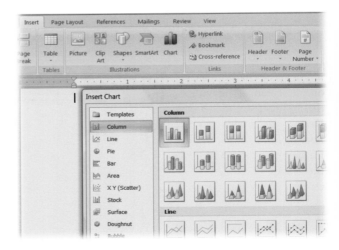

● Now look what happens. Demonstrating the power that integrated programs have in Office 2007, the Excel program opens.

● We'll be looking in detail at Excel in the next chapter, but we can see here a group of cells into which we're invited to key our data.

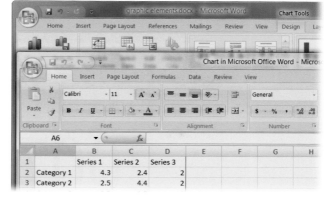

● Here, we are inputting the passenger figures that were used in the table we created earlier.

● Data can be pasted into Excel from a Word table, but if you know you want both a table and a chart, it is easier to start the process in Excel and then export both into Word.

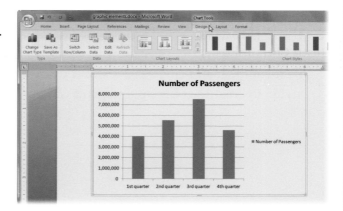

● With the data keyed in, close the Excel spreadsheet.

● The basic chart appears on the screen, along with three Chart Tools tabs–**Design**, **Layout**, and **Format**–with which to fine tune every aspect of the graphic. These are essentially Excel toolbars, and we will look at these in the next chapter.

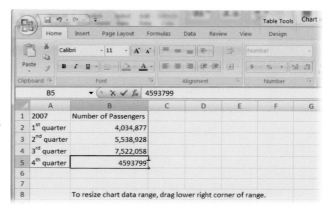

EXCEL®
2007

THE KEY FEATURES OF EXCEL are presented section by section in this chapter. This spreadsheet program has become an essential business tool, with the power to organize and analyze large amounts of data, and to present the results in clear and eye-catching visual forms. For the home user, Excel is the ideal way to deal with accounts and budgeting, team lists and project schedules. If you are new to Excel, this chapter explains how to create a worksheet, input data, manipulate text, numbers, and worksheet cells, and use Excel's mathematical formulas. If you already know the ropes, you'll discover the layout of the Ribbon toolbar, and the ease with which text and cells can now be formatted, and charts, tables, and whole worksheets can be styled to create a coherent and professional look.

EXCEL ON SCREEN

Excel is a spreadsheet program, designed for storing and manipulating numerical data, carrying out complex calculations, and presenting the data visually.

WHAT CAN EXCEL DO?

Storing spreadsheet data is only the beginning as far as Excel is concerned. The wide range of features it contains lets you manipulate and present your data in almost any way you choose. Excel can be used as an accounts program; it also works as a sophisticated calculator capable of utilizing complex mathematical formulas; it can also be a diary, a scheduler, and much, much more besides. Excel has many of the design capabilities of Microsoft Word, using fonts, colors, borders, and text formatting to present textual and numerical information in a clear and professional style. Data can be also be presented in highly visual ways using Excel's wide range of pre-designed graphs and charts.

WHAT IS A WORKSHEET?

● At the heart of Excel is a two-dimensional grid of data storage spaces called a worksheet (right).
● This is where you input the data that you want to store, manipulate, or analyze. The individual spaces are called cells.
● To begin with, all the cells are empty. As you enter data into the cells, you build and develop the individual worksheets.

	A	B	C	D	E	F	G
1		Jul-07	Oct-07				
2	Canada	32,976,026	33,091,228	0.35			
3	Newfoundland and Labrador	506,275	507,475	0.24			
4	Prince Edward Island	138,627	139,103	0.34			
5	Nova Scotia	934,147	935,106	0.1			
6	New Brunswick	749,782	750,851	0.14			
7	Quebec	7,700,807	7,719,993	0.25			
8	Ontario	12,803,861	12,850,636	0.37			
9	Manitoba	1,186,679	1,190,400	0.31			
10	Saskatchewan	996,869	1,003,299	0.65			
11	Alberta	3,473,984	3,486,767	0.37			
12	British Columbia	4,380,256	4,402,931	0.52			
13	Yukon	30,989	31,115	0.41			
14	Northwest Territories	42,637	42,425	-0.5			
15	Nunavut	31,113	31,127	0.04			
16							
17							
18							
19							
20							

FORMATTING TEXT AND CELLS

● Using all the formatting power that we've seen in the Word toolkit, Excel lets you control every aspect of the fonts you use, as well as alignment, cell background colors, and borders.

STYLES AND THEMES

● The same ready-made text Styles and design Themes are also available, giving an instant branded feel to worksheets to match your Word documents.

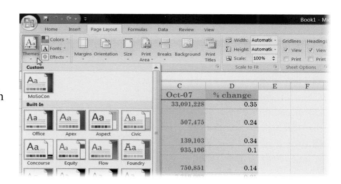

CHARTS AND GRAPHS

● Excel's chart-making tools turn selected data into high-impact visuals at the click of a button, while dedicated tabs on the Ribbon for Design, Layout, and Format make it easy to personalize the look.

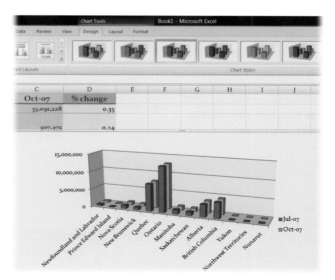

THE EXCEL WINDOW

When Excel launches, the window that appears on your desktop will be called Book 1–Microsoft Excel. The main part of the screen is the worksheet–a grid of blank rectangular cells. Letters and numbers label the columns and rows of the grid, and each cell has a unique address, such as A1, that specifies its position on the grid.

Along the top of the screen runs the Ribbon toolbar, which, if you've read the preceding chapter, will look very familiar. The left-hand end of the Home toolbar, shown here, contains the very same tools that are found in the Word Ribbon. Many of the commands found in the other Ribbon tabs are specific to Excel.

FEATURES KEY

❶ Office Button

❷ Home Tab
Contains the most commonly used text formatting commands.

❸ Quick Access Toolbar
A handy set of tools that can be customized to suit your needs.

❹ Other Tabs
Clicking on any of these brings up a specific ribbon of commands.

❺ Minimize Excel

❻ Restore Excel

❼ Close Excel

❽ Excel Help
Click here for online help and advice from Microsoft.

❾ Minimize Window

❿ Restore Window

⓫ Close Window

⓬ Expand Formula Bar

⓭ Scroll-up Arrow
Moves up the document.

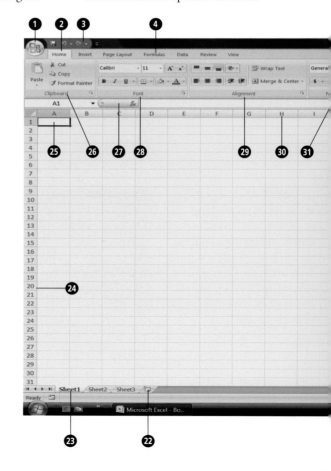

THE COLLAPSING TOOLBAR

The Excel window shown here is displayed full screen on a fairly high resolution monitor. On a lower resolution screen, or if the window has been reduced down to occupy only part of the screen, some of the command groups will be compressed down to a small icon, or even a single button that opens the command group. In this chapter, we have reduced the window size in some instances to display the relevant tools as close to the work area as possible.

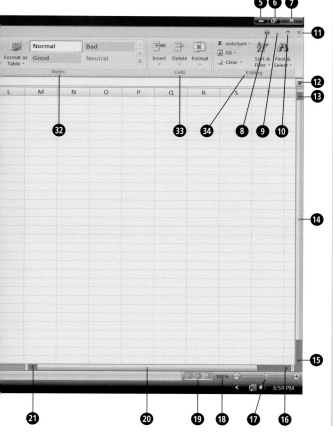

EXCEL ESSENTIALS

In this section, we look at opening and naming Excel spreadsheets, at saving a newly created Excel file, at using installed and online templates, selecting cells, and inputting data.

STARTING A NEW WORKBOOK

Anything you create using Microsoft Excel is stored on your computer as a file called a workbook. A workbook contains one or more separate worksheets. When you first open Excel, you are presented with an unused workbook called Book1. This contains blank worksheets, initially labeled Sheet1, Sheet2, and Sheet3.

NAMING WORKSHEETS

● Once you start putting data into a worksheet, you'll want to give the worksheet a short name to indicate what it contains.
● To do this, double-click on the existing name, so that it becomes highlighted.

● Now type in the new name for the worksheet– preferably one that will identify it easily. This is especially important once you have a large number of sheets within a workbook.
● Press Enter ⏎ to complete the name.

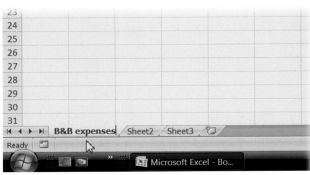

- You can switch between worksheets by clicking on the tabs at the bottom of the workbook window.
- To add further sheets, click on the **Insert Worksheet** button to the right of the worksheet tabs.

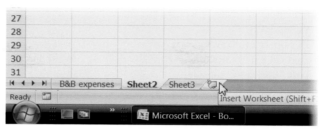

SAVING THE WORKBOOK

- To save the workbook in the default Excel Workbook file format, simply click on the **Save** disc icon in the Quick Access toolbar.
- The **Save As** dialog box opens. Name your file by typing over the default name in the **File name** field, choose a location in which to save it, and click on **Save**.

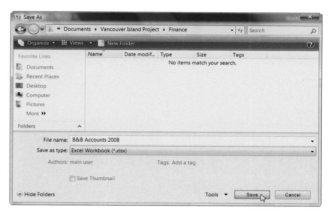

- If you wish to save the workbook in a particular format, for example as a file that can be opened on a computer running an earlier version of Excel, click on the Office button, move your cursor over the **Save As** button, and select from the options there.

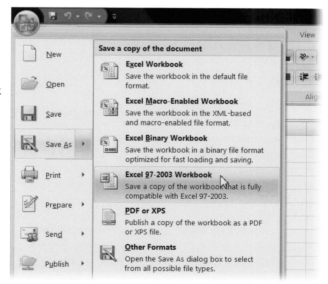

OPENING A NEW WORKBOOK

● To open a new workbook based on Excel's normal Blank Workbook template, click on the Office button and then on **New**.

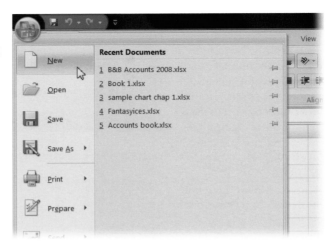

● In the **New Workbook** panel that opens, select the **Blank and recent** tab.
● Click on **Blank Workbook** and then click on the **Create** button at the bottom.
● A new blank workbook will open on the screen.
● You can also open a new workbook by using the keyboard shortcut Ctrl N.

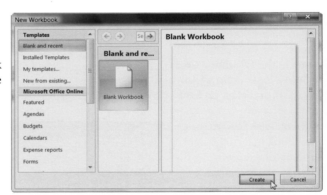

MAKE YOUR OWN TEMPLATE

Once you have created a workbook that fulfils your requirements, you can save the document as a template and base future documents on this. Go to the Office button and click on **Save As** (or hover over the button and select **Other** Formats at the bottom of the panel). In the **Save As** dialog box, click on the downward pointing arrow at the right-hand end of the **Save as type** text panel and select **Excel template** from the drop-down list. Name your template and click **Save**, and Excel will save it in the **Templates** folder. If you now click on the Office button and then on **New**, and then click on **My templates** in the **New Workbook** panel, you will find your new template there, ready for use.

USING AN INSTALLED TEMPLATE

● Excel has a number of ready-made templates that may save you the trouble of creating your own. Simply click on **Installed Templates** in the **New Workbook** panel, and look through the range of worksheets there.

● Each one contains labels and placeholder text to make filling the worksheet easy, and all the formulas and functions 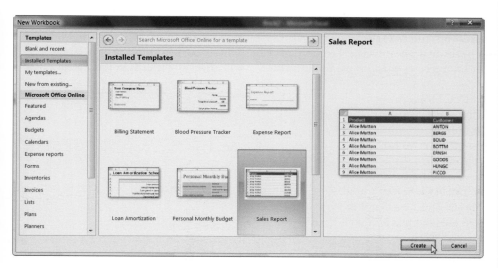 are already in place to analyze and calculate your data.

● If a template looks as though it might be suitable, select it, click on **Create**, and check it out in detail.

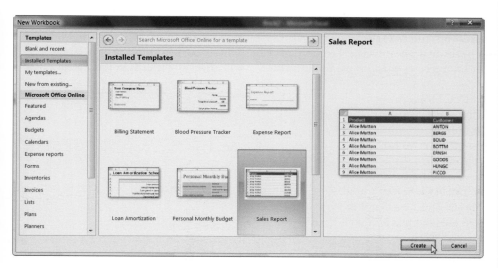

SEEKING EXCEL TEMPLATES ONLINE

● For a far wider range of useful templates, you can visit, as we did in Word, Microsoft Office Online.

● Click on one of the categories below the Microsoft Office Online heading to see what is available, and you'll be amazed at what you find.

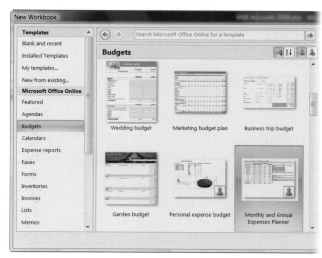

 Formulas and
334 Functions

Templates
284 Online

SELECTING WORKSHEET CELLS

Before performing any operation in Excel, such as typing data into cells, coloring cells, or deleting them, you need to choose the cells on which you are going to perform the action. This process is called cell selection. You can select a single cell, a horizontal row or vertical column of cells, or several rows or columns. You can also select a block of cells, or several separate blocks. When a block is selected, the cells appear within a black border with a blue tint, except for the "active cell," which remains white. Anything you type will appear only in the active cell, but other actions, such as coloring or deleting, will affect all the cells in the selected area.

SELECTING A SINGLE CELL

● Move your mouse pointer over your chosen cell and click the left mouse button.

● The black border round the cell indicates that it is selected, and this is now the active cell.

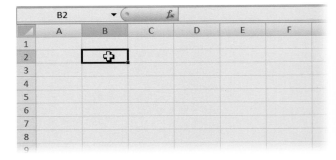

SELECTING A SINGLE COLUMN

● Click on the column header button at the top of your chosen column.

● Click and drag across the header buttons of several columns to select them all.

SELECTING A SINGLE ROW

● Click on the row header button to the left of your chosen row.

● Click and drag down the header buttons of several rows to select them all.

SELECTING A BLOCK OF CELLS

- Click on a cell at one corner of the block you wish to select, and drag the cursor to the opposite corner of the block.
- Alternatively, click on one corner, hold down the ⇧ Shift key, and click on the opposite corner.

SELECTING SEVERAL BLOCKS

- Holding down the Ctrl key, click and drag to select a block, and then repeat for subsequent blocks, which will all remain selected.

SELECTING THE WHOLE WORKSHEET

- The small square in the top left corner of the worksheet is the **Select All** button.
- Click here to select all the cells in the worksheet. Cell A1 will be the active cell.

- Alternatively, use the keyboard shortcut Ctrl A; in this case, the active cell will be the cell that was active before all the cells were selected.

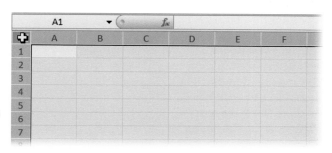

ENTERING TEXT

There are three categories of data that you can put into a worksheet–text, numbers, and formulas. Worksheets usually take a tabular form, and text is used most often as labels for the table's rows and columns. It makes sense to enter these text labels first, in order to provide a structure for the numerical data and formulas. To demonstrate the principles, we are using the simple example of accommodation revenue at the B&B. It may be helpful to follow our worked example step by step.

SELECTING THE FIRST CELL FOR TEXT

● Click on cell A2 to select this cell. Cell A2 is now the active cell and anything you type on the keyboard will appear in this cell.

● Note that A2 appears in the name box at the top left of the worksheet.

TYPING IN THE TEXT

● To follow this example, type the word **Room**.

● Note that the insertion point stays just to the right of the last letter you typed, marking where the next letter you type will appear.

COMPLETING THE ENTRY

● Once you have typed your text, press Enter↵. This completes the data entry into the cell, and the active cell now moves down a single cell to A3. Further entries can be made in the same way.

CREATING COLUMN HEADINGS

● To add column headings for the numerical data, select the cells B2 to D2 ◻.
● Type in **Number of nights**, which appears in the current active cell, B2.

B2		▼	× ✓ ƒx	Number of nights	
	A	B	C	D	E	F
1						
2	Room	Number of nights				
3	Single room					
4	Double room					
5	Family apartment					
6						

● Complete the entry by pressing the Tab⇄ key. This time, the active cell moves one cell to the right.
● Type **Cost per night ($)** into C2, press the Tab⇄ key, and type **Room revenue** into D2.

D2		▼	× ✓ ƒx	Room revenue	
	A	B	C	D	E	F
1						
2	Room	Number ol	Cost per ni	Room revenue		
3	Single room					
4	Double room					
5	Family apartment					
6						

● Select cell C6, and type in **Total revenue**.

	A	B	C	D	E	F
1						
2	Room	Number ol	Cost per ni	Room revenue		
3	Single room					
4	Double room					
5	Family apartment					
6			Total revenue			

ADJUSTING THE COLUMN WIDTHS

● We can see that the text extends beyond the cells, but there are some quick methods for adjusting the widths of columns to fit cell data. For this example, move the mouse pointer over the line that divides column headers A and B. The pointer should form a bar with arrows pointing to either side.

Q30		▼	
	A	↔ B	C
1			
2	Room	Number ol	Cost per
3	Single room		
4	Double room		
5	Family apartment		
6			Total re
7			
8			
9			
10			
11			
12			
13			
14			

TYPING ERRORS

If you mistype a letter, press the ← Bksp key on your keyboard to delete the last letter you typed. If you want to start the data entry into a cell from scratch, press the Esc key at the top left of your keyboard. Even if you have completed entering data, it's easy to make changes later.

323 Selecting a Block of Cells

- Click and drag the mouse pointer to the right.
- A dotted vertical line shows the position of the new column divider.
- Drag this line to the right of the words **Family apartment**, and the column widens to that extent.

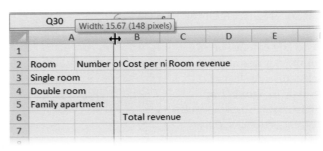

- With the mouse pointer on the line that divides column headers B and C, double-click the mouse.

- This method widens column B automatically to display the longest line of text in that column. Now widen columns C and D.

ENTERING NUMBERS

Numerical values include integers (whole numbers), decimal numbers (such as 3.25), fractions, monetary amounts, percentages, dates, and times. Excel applies various rules to detect whether a string of characters constitute a numerical value and, if so, what type (for example, integers, date, or time). If Excel recognizes the typed-in expression as a numerical value, it will align it ranged right in the cell.

ENTERING WHOLE NUMBERS

- To select the cell in which you wish enter the number, click on it.
- In this example, click on cell B3 and type in any whole number.

NUMBER FORMATS

The way in which a number or numerical expression is displayed in a cell is affected by what format that cell has. By default, cells have a "general" number format. When you type any numerical expression into a cell that has this "general" number format, Excel analyzes what type of expression it is and then displays it in an appropriate standard way, usually, though not always exactly, as it is typed. For example, an integer will be displayed as an integer, a date will be given a date format, and so on.

● Press Enter ↵ to complete the entry.
● Now enter further whole numbers into cells B4 and B5, pressing Enter ↵ after each entry.
● These numbers represent the number of nights each guest room is occupied.

B6			f_x	
	A	B	C	D
1				
2	Room	Number of nights	Cost per night ($)	Room reve
3	Single room	97		
4	Double room	140		
5	Family apartment	56		
6			Total revenue	
7				
8				

ENTERING DECIMALS

● Enter decimal numbers into cells as you would write them, using a period to represent the decimal point.
● Here we are have typed the cost per room in the cells C3 to C5, pressing Enter ↵ each time to move to the cell below.

C6			f_x	Total revenue
	A	B	C	D
1				
2	Room	Number of nights	Cost per night ($)	Room reve
3	Single room	97	50	
4	Double room	140	95.5	
5	Family apartment	56	125.75	
6			Total revenue	
7				
8				
9				
10				

IS IT A NUMBER?

Excel interprets various sorts of expression (not just strings of digits) as numerical values. For example $43, or 43%, or 4.3, or 4,300, or 4.3E+7 (standing for 43,000,000) are all recognized as numerical values. Both -43 and (43) would be recognized as negative or debit numbers.

COPYING DATA BY FILLING

Putting the same data into adjacent cells is a common Excel task. Instead of typing the data into every cell, you can type it once and then copy it using Fill and Auto Fill. This works for copying the content of a single cell or, in the case of Auto Fill, a range of cells. Here, we will work through two simple examples.

COPYING THE DATA IN A SINGLE CELL

● Start by selecting the cell that contains the data you wish to copy.

● In this example, we intend to copy the text in cell M2 into the three cells below it.

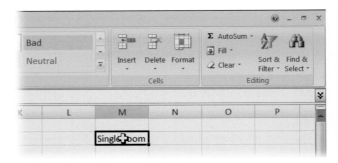

● Now drag the cursor down to select the three cells M3 to M5 as well.

● Click on the **Fill** button and select **Down**.

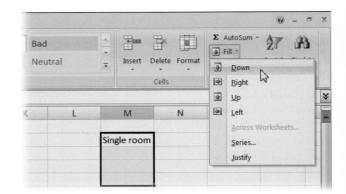

● The content of M2 is automatically copied into the other selected cells.

● The same method can be used to copy the contents of all four cells into the four cells to the left or right.

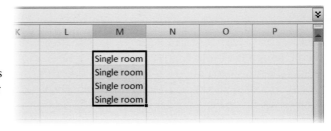

COPYING DATA USING AUTO FILL

● To copy data from one or more cells, start by selecting the cells, and then roll your cursor over the Auto Fill handle at the bottom right corner of the cell or cells. It will turn into a fine cross.

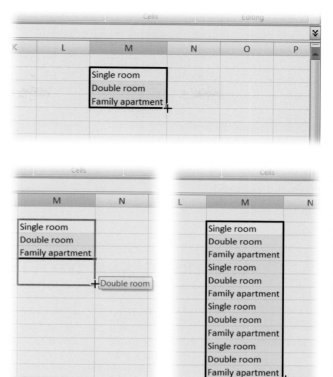

● Now drag down over the cells into which you are copying. As you do so, a label appears telling you what is being copied into the cell you are over.

● Release the mouse button when the cells you want to fill have been included.

● We will look at the little icon that has appeared at the bottom right-hand corner of the cell block in the next section ⌐.

CREATING DATA SERIES

The Auto Fill feature recognizes certain types of sequence and can be used to create data series across all cell ranges. These include number series (1, 2, 3...), days of the week (Mon, Tue, Wed), dates (such as Jan 1, Jan 2, Jan 3 etc.), and months (Jan, Feb, Mar...). It also recognizes series with regular intervals (such as 5, 10, 15...).

CREATING A SERIES OF MONTHS

● Start by typing in the first term in the series.

● In this case, we're starting a list of months.

◢ **The Auto Fill**
338 **Options Menu**

● Position the cursor over the Auto Fill handle and drag down over the cells below. The terms being pasted appear in a label at the side of the column.

● Once the Auto Fill series is complete, release the mouse button. For as long as you continue to drag down, the series will continue to be repeated.

CLEARING AND MOVING CELLS

As a worksheet grows and evolves, you will need to clear the content from cells, add new cells, remove cells entirely, or move them to a new position. Excel makes it easy to do this, but you'll need to plan ahead to avoid unexpected consequences.

CLEARING CELL CONTENTS

● To empty cells of their content, start by highlighting them.
● Then right click in the selected cell or block and select **Clear Contents** from the pop-up menu.

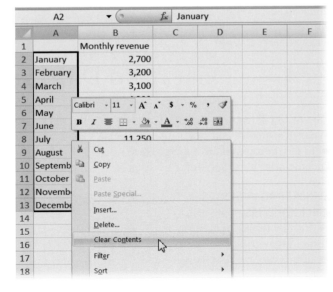

● This leaves the cells empty, but does not remove the cells themselves or cause any other cells to move. The Monthly revenue column remains where it is.

DELETING CELLS

● To delete cells, again highlight the cells in question, right click, and this time select **Delete** from the drop-down menu.
● This time the actual cells themselves will be removed, which raises the question of what will take their place.

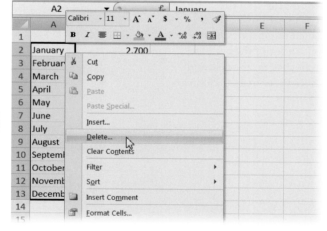

● To get the answer, the **Delete** dialog box appears. Here you can choose which of the surrounding cells should move to fill the gap.

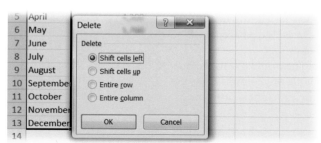

CUTTING AND PASTING CELLS

● Cutting and pasting is a good way to move cell content into a new group of cells, but it needs to be used with care, as the content will overwrite the content of the cells it takes over.

● Select the cells, right click, and select **Cut**.

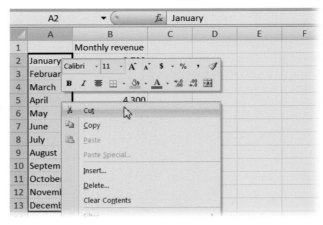

● A flashing border appears around the cut cells.

● Choose a new cell in which to position the top left corner of the cut block, right click on the cell, and select **Paste** from the pop-up menu.

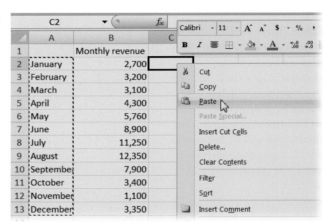

● As you can see, the content of the cut cells has been pasted into our chosen cell and the adjacent cells below it.

● The original cells are now blank, but column B has not moved from its position.

DRAGGING AND DROPPING CELLS

- To move a cell or block of cells by using "drag and drop," select them and then move your cursor over the border. The cursor becomes a four-headed arrow, and you can now drag the block to its new position.

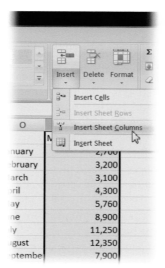

INSERTING CELLS

- To insert cells, rows, columns, or an entire worksheet, select a cell, row, or column, click on the **Insert** button in the **Cells** group on the Home toolbar, and select from the drop-down menu.
- Columns are inserted to the left of selected columns, as we see here, and rows are inserted above selected rows. If you select **Insert cells**, a dialog box will ask which way you wish to move the surrounding cells.

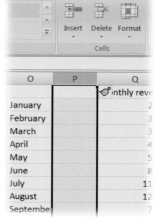

DELETING CELLS

- The **Delete** button offers a similar range of choices, and, again, you will be asked which way to shift the surrounding cells if you delete cells.
- Columns, of course, move in from the right when a column is deleted. Rows move up to fill the place of a deleted row.

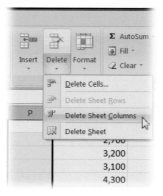

FORMULAS AND FUNCTIONS

The key to Excel's powers of analysis lies in the way
it uses formulas, functions, and cell references. Here we look
at performing simple calculations using formulas.

USING SIMPLE FORMULAS

For even the simplest Excel worksheets, you will soon want to use formulas. A formula returns (calculates and displays) a value in a cell based on numbers you supply it with, arithmetic operators (such as add or multiply), and cell references (the addresses of other worksheet cells containing numerical values). Much of Excel's power derives from the use of cell references in formulas, because if you later decide to change a value in a referenced cell, all formulas in the worksheet that depend on that reference are automatically recalculated.

MULTIPLYING TWO CELL VALUES

● For one cell to contain the result of multiplying the values of two other cells, you can type an = sign into the cell followed by the address of the first cell, then the multiplication operator *, and then the address of the second cell.

● Here we want cell D3 to contain the revenue from the B&B's single room.

● This is the product of the number of nights (cell B3) multiplied by the cost per night (cell C3).

● So, select cell D3 and type: =B3*C3.

● As you type each cell address, you will see a border appear around that cell. As you compose it, the formula appears in the Function bar that sits above the header buttons.

	SUM	▾	X ✓ fx	=B3*C3			
	A	B	C	D	E	F	G
1							
2	Room	Number of nights	Cost per night ($)	Room revenue			
3	Single room	97	50	=B3*C3			
4	Double room	140	95.5				
5	Family apartment	56	125.75				
6			Total revenue				
7							
8							

● Press Enter ↵ , and you will see the result of the calculation displayed in D3.
● Now select D3 again and look again at the Function bar above it. There is now a difference between what D3 actually contains (the formula, as shown in the Function bar) and what it displays (the value that is calculated by that formula).

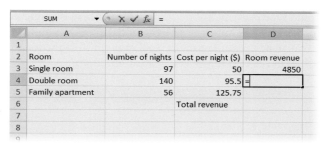

FORMULAS USING THE MOUSE

● Instead of typing, you can use the mouse to help you construct formulas.
● We're going to enter the formula =**B4*C4** into cell D4.
● Start by selecting cell D4 and type the = sign.

● Now click on cell B4. D4 now contains the expression: =**B4**.

● Type an asterik (*) and then click on cell C4.
● Finally, press Enter ↵ .

COMPLETING THE FORMULAS

● Now use either entry method to calculate the family apartment revenue in cell D5, and press [Enter ⏎].

	A	B	C	D
1				
2	Room	Number of nights	Cost per night ($)	Room revenue
3	Single room	97	50	4850
4	Double room	140	95.5	13370
5	Family apartment	56	125.75	7042
6			Total revenue	
7				

ADDING VALUES IN SEVERAL CELLS

● To add together the values in several cells, you could type in an addition formula. For example, to calculate the sum of the values in cells D3 to D5, you could key in the formula =D3+D4+D5.

● However, when the cells are adjacent in the same row or column, there is a quicker method. Excel has a built-in tool to do this–a function called AutoSum.

● In cell D6, we want to put the sum of the revenues generated by all the rooms, held in cells D3 to D5.

● To do so, select cell D6, and then click the **AutoSum** button in the **Editing** group on the **Home** tab.

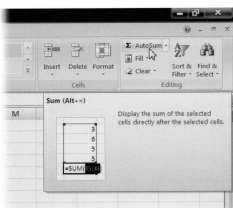

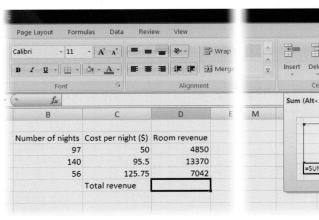

MATH OPERATORS

The math operators available in Excel are: % (percent); ^ (raising to the power); / (division) * (multiplication);

+ (addition); - (subtraction). These follow the standard order of operations, which can be overruled by using brackets.

For example, if you want to subtract A2 from 5, and then multiply the result by B2, you should type: =(5-A2)*B2.

● A flashing border appears around cells D3 to D5, and the term: **=SUM(D3:D5)** appears in cell D6 and in the formula bar. This indicates that a function (a special type of formula) called SUM, is adding the values in cells D3 to cell D5.

	X ✔ fx	=SUM(D3:D5)				
	B	C	D	E	F
	Number of nights	Cost per night ($)	Room revenue		
	97	50	4850		
m	140	95.5	13370		
tment	56	125.75	7042		
		Total revenue	=SUM(D3:D5)		
			SUM(**number1**, [number2], ...)		

● Press [Enter ↵], and the figure for total revenue appears in cell D6.
● It's worth noting that, here, the SUM function is adding the values of cells that themselves contain functions, not values that have been directly input, and this is the basis on which complex and effective worksheets are constructed.

		fx			
	B	C	D	E	F
	Number of nights	Cost per night ($)	Room revenue		
	97	50	4850		
m	140	95.5	13370		
tment	56	125.75	7042		
		Total revenue	25262		

PASTING A FORMULA

● We need a record of the sales tax that we've charged and that we have to pass on the tax man, so in cell E2 we've typed the heading for a new column, and in E3 we've typed the formula: **=D3*5%**.

	X ✔ fx	=D3*5%		
	B	C	D	E
	Number of nights	Cost per night ($)	Room revenue	Sales tax @ 5%
	97	50	4850	=D3*5%
m	140	95.5	13370	
tment	56	125.75	7042	
		Total revenue	25262	

QUICK MATH IN EXCEL

Excel can be used for one-off calculations. If you want to perform a quick calculation and you don't have a calculator, you can use any cell in Excel instead. Suppose you want to add 23 to 31 and multiply the result by 27. Select a blank cell, type: **=(23+31)*27**, and then press [Enter ↵]. If you don't want to leave your calculation on display, you should then clear the cell.

• We could now type in the same formula, but with different cell references, for the next two rows, but there's an easier way.

• Excel allows us to Auto Fill the formula into adjacent cells, and will automatically substitute the correct cell references. Select the cell with the formula in it (E3), and then drag the Auto Fill handle in the bottom right corner of the cell down across the two cells below it.

E3			f_x =D3*5%				
	A	B	C	D	E	F	G	H
1								
2	Room	Number of nights	Cost per night ($)	Room revenue	Sales tax @ 5%		
3	Single room	97	50	4850	242.5		
4	Double room	140	95.5	13370			
5	Family apartment	56	125.75	7042			
6			Total revenue	25262			
7							
8							

• When you release the mouse button, the formula will have been pasted into the cells and they will be displaying the results. (You can double check that the correct formula is there by selecting one of the cells and looking at the Function bar.)

• Note that a small icon has appeared next to the cursor cross. This is the **Auto Fill Options** icon.

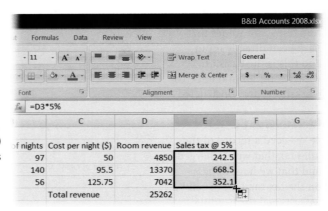

THE AUTO FILL OPTIONS MENU

• Click on the arrow next to the Options icon to open a drop-down menu. By default. Auto Fill is set to **Copy Cells**, but we could also choose to copy only the formatting or only the content from here.

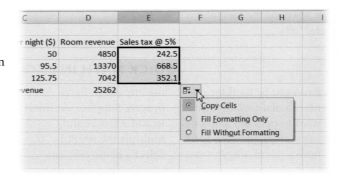

CHANGING CELL CONTENTS

• Just to prove the power of cell references, let's change the value of the number in cell B3 from 97 to 99. Select the cell and then double click in the cell or in the Function bar to highlight the number. Type in 99, and press the Enter ⏎ key.

• You will see that the figures in the Room revenue and Sales tax columns have changed in response and now reflect the new value.

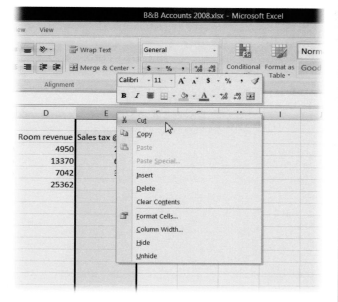

MOVING CELLS AND FORMULAS

• What happens, however, if a cell that contains a formula or is referred to in a formula is moved? Fortunately for us, Excel simply takes this change of position into account, and any formula that refers to a cell that has been moved is automatically updated.

• To test this, right click on the header button of column E, and select **Cut** from the pop-up menu.

- The cut column now has a flashing dashed border.
- Right click on the column D header button and select **Insert Cut Cells** from the menu.

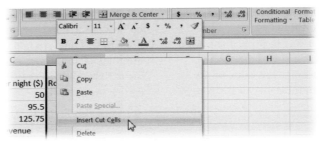

- The cut Sales tax column becomes the new column D, and Room Revenue becomes column E. Now click on cell D3 and look at the Function bar. Instead of D3, the formula now refers to E3, which is where the referenced cell has moved to.
- Now return the columns to their original positions.

	C	D	E	F	G
of nights	Cost per night ($)	Sales tax @ 5%	Room revenue		
99	50	247.5	4950		
140	95.5	668.5	13370		
56	125.75	352.1	7042		
	Total revenue		25362		

VIEWING ALL FORMULAS

- It is possible to see all formulas in cells by changing to the **Show Formulas** view.
- To do this, click on the **Formulas** tab at the top of the Ribbon, and then click on **Show Formulas**.
- As we can see here, columns D and E now display the functions that we inserted, rather than the results of those formulas.
- To return to the normal view, click again on the **Show Formula** button.

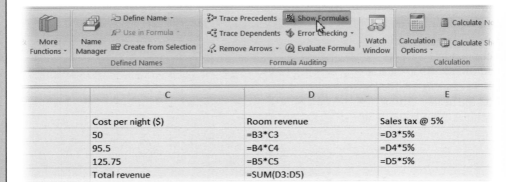

C	D	E
Cost per night ($)	Room revenue	Sales tax @ 5%
50	=B3*C3	=D3*5%
95.5	=B4*C4	=D4*5%
125.75	=B5*C5	=D5*5%
Total revenue	=SUM(D3:D5)	

PRECEDENTS AND DEPENDENTS

● To check that your spreadsheet is working logically, it can be helpful to trace the relationships between cells–to see which cells contribute to or are dependent upon a particular cell. Start by highlighting the cell in question (in this case, cell D6). In the Formulas toolbar, click on the **Trace** **Precedents** button in the **Formula Auditing** group. A blue arrow and a blue cell group border tell us that D3, D4, and D5 are contributing to the result in D6.

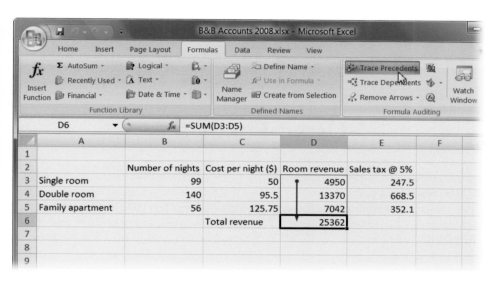

● Now click again on the **Trace Precedents** button. The trail now extends back to include the input of the values in columns B and C.
● When you've finished, click on the **Remove Arrows** button at the bottom left of the **Formulas Auditing** tools.

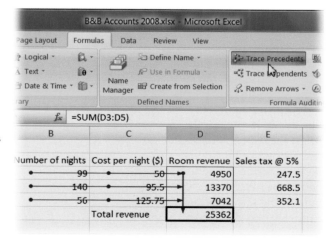

● To work in the opposite direction and discover which cells depend upon a particular cell, highlight the cell (in this case, B3) and click on the **Trace Dependents** button, below **Trace Precedents**.

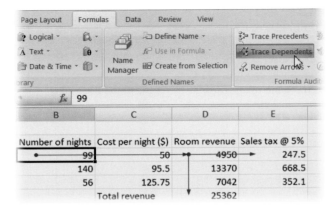

USING FUNCTIONS

Formulas are sequences of instructions that you type into a cell to perform a calculation. Functions are ready-made mathematical calculations that Excel provides for you to use "off the shelf"

in your formulas. We have already seen one in action–when we added figures using the AutoSum feature. Here we look at the other functions available in AutoSum, and at the range of functions in the Excel toolbox.

AUTOSUM FUNCTIONS

● We've already used the **AutoSum** function button in the **Home** tab.
● Now click on the **Formulas** tab, which contains the same **AutoSum** tool.
● Type in a column of figures and leave the cell below the last entry selected (in this case, cell B9).
● Now click on the bottom half of the **AutoSum** button, and select **Average** from the drop-down menu.

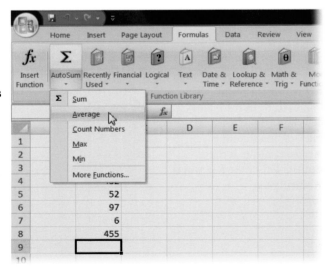

● Cell B9 now contains a formula that gives us the average of the values in the range of cells B1 to B8.
● Press the [Enter ←] key and the result will be displayed.

1	46
2	47
3	59
4	432
5	52
6	97
7	6
8	455
9	=AVERAGE(B1:B8)
10	AVERAGE(**number1**, [number2], ...)
11	

● To carry out further operations on these same cells, but without including the newly calculated average figure, select cells B1 to B8, click again on the lower part of the **AutoSum** button and select **Max**.
● Cell B10 now displays the highest value in the range, 455 (the Maximum value).

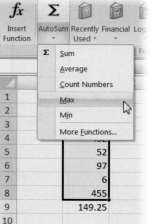

● The value in cell B9 has not been included in the calculation, even though the cell is now included in the selected block.
● We can prove this by double clicking on cell B10, which then displays the formula it contains. Also, the range of cells included in the calculation now has a blue border.

DOLLARFR	▾	× ✓ ƒx	=MAX(B1:B8)			
	A	B	C	D	E	F
1		46				
2		47				
3		59				
4		432				
5		52				
6		97				
7		6				
8		455				
9		149.25				
10		=MAX(B1:B8)				
11		MAX(**number1**, [number2], ...)				
12						

ERROR ALERT
● Excel is good at identifying when and where you have introduced an error into a formula, and telling you.
● Select just cells B1 to B6, click again on **AutoSum** and select **Min**.

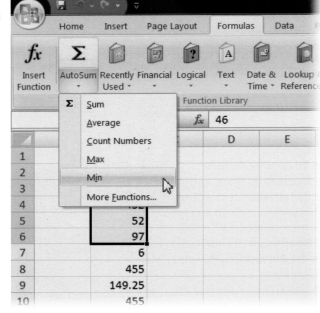

● The minimum value in the range, 46, is now displayed in cell B11, but there is a small triangle in the top left corner of the cell, alerting us to a possible error.

● Click on the cell and an exclamation mark appears in the cell to the left.

- When we click on the exclamation mark, a drop-down menu tells us that we have omitted adjacent cells from the range. This was deliberate, but if it wasn't we could choose to update the formula to include them or choose other options.
- The warning triangle disappears when you choose the **Ignore Error** option.

7	6
8	455
9	149.25
10	455
11	46

Formula Omits Adjacent Cells
Update Formula to Include Cells
Help on this error
Ignore Error
Edit in Formula Bar
Error Checking Options...

ERROR CHECKING

- You can ask Excel to look for errors that you may not have spotted.
- Repeat the sequence that we just carried out above,

choosing part of the cell range and then selecting **Min** in the **AutoSum** menu.
- Now click on the **Error Checking** button in the **Formula Auditing** group

in the Formulas toolbar. Excel pops up the **Error Checking** dialog box, in which it identifies the same potential error and offers the same options.

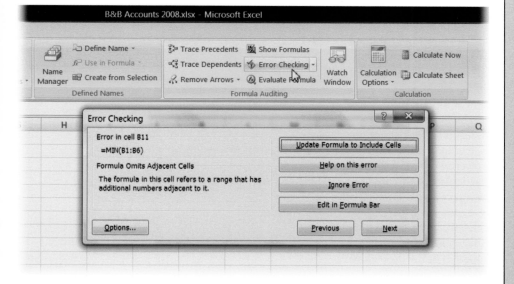

INSERT FUNCTION

● At the bottom of the AutoSum drop-down menu you will have seen the option **More functions**.

● Click on this, or on the **Insert Function** button at the left-hand end of the Formulas toolbar, and the **Insert Function** dialog box appears. This is the doorway to all the functions that Excel has to offer.

● Type what you want to do into the top panel to have Excel search for the right function, or click on the arrow at the end of the **select a category** panel and choose one to open a list of functions in that category.

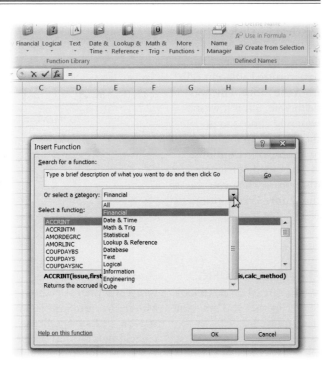

● These function categories correspond with the buttons in the **Function Library** group of tools that are on the Formulas toolbar, and which open the same long lists of functions.

● The **Function Library** deserves serious attention, as it contains a wealth of powerful functions. It is particularly useful if you have a complex spreadsheet.

● Click on any of the category buttons and then hover your cursor over a function in the drop-down list to see what it does.

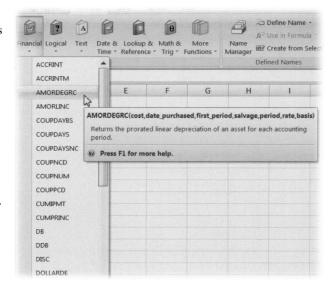

- If you think a function does the job you want, click on it to open the **Function Arguments** box for that function.
- Here you will find panels into which to type your data, or "arguments." An explanation of what data each panel requires is given in the dialog box.
- When a panel requires a cell reference or range, you can input this by selecting the cell or range of cells in the worksheet. If the **Function Arguments** box itself is obscuring the worksheet, you can minimize it by clicking on the range selector button at the end of a each panel.
- If the data has been input correctly, the function will return the result of the calculation in your selected cell when you click on **OK**.

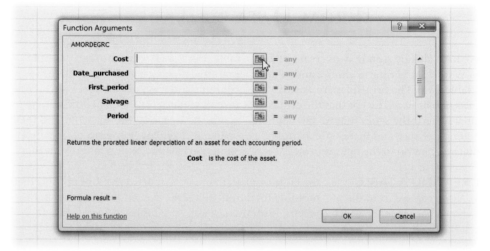

- If the function is outside your area of expertise, or you get an error message, you can click on the **Help on this function** link at the bottom left-hand corner of the dialog box.
- This takes you to a full explanation of the specific function in Office Online's Excel Help, which includes detailed advice on filling in the function arguments.

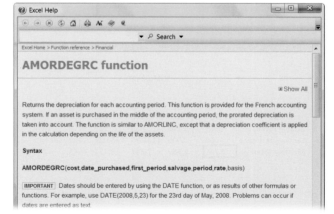

TABLES AND CHARTS

The capability to present numerical data in a clear and visual form is one of Excel's great strengths. Here we look at how to turn your data into a table or a chart, and how to make it look good.

FROM DATA TO TABLE

We have already seen how to create a table in Word ⌐, and how to choose and adjust a table style. The principles are exactly the same in Excel, except that the grid is already here, the styles that we saw actually belong to Excel, and there's much more that you can do to the figures in an Excel table. Here, we'll work through a simple example, turning a grid that contains columns and rows of data–the year's revenue figures for the B&B business, by room and by month–into a table, and then styling it. To follow this example, create a similar grid with column and row headers.

CREATING A TABLE

● As we can see from the formula bar when we select cell B5, the bottom row of the table displays the monthly total from all three rooms. With this cell still selected, click on the **Insert** tab on the Ribbon, and then on the **Table** button in the **Tables** group at the left-hand end of the toolbar.

	A	B	C	D	E	F	G	H	I	J	K	
1	Monthly Income	January	February	March	April	May	June	July	August	September	October	Nove
2	Single room	300	400	550	800	850	650	600	650	400	300	
3	Double room	955	1146	955	1528	1719	1910	2674	2483	1623.5	668.5	
4	Family apartment	1006	1006	1131.75	1383.25	1509	1886.25	2892.25	3898.25	1886.25	1257.5	8
5	Monthly totals	2,261	2,552	2,637	3,711	4,078	4,446	6,166	7,031	3,910	2,226	
6												
7												
8												
9												

B5 ⟶ =SUM(B2:B4)

● The **Create Table** dialog box opens. Excel has identified the part of the grid that forms the basis of a table (the block defined by cells A1 to M4), and has excluded the totals row from the selection, which has a flashing border around it. Tick the check box if the table has headers (which it does), and click on **OK**.

	A1			f_x	=SUM(B2:B4)							
	A	B	C	D	E	F	G	H	I	J	K	
1	Monthly Income	January	February	March	April	May	June	July	August	September	October	Nove
2	Single room	300	400	550	800	850	650	600	650	400	300	
3	Double room	955	1146	955	1528	1719	1910	2674	2483	1623.5	668.5	
4	Family apartment	1006	1006	1131.75	1383.25	1509	1886.25	2892.25	3898.25	1886.25	1257.5	8
5	Monthly totals	2,261	2,552	2,637	3,711	4,078	4,446	6,166	7,031	3,910	2,226	

Create Table

Where is the data for your table?

=$A$1:$M$4

☑ My table has headers

OK Cancel

● The grid in the worksheet now takes on the form of a table, and the Table Tools **Design** tab has appeared on the Ribbon at the top of the screen. The **Table Style Options** and **Table Styles** groups available in this tab are the same as those we've already seen in Word ⌂, but the other tools are specific to Excel. Also, in Excel, the table itself has a drop-down arrow in the first cell of each column.

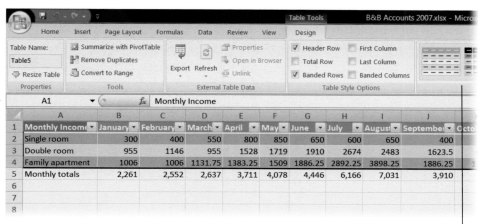

Table Styles group of commands

SORTING TEXT COLUMNS

● These arrows are for sorting or filtering the data in each column. In a column containing text (such as column A), the order in which the rows appear can be rearranged by sorting the data alphabetically. This will affect the order of the rows across the whole table.

● Removing the tick from a check box in the bottom panel will remove that row from the table.

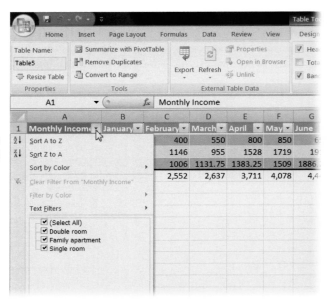

● In a column containing numerical data, such as column B, the rows in the table can be ordered by sorting the data according to numerical value, or a row containing a specific value in the selected column can be removed from the table.

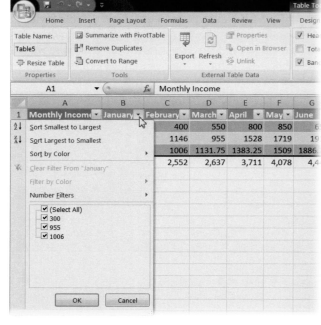

CONVERTING FROM A TABLE

● If you no longer need this table functionality, you can convert the table to a normal range of cells but keep the styling by clicking on the **Convert to Range** button in the **Tools** group on the **Design** tab.

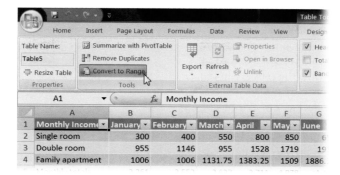

REMOVING THE CELL STYLING

● To return the cells to their normal formatting, highlight them, select the **Home** tab, and click on **Normal** in the **Styles** group.

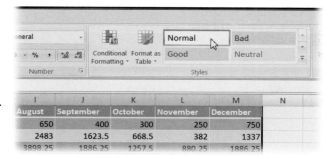

● The styling in the selected cells returns to being that of normal worksheet cells.

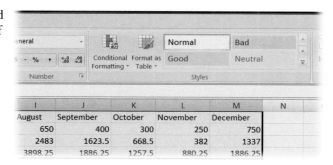

DEACTIVATING SELECTED CELLS

When you carry out certain actions on selected cells, such as cutting or copying them, a flashing border appears around the block. If you decide not to complete the sequence of actions, or the flashing border remains when you have finished, press the [Esc] key on your keyboard to deactivate the cells.

CHOOSING A NEW STYLE

● Just as a reminder of what we saw in Word , while the cells are in the form of a table, you can select a new style by clicking on the bottom right arrow in the **Table Styles** group on the **Design** tab.

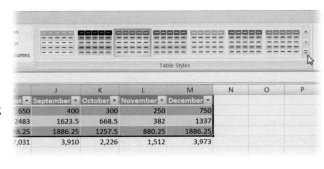

● The Table Styles gallery opens and you can preview the look of each style by rolling your cursor over each one to see how it looks.
● Click on one to select it for your table.

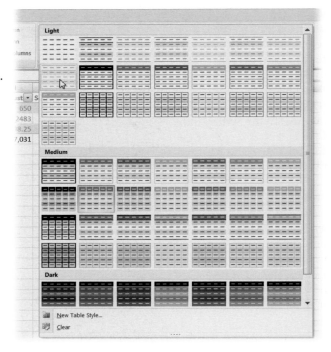

● Alternatively, you can keep the cells in the form of a table but remove all formatting by clicking on the **Clear** option at the bottom of the gallery.

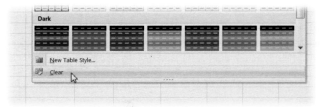

FROM DATA TO CHART

Tables have an important role in studies and reports when you need to highlight exact numbers. However, a more visual "snapshot" of the data can often be more effective and make the information easier to grasp. That's where charts come in, and Excel has a wealth of different types to offer you. The important thing is to choose a chart that suits the data you're presenting and that brings out the point you're trying to see or make. Here we'll look at just a few of the many possibilities.

USING A PIE CHART

● Let's suppose we want to see the relative contributions to January's revenue made by the three rooms.

● Select cells A1 to B4, select the **Insert** tab, click on the **Pie** button in the **Charts** group, and select the **Exploded pie in 3-D** from the drop-down menu.

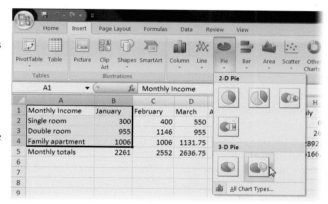

● The chosen chart appears on the worksheet, and three **Chart Tools** tabs–**Design**, **Layout**, and **Format**–have been added to the Ribbon.

● The **Design** tab includes the tools to select a new chart type, alter the data, select from a range of layouts, refine the style of the chart, or move it to another worksheet.

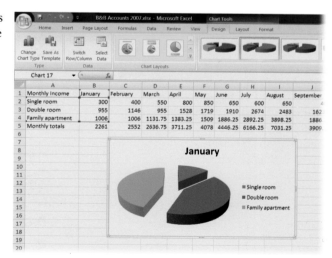

● With just a few clicks on the commands in each of the **Chart Tools** tabs, we can change the color, the shadow, the perspective, and the bevel of the pie slices and the border, and ask Excel to label the percentage that each room contributes rather than the actual revenue. We can use the cursor to change the proportions of the chart or to drag it to a new place on the worksheet.

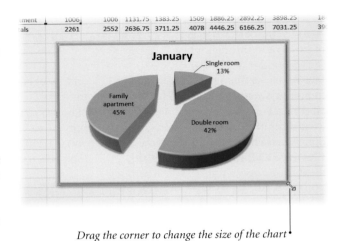

Drag the corner to change the size of the chart

THE AREA CHART

● Now we want to see how the relative contributions of the three rooms fluctuate throughout the year.

● We have highlighted the first four rows of the grid, and we're clicking on the **Area** chart in the **Charts** group on the **Insert** tab and choosing **Stacked Area**.

● This displays the information in a totally different way, and again we have all the tools that we need to add the information and create the look that we want.

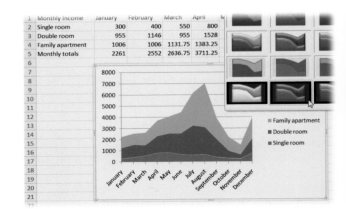

THE COLUMN CHART

● To see the performance of each room throughout the year and to see how the revenue varies from month to month, we have selected all the data and we're clicking on the **Column** option and choosing **Clustered Cylinder** from the drop-down menu.

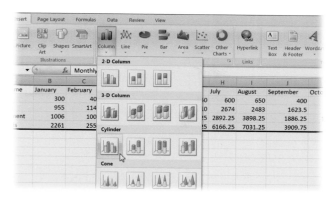

● The resultant chart displays the information, but we'd prefer to see the performance of each room and the monthly totals separately, so we're clicking on the **Switch Row/Column** button in the **Data** group in the **Design** tab.

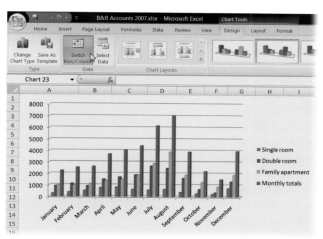

● That separates the four categories and tells us more clearly what we need to know–turn the single room into a double, and take a vacation in November!

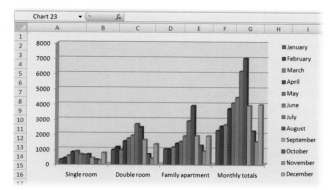

STYLING WORKSHEETS

**Even without charts or tables, the cells and
the text in a worksheet can be made to look structured
and attractive. In this section, we find out how.**

FORMATTING CELLS

In the second section of this chapter we saw two ways to adjust individual column widths 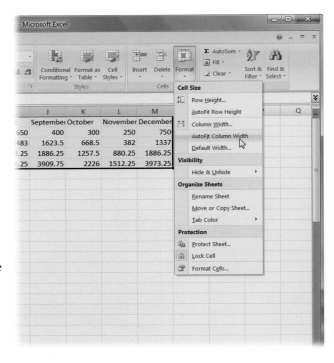 in a worksheet, but here we are going to look at ways to alter the complete look of a selected blocks of cells or a whole worksheet. Excel has many different options for making global changes, not only to cell sizes, but also to the position, and even the angle, of text within the cells.

WIDENING SELECTED CELLS

● We return to our earlier example of monthly B&B figures, at the stage when the data has just been keyed in. All the cells have the standard column width (which is just over eight characters in the standard font and size), and we can see that some of the columns, such as column J, are too narrow to hold the text that's been keyed into them. With all these cells selected, we can widen these to fit the text by clicking on the **Format** button in the **Cells** group on the **Home** tab and selecting **AutoFit Column Width**.

325 **Adjusting the Column Widths**

• The width of the data columns varies, so to make them all the same, which would be tidier, select them and click on the **Format** button again, but this time select **Column Width**.

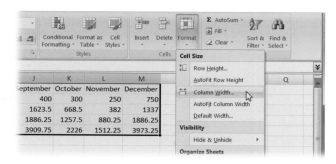

• In the box that opens, you can specify the column width. This width must be specified in the default units of characters, and we are setting it at 10 characters.
• Click on **OK** to implement the change.

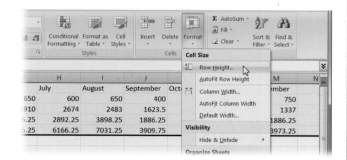

CHANGING THE ROW HEIGHT

• To change the height of the rows, select them first, and then click on the **Format** button and select **Row Height**.

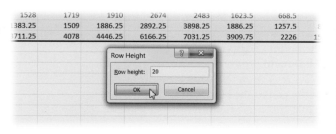

• The **Row Height** dialog box opens, and here the row height is specified in points (one point being about $1/72$ in or .035 cm).
• We're going to make the rows 20 points high. Click **OK** to confirm the change.

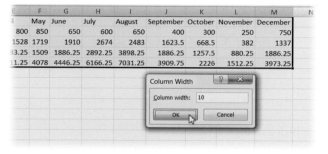

POSITIONING TEXT AND NUMBERS

By default, cells have General formatting, which means that all text within the cells is automatically ranged left, and all the numbers within the cells are ranged right. Both are positioned at the bottom of the cell. Most of the time this looks fine, but sometimes it can lead to a slightly ragged appearance. Here we will look at ways to reposition text and numbers horizontally and vertically within the cells.

ALTERING VERTICAL ALIGNMENT

● To center both text and numbers vertically within cell, select the cells (in this case we are selecting all the cells) and, in the **Home** tab, go to the **Alignment** group. You will see that the **Bottom Align** option is already highlighted. Now click on the next option to the left–**Middle Align**.

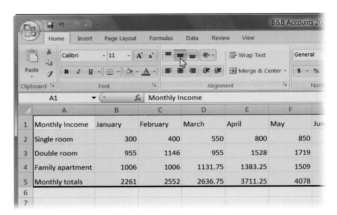

ALIGNING TEXT HORIZONTALLY

● Rather than using the horizontal alignment buttons (in the **Font** group, below the vertical alignment button) to center the headers, we're going to use the **Format Cells** dialog box.
● First, select the headers, then click on the arrow at the bottom right of the **Alignment** group.
● Now click on the arrow at the end of the **Horizontal** panel and select **Center**.
● Click on **OK** to confirm.

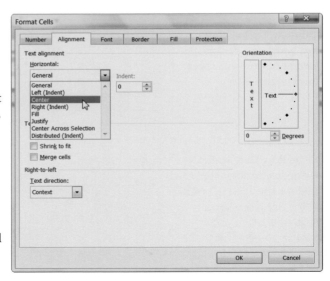

ALIGNING THE NUMBERS

● Now the headers are centered. As we have seen, the numbers are aligned right, but because some figures have no decimal places, some have one, and some have two, they don't align with each other. We can put this right.

● First of all, select the cells with figures in them.

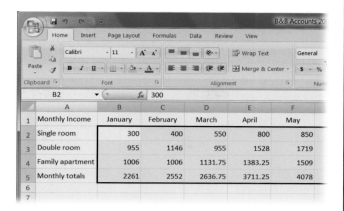

● Click on the arrow in the **Number** group, and the **Format Cells** dialog box opens again, but this time with the **Number** tab open.

● Click on **Number** in the category list. We're leaving the **Decimal places** setting at **2**, ticking the **Use 1000 Separator** check box, and clicking on the second option in the **Negative numbers** panel so that, if we have any, negative numbers will appear red.

● Click on **OK** to finish.

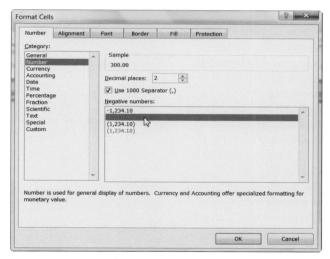

● Now we have clicked outside the selected cells. The numbers in the worksheet are all ranged right and they align with each other, so the figures in each column can be compared more easily.

REORIENTATING CELL CONTENTS

To add visual interest to your worksheet, or to reduce the overall width of the grid when there are long labels on columns or rows, it can be useful to have text running at an angle or even vertically. Excel offers two ways to do this. Of course, turning the text at an angle increases the vertical height of the content and requires deeper cells. Here, we have increased the height of the cells in the top row to make room.

USING THE ORIENTATION TOOL

● Start by selecting the cells whose contents you intend to reorientate.

● Now click the **Orientation** button in the **Alignment** group on the **Home** tab. The options in the drop-down menu are fairly clear, and each of them also has an small explanatory symbol next to it. Here, we're selecting the **Angle Clockwise** option.

● The text in the selected cells now slopes diagonally down at an angle of 45°.

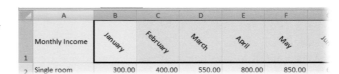

USING THE FORMAT CELLS DIALOG

● With the cells still selected, click again on the **Orientation** button and then on **Format Cell Alignment** at the bottom of the drop-down menu.

• The **Format Cells** dialog box opens, and here we can see that the text in the selected cells is at an angle of **-45°**. By moving the "clock" pointer or clicking on the up and down arrows, it is possible to slope text at exactly the angle you want.

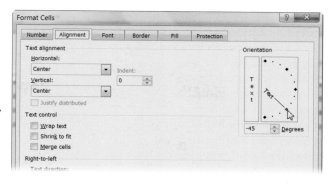

• Here, we have adjusted the text to an angle of +30°.
• Before moving on, we'll return the text to 0° in the **Format Cells** box.

TRANSPOSING ROWS AND COLUMNS

Depending on the data involved and the kinds of categories that make up the labels for the rows and columns, you may find that you wish the grid had been planned with the columns and rows the other way round. In this example, for instance, we might decide that we'd prefer to have the months down the side and the rooms across the top. We don't have to start again–there's an easy way to do this.

• Start by highlighting all the cells, and then click the **Copy** button at the top left, in the **Clipboard** group.
• A flashing border appears around the selected cells.

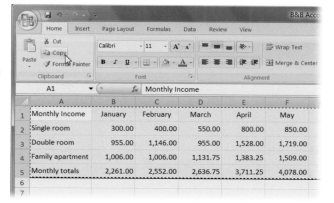

● We're now going to paste the cells and transpose them, but the pasted version cannot overlap the original block, so select a cell further down the worksheet (in this case, A6, which is directly below the selected block).

● Now click on the bottom half of the **Paste** button and select **Transpose** from the drop-down menu.

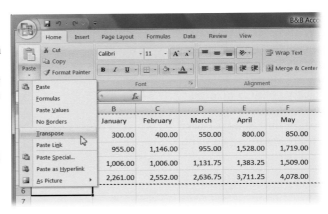

● In the new version, the rows and columns have been transposed. We can compare the two versions and choose which one we want to keep.

	A	B	C	D	E	F
1	Monthly Income	January	February	March	April	May
2	Single room	300.00	400.00	550.00	800.00	850.00
3	Double room	955.00	1,146.00	955.00	1,528.00	1,719.00
4	Family apartment	1,006.00	1,006.00	1,131.75	1,383.25	1,509.00
5	Monthly totals	2,261.00	2,552.00	2,636.75	3,711.25	4,078.00
6	Monthly Income	Single room	Double room	Family apart	Monthly totals	
7	January	300.00	955.00	1,006.00	2,261.00	
8	February	400.00	1,146.00	1,006.00	2,552.00	
9	March	550.00	955.00	1,131.75	2,636.75	
10	April	800.00	1,528.00	1,383.25	3,711.25	
11	May	850.00	1,719.00	1,509.00	4,078.00	
12	June	650.00	1,910.00	1,886.25	4,446.25	
13	July	600.00	2,674.00	2,892.25	6,166.25	
14	August	650.00	2,483.00	3,898.25	7,031.25	
15	September	400.00	1,623.50	1,886.25	3,909.75	
16	October	300.00	668.50	1,257.50	2,226.00	
17	November	250.00	382.00	880.25	1,512.25	
18	December	750.00	1,337.00	1,886.25	3,973.25	

● We'll keep the transposed version, so select all the cells in the top block and then click on the **Delete** button in the **Cells** group.

● In the drop-down menu, select **Delete Sheet Rows**.

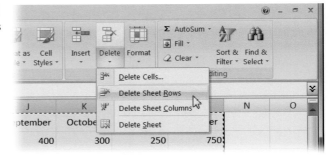

● As our new version was directly below the original block of cells, it moves up into position at the top of the worksheet.

● All we need to do now is widen columns B to E to make room for the headers.

	A	B	C	D	E
1	Monthly Income	Single room	Double room	Family apartm	Monthly
2	January	300	955	1006	2
3	February	400	1146	1006	2
4	March	550	955	1131.75	263(
5	April	800	1528	1383.25	371
6	May	850	1719	1509	4
7	June	650	1910	1886.25	444(
8	July	600	2674	2892.25	616(
9	August	650	2483	3898.25	703
10	September	400	1623.5	1886.25	390(
11	October	300	668.5	1257.5	2
12	November	250	382	880.25	151

MERGING CELLS

There will be times when you need to have information running right across the width of two or more cells, for example to insert a heading over multiple cells. This is quite straightforward to do, but be aware that if you try to merge several cells that already contain text or numbers, only the content of the top left cell will be retained.

INSERTING A ROW

● We're going to add a heading to our grid that runs across all the cells, and we need to make space to do this, so we'll start by inserting a row at the top. Select the current top row by clicking in its row header button, and then click on the bottom half of the **Insert** button in the **Cells** group. From the drop-down menu, select **Insert Sheet Rows**. (Or, if you click on the top half of the button, Excel will automatically insert a row because a row has been selected.)

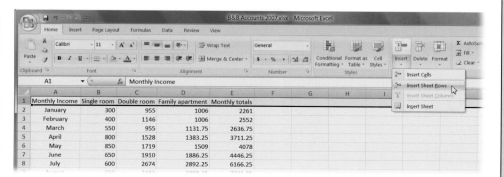

● A row is inserted above the selected row, and the **Format Painter** icon appears at the left-hand end. Click on it to view the formatting options in the drop-down menu.

● If we were working in the middle of a worksheet with complex formatting, these options could be important, but as we'll be changing the formatting, we're content to accept the default option here.

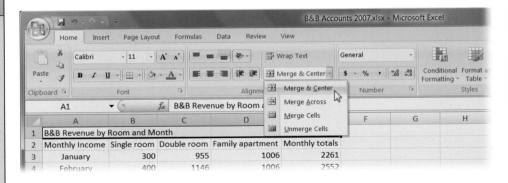

● Double click in the left-hand cell in the new row and type a heading into it.

● Now select the five cells across the grid, click on the arrow next to the **Merge &**

Center button in the **Alignment** group, and then click on **Merge & Center**.

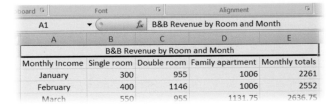

● The new heading is now centered across the five columns.

USING CELL STYLES

If you are familiar with formatting text in Word ⬜, you'll recognize the Font group of commands at the left-hand end of the Home tab, because these are the very same tools. Using these, you can change the font, font size, styling, and color of text that you have highlighted by double clicking in the cell and then dragging with the cursor. However, Excel also has a gallery of Cell Styles that affect the look of not just the text but the cells as well, and this is a much quicker way to add flair to your worksheet.

CREATING A HEADING

● To implement a cell style, text does not need to be highlighted–just select the cells you wish to affect. Here we have clicked in the merged cell that contains the heading at the top of the data. Now go to the bottom right-hand end of the **Styles** group and click on the drop-down arrow.

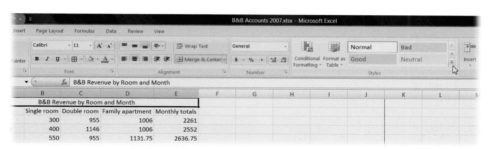

● As you roll the cursor over each of the **Titles and Headings** options, the style of the text in the cell changes.

● Here we are trying out the **Heading 1** style. Click on it to implement it. Bear in mind that changing the style may increase the size of the font and you may have to increase the size of some cells to fit.

COLORING CELLS

● Cells can be colored by using the **Themed Cell Styles** in the same gallery.
● Here we are selecting the 20% tint of the Accent4 color for the cells that contain our figures.

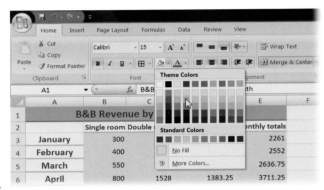

● You can't use a Themed Cell Style and a Title or a Heading style at the same time, but it is possible to color the cells containing headings by using the **Fill Color** button in the **Font** group (or the **Fill** tab in the **Format Cells** box □). Select the cells, click on the button arrow, and select a color from the drop-down palette.

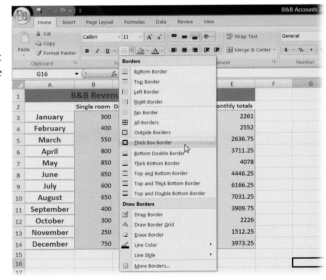

ADDING BORDERS

● To add a border to individual cells or blocks of cells, click on the arrow next to the **Borders** button in the **Font** group and make your selections. To remove the border, click on **No Border**.
● Clicking on the **More Borders** option at the bottom of the drop-down menu will open the **Format Cells** dialog box with the **Border** tab open. Here you can create a custom border in the color of your choice.

USING THEMES

The Themes that are found throughout several of the Office programs are a very powerful tool for completely changing the visual tone of your work. Even if you are totally pleased with your finished worksheet, it's worth running your cursor through the Themes options just to see what the effect will be. As we have seen [ ], each Theme comprises a complementary set of fonts, colors, and effects. All the styling on this worksheet so far has been done using the default Office Theme.

ALTERING THE LOOK

● The Accent colors in the **Themed Cell Styles** and **Fill Color** palette, as well as all the colors and fonts used in headings, charts, and graphs belong to this Theme. Let's see what happens when we change the Theme.

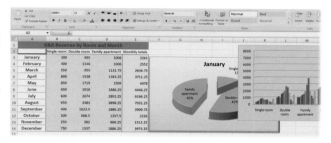

● Here, we have selected the **Page Layout** tab, clicked on the **Themes** button, and there, right at the top of the gallery, is the **Custom** theme we created in Word.

This is another example of the clever integration of programs in Office 2007.

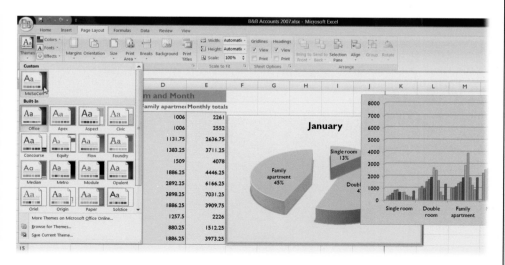

DISTRIBUTING

In this section, we look at way of presenting your
Excel worksheet to other people as a printout, in other
kinds of document, or electronically.

PRINTING YOUR WORKSHEET

Whereas printing a Word document or other single page format is a simple matter, the potential extent of the working area in an Excel worksheet makes the process slightly more complicated. Here we'll look at moving elements into position to fit the page extent, at moving elements to separate worksheets, and at printing part of a page.

ARRANGING THE PAGE

● To see how a worksheet will appear when printed, start by making sure that the page orientation and the size are set correctly by clicking on the **Orientation** and **Size** buttons in the **Page Layout** tab. In this example, the page is **Letter** size, **Portrait** orientation.

● Now click on the **Office** button in the **View** tab, select **Print**, and then click on **Print Preview**.

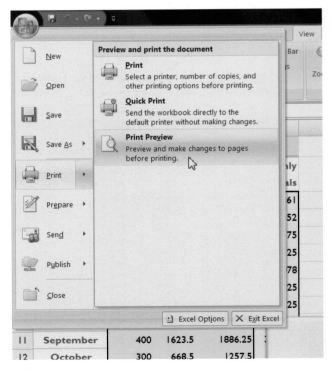

● It's immediately obvious in this view that the first chart is split across two pages, and when we scroll down we find that the second is on another page. We can move the first onto a single page by clicking and dragging it, but not in this view, so click on the **Close Print Preview** button to return to the **Normal** view.

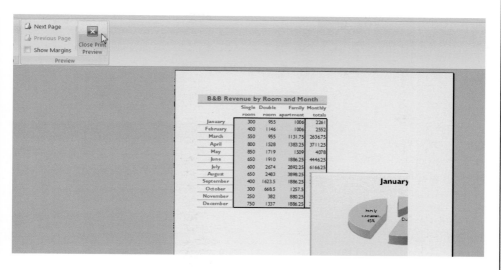

● Back in the **Normal** view, click on **Page Layout**. In this view, the pages are seen at a size that will fit within the screen–in this case, 50%. In this view we can drag the items into new positions within the bounds of the page or pages.

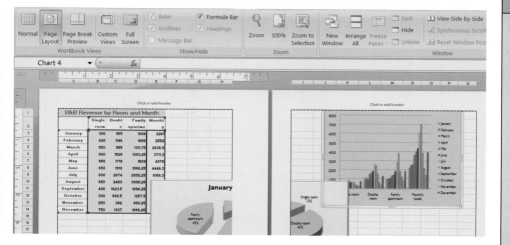

SENDING TO THE PRINTER

● When everything is in position, we can open the **Print** dialog box by clicking on the **Office** button and selecting **Print**, or using the keyboard shortcut [Ctrl] **P**.

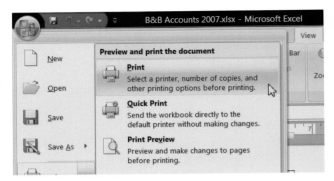

PRINTING GRAPHIC ITEMS

● To print an individual chart or graph, simply click on the item and then print.
● You can first check what will be printed by going to the **Print Preview**.
● Here we have selected the January pie chart and we're clicking on Print Preview.

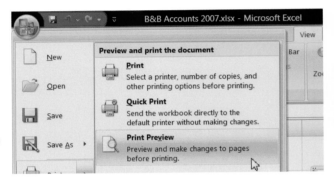

● In this view, we can see that the chart is the only element being printed.

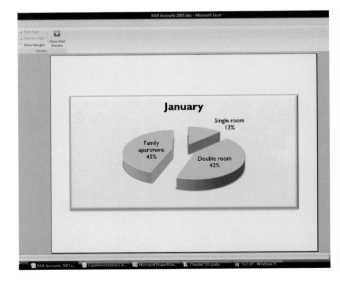

MOVING A CHART

● If you wish to move a chart from a worksheet (for example, so that it does not print with the rest of the sheet), right click on the Chart Area (not on any sub-element within the chart), and select **Move Chart** from the pop-up menu.

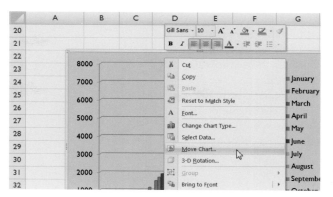

● In the **Move Chart** dialog box, you can opt to send the chart to a new sheet within the workbook by clicking on the *New sheet* radio button, or you can choose **Object in** and use the drop-down arrow to select an existing sheet within your workbook. Click on **OK** to move the chart.

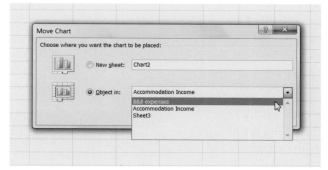

PRINTING WORKSHEET PARTS

● Printing just part of a worksheet can't be done by simply selecting and sending to the printer, as it can for a chart, but it isn't much more complicated.

● Start by selecting the cells that you want to print. In this case, we have selected the Revenue table.

● Then, in the **Page Layout** tab, click on the **Print Area** button and select **Set Print Area** from the menu.

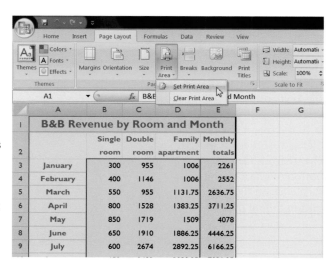

● A dotted border appears around the area selected for printing, indicating that only these cells will be printed.

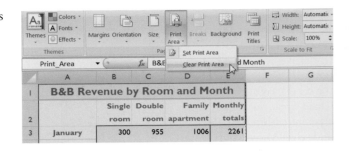

● To deselect the block of cells, click again on the **Print Area** button and select **Clear Print Area**.

EMBEDDING AN OBJECT

Many of the Office 2007 programs share Object Linking and Embedding (or OLE) capabilities. This means that you can take an element from one program, such as a paragraph from Word, a slide from Powerpoint, or a table from Excel, and place it in a document in another program for distribution. In this section we are going to look at an example of using an Excel item in PowerPoint.

COPYING A TABLE INTO POWERPOINT

● To import an Excel table into PowerPoint, we'll start by opening Powerpoint, creating a new slide, and giving it a suitable heading.
● Now click in the main slide area, select the **Insert** tab, and click on **Object** in the **Text** group.

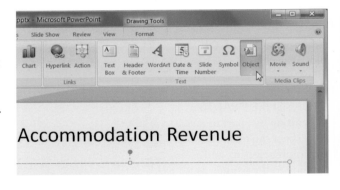

● In the **Insert Object** dialog box, click on the **Create from file** radio button to select it, and then click on the **Browse** button to find the file.

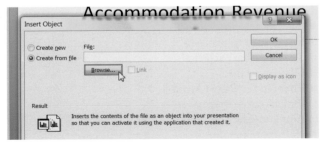

● Navigate to the Excel file that contains the table, select it, and click on **OK**.

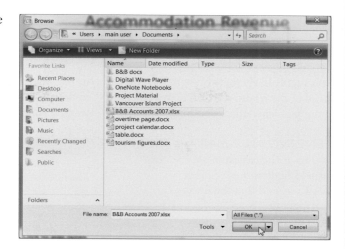

● The table appears on our PowerPoint slide. When working in PowerPoint, if you now click on this chart, the Excel column and row headers, together with the Excel Ribbon tabs, will appear, and you will be able to manipulate the table as if it were still in Excel.

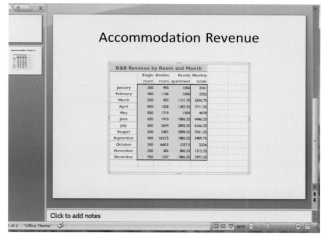

LINKED OBJECTS

An embedded chart or table, although it can still be opened in the program in which it was created, is no longer connected to the original data on which it is based. A linked object, on the other hand, still has this connection. As an experiment, copy and paste a chart from Excel into Powerpoint. Now go back to Excel and change the data on which the chart is based. The chart changes in Excel, of course, but you will find that the version in PowerPoint is also updated.

SENDING ELECTRONICALLY

It is highly likely that you will find you need to distribute your Excel worksheet in a digital form, either sending it by e-mail or placing it on a server for someone else to download and use. There are several ways in which you can do this.

SENDING AN E-MAIL

● This is the easiest of all, providing that the recipient has Excel and that the file is not gigantic.

● With the Excel worksheet open, click on the **Office** button, select **Send**, and then click on **E-mail**.

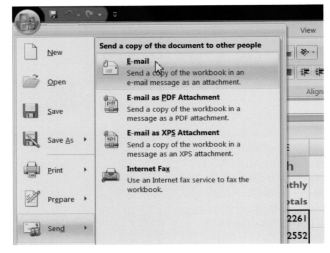

● The Outlook "new message" window opens with the Excel file already attached, ready for you to fill in the recipient's details and add your message.

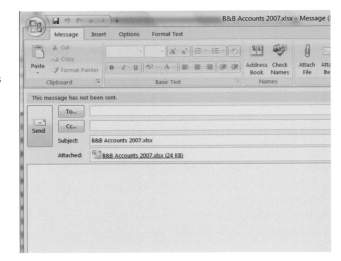

SENDING AS A PDF

● A pdf has the advantage of being readable by anyone who has Adobe's free pdf reader, and the file size will be fairly small, but the file can no longer be opened in Excel. Assuming you have already downloaded the Microsoft pdf-making add-in 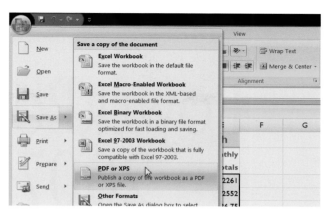, go to the **Office** button **Save As** option and select **PDF or XPS**.

● In the dialog box that opens, select a location in which to save it and click on the **Publish** button.
● The pdf can then be placed on a server or attached to an e-mail.

VIEWING WITH A WEB BROWSER

● An interesting option can be found by clicking on **Other Formats** at the bottom of the **Save As** list.
● In the **Save as type** panel, select **Web Page**, choose a location in which to save it, and click on **Save**.

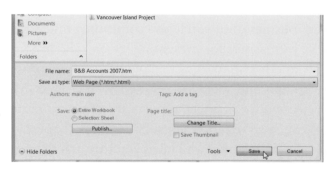

● When you–or anyone else–double clicks on the saved file, it will now open, not in Excel, but in the web browser program, in this instance Internet Explorer, and the page can be posted on the Internet in this form.

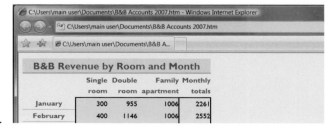

177 **Sharing OneNote Files**

POWERPOINT® 2007

IN RECENT YEARS, PowerPoint has been transformed from aXhumdrum business slide show program into a versatile presentation powerhouse that can be used to persuade in the widest sense. It remains the program of choice for big business, but you'll also commonly find it being used in schools by teachers for presenting lessons and by students for projects and homework, or making up part of a promotional package for clubs and societies seeking new members. Micro businesses also use it for financial reports, to secure more capital, or to promote themselves and their services. This chapter looks at PowerPoint's main features, and takes you through the process from creating a basic slide presentation to presenting a show complete with text, images, animation, sound, and video.

POWERPOINT ON SCREEN

In this section, we'll introduce you to PowerPoint, a powerful and versatile program for getting any kind of information across to an individual or a group of people.

WHAT IS POWERPOINT?

PowerPoint is a program designed to create electronic slide shows that small groups or individuals can watch on a computer, or that large groups can watch on a big screen projector. Originally intended for bigger businesses, PowerPoint is now routinely used in classrooms, waiting rooms, kiosks, and on exhibition stands–in fact, in any environment where you need to get a sales or information-based message across.

WHAT CAN I DO WITH IT?

- Persuade people with simple, colorful slide shows.
- Display your PowerPoint presentation in person or let it run unattended in a kiosk or on an exhibition stand.
- Include information from other Office programs, such as Excel.
- Package the presentation onto a CD to send through the post.

QUICK PHOTO ALBUMS

PowerPoint includes a neat feature that allows you to create an instant slide show from any folder on your PC that contains photos. Just start the program, click the **Insert** tab, then the **Photo Album** button and navigate to the folder where the photos are stored. Select what you want to include, click **Insert**, then **Create**.

KEY POWERPOINT FEATURES

RICH CONTENT

- Use PowerPoint to collate information and content from different sources and then assemble them into a powerful presentation that features, text, tables, charts, photos, diagrams, video, sound effects, animation, narration, and background music.

ATTRACTIVE GRAPHICS

- Thanks to improved displays and the slicker screen "furniture" provided by Windows Vista and Office 2007, PowerPoint slides are better looking than ever; expect more detailed graphics, smoother gradients, more engaging animations, better video performance, and a great collection of Clip Art.

THEMES

- Take the effort out of designing slides with PowerPoint's themes. Used in conjunction with other settings for backgrounds, color palettes, and fonts, these allow you to apply an entire "look" to a slide show with a few mouse clicks. The various elements that go to make up a theme– slide background, color schemes, fonts, etc.–have all been chosen to compliment each other to produce a consistent look and feel that makes sense in design terms. By applying themes in real time, PowerPoint lets you see instantly whether the design works.

SMARTART

- Much more than a collection of pre-drawn shapes, SmartArt graphics can also incorporate many of the sophisticated visual elements that are applied elsewhere in the program. An organization chart, for example, can quickly be transformed from a series of simple lines, arrows, and boxes into a much more attractive diagram that includes three dimensional shading and gradients, reflections, beveled edges, fancy text styles, and so on. SmartArt can also be animated so that different parts of the diagram appear on screen when you click the mouse, or at pre-determined intervals, thus allowing time for a synchronized narration.

MULTIMEDIA

- More than ever before, PowerPoint is at home with sound and video. You can use the many built-in sound effects to make a point, record background music from a CD, and add narration using a microphone. PowerPoint mixes all three types of sound together and stores them alongside your presentation so the show can play unaccompanied if necessary.

SORTING SLIDES

- PowerPoint 2007 makes it easy to re-arrange the order in which slides are shown. Using the Slide Sorter view, it's possible to drag and drop slides into a new order in a few moments; you can also temporarily hide slides so that they stay safely stored with the rest of the presentation but aren't displayed on screen when you come to give the slide show. This allows you to create a single presentation and then filter out those elements that aren't appropriate to your audience at any one time.

POWERPOINT IN ACTION

PowerPoint shares the familiar Office interface and includes a wide range of styles, designs, and templates, so it's pretty easy to get going and produce slide shows straight away. The latest version includes many more pre-defined themes, styles, and templates, making it easy to put together slick, persuasive presentations. It integrates well with other Office programs and is able to import pictures, sounds, and video to use alongside its own collection of Clip Art and design tools; the SmartArt feature is particularly effective, as we'll see later on in this chapter. Your finished presentation can be shown directly from your computer, or distributed by e-mail or on a CD-ROM.

FEATURES KEY

❶ Office Button
Access PowerPoint's basic file commands.

❷ Tabs
Each tab has a specific set of commands and menus.

❸ Themes
A gallery of ready-made designs to transform your slides with a mouse click.

❹ Colors, Fonts, Effects
Each button opens a gallery of color schemes, font styles, and graphic effects.

❺ Background Styles
Offers colors and textures to change slide background.

❻ Hide Background Graphics
Switches off background images and colors.

❼ Task Pane
Contains extra commands and options specific to the task in hand.

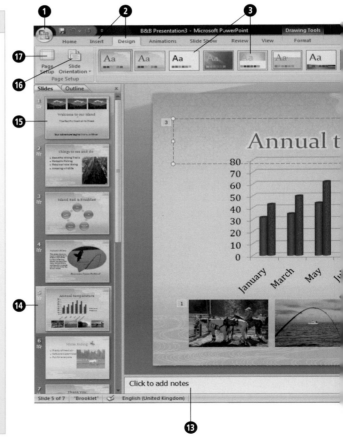

INSTANT SLIDE SHOWS

Microsoft Office Online has a range of templates that you can download and use as the basis for your own presentation. Make sure you're connected to the Internet, start PowerPoint, click the Office button and choose **New**. At the dialog box, select **Presentations** and click one of the categories (for example, **Business**) in the main window. Click on a template to select it and then click the **Download** button to bring it into PowerPoint.

FEATURES KEY

❽ Add Effect
Allows you to animate items on the slide.
❾ Animation List
A selection of numbered animations that have been applied to this slide.
❿ Zoom
Drag the slider right or left to make slides in the main window bigger or smaller.
⓫ Speaker Icon
Indicates that this slide includes a recorded narration.
⓬ Chart
This chart was created using Excel and then added to PowerPoint.
⓭ Notes Panel
Click here to add notes to the slide.
⓮ Current Slide
The slide in the main window is highlighted in orange.
⓯ Slide Thumbnails
This list gives you an overview of other slides in the show while you work on the one in the main window.
⓰ Slide Orientation
Switch between landscape and portrait formats.
⓱ Page Setup
Change the way each slide is presented on the screen.

INTRODUCING POWERPOINT

As we're about to demonstrate in this section, the principles behind creating a good presentation are quite simple and good results can be achieved surprisingly quickly.

THE FIVE-MINUTE PRESENTATION

Although PowerPoint positively bristles with all kinds of tools that allow you to create slide shows brimming with special effects and animations, it's always best to start your presentation simply. One of the most effective ways of doing this is to limit the time you take or the number of slides you use in order to create your presentation. Over the next four pages, we'll show you how to make a presentation in 14 steps that uses just two slides to get a message across.

CHOOSING A THEME
● Open PowerPoint. You'll see an empty slide in the main window and the now familiar Ribbon Toolbar along the top.

● Let's start by finding a good "look" for our slide show. Click the **Design** tab.

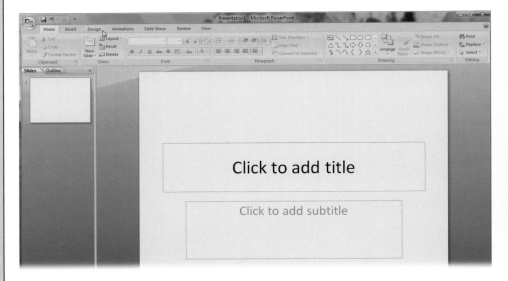

● Roll the cursor along the miniature slides on the toolbar and watch what happens to the slide in the main window.

● As you do, the slide takes on the formatting of each theme in turn, displaying different colors, fonts, and graphics. This one, for example, is called **Apex**.

ADDING TEXT

● However, we're going to choose **Metro** because we like the dark blue look and the way the title is reflected.

● PowerPoint makes it pretty clear what we have to do next.

● To add our own title, we need to move the cursor over the **CLICK TO ADD TITLE** text that's already there (this is called a place-holder) and then click.

● When we do, the place-holder text disappears and we can start typing in our own title.

● Finish the title and then click on the subtitle above it and type in something there to complete the first slide.

ADDING A NEW SLIDE

● Having completed the first slide, let's add a second. There are several ways of doing this, but this is the quickest way.

● Move the cursor under the miniature slide in the left-hand column and right click there.

● Choose **New Slide** from the menu.

● PowerPoint creates a new slide and displays it in the main window. In addition, it puts a miniature version in the column on the left-hand side of the screen.

● Along with the title, you can see that this slide also has bullet points and a selection of icons in the middle that allow us to add different kinds of content.

- Here we've completed the slide in the same way as the first one.
- When you press the ⟨Enter ⏎⟩ key after typing the first bullet point, PowerPoint automatically creates the next one, ready for you to carry on.

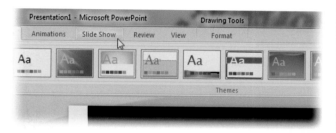

RUNNING THE SHOW

- Having finished your second slide, move the cursor up to the **Slide Show** tab at the top of the Ribbon Bar and click on it.

- Leave all the settings as they are and move the cursor over to the **From Beginning** button as shown here and click it once.

- Here's the first slide of the presentation, running full screen on our PC.
- To move to the next slide we can either press the ⟨Spacebar⟩ on your keyboard or click the left mouse button.
- When the slide show has finished running, press the ⟨Spacebar⟩ or click the mouse button to exit and return to PowerPoint.

SLIDE DESIGN

Of course, content is king when it comes to presentations, but it's also important to make sure that your slides look their very best. PowerPoint makes this easy to achieve.

THEMES AND BACKGROUNDS

We've already seen that PowerPoint comes with a number of pre-formatted designs that you can use to create slides quickly and easily. The program also includes design layouts, as well as many different ways to adjust the background to change the look of your presentation with very little effort; and none of it requires any artistic skill.

SAVING YOUR PRESENTATION

● Before we go any further, save what we've already done by clicking the disc icon at the top left corner.

● When the **Save As** dialog box opens, navigate to the folder where you want to store the presentation and then type in a name for it.
● Click the **Save** button to continue.
● The presentation is now safely stored on the PC.

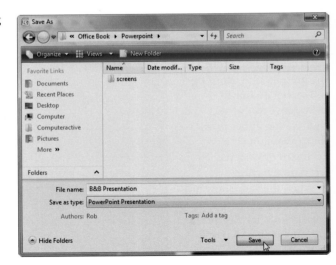

CHOOSING ANOTHER THEME

- Now slide the cursor over to the right-hand end of the row of themes, where you'll see a little arrow. The fact that this isn't grayed out indicates that there are more themes to choose from. Click the arrow once.

- The line of themes "rolls up" to reveal another line below. Move the cursor along these thumbnails, checking out how they change the look of the slide in the main window as you go. Choose one by clicking on it. Note how both slides in the left-hand column change to reflect your new choice.

DEATH BY POWERPOINT

This has become a phrase commonly used in the business world to describe presentations that are either interminably long or that feature too many eye-popping colors, fonts, animations, and videos. Either fault may result in audiences switching off, zoning out, or even walking out. In this chapter, we'll explain how, by following a few simple design rules, you can make presentations that get your message across, rather than getting in the way of it.

CHANGING THE BACKGROUND

- Having chosen a new theme, there's all sorts we can do with it.
- Slide the cursor over to the right-hand end of the theme thumbnails where you'll see controls to change the background, colors, and fonts, and also one for something called **Effects**.

- Let's start by looking at the different backgrounds available for this particular theme. Move the cursor over to the arrow next to

Background Styles and click it once to open the background palette.
- Move the cursor over the different backgrounds in

the box and watch as the main slide changes to reflect your choice. This preview is a really helpful way to decide on a slide layout.

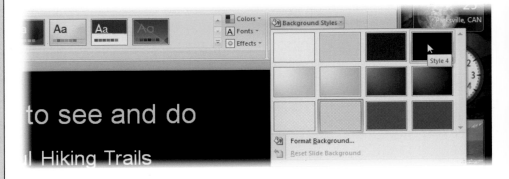

HIDE BACKGROUND GRAPHICS

You can see this option beneath the **Background Styles** command on the Ribbon Toolbar, and you might wonder what it's for. If you've got an older machine, or perhaps one with not much memory, creating a fancy slide show can slow everything down. If that's the case, click this button to turn off any background graphics while you're preparing the actual slide content–the PC will have less screen "furniture" to process and will run more smoothly. Just switch it on again when you're ready to play the actual slide show.

● Once you've found a background you like, click on it once to select it and change the slides you've created so far.

CHANGING FONTS AND EFFECTS

● Next, move the cursor over to the arrow next to **Fonts** and click it to open PowerPoint's selection of font styles.
● Preview the fonts by sliding the cursor over each of them in turn and then select one you like.
● In this example, we're selecting **Office 2**.

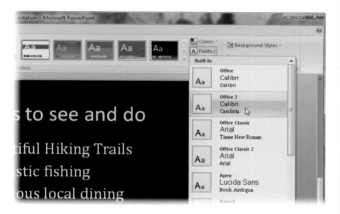

● Finally, click the arrow next to **Effects**. You'll see a range of subtle effects that can be added to your slides.
● Note that they're not always visible, depending on the slide layout and its components. We'll return to **Effects** later in the book.

SLIDE LAYOUTS

As well as allowing you to select from a wide range of pre-defined themes, background styles, color palettes, and fonts, PowerPoint also provides a selection of ready-made layouts. These take all of the elements we've looked at so far and then arrange them in different ways that are best suited for the type of information being displayed. By allowing you to pick from a selection of pre-defined layouts, PowerPoint can help you save lots of time when preparing your presentation.

CREATE A NEW SLIDE

● Start by opening the **Home** tab, and then click on the **New Slide** button.
● Be sure to click the top half of the button where the icon is, rather than clicking on the text and the drop-down arrow.

● This produces another new, blank slide with the same formatting as before, and another miniature slide in the left-hand panel.
● Each of the miniature slides is numbered.
● Whenever you have second thoughts about a new slide, you can always get rid of it and try again.
● Simply move the cursor over the miniature version in the left-hand column and click on it with the right mouse button. Then choose **Delete Slide**.

CHOOSING A SLIDE LAYOUT

● Now, move the cursor back up over the **New Slide** button. This time, click on the arrow at the bottom of the button. This opens a small gallery of commonly used slide layouts.

● We're going to move the cursor down to the slide layout called **Two Content**. Click on it to select it.

● This adds a third slide with a different layout to our presentation.

● If you don't like it, you can easily change it.

● Right click on the slide in the left-hand column and choose **Layout** from the pop-up menu. Then select a different layout.

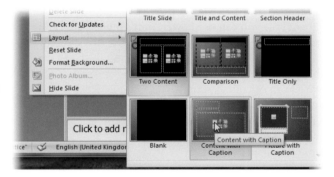

● Here's the new slide in place, ready for us to add some content.

ADDING CONTENT

We've seen already how easy it is to create a couple of effective, basic slides using PowerPoint 2007. In this section, we'll look at adding some proper content of our own.

ADDING TEXT

The message of your presentation should be clear to the audience. Although your design should be attractive, it should not be so startling as to compete with the content of your presentation. We've already shown how you can use PowerPoint's built-in layouts to add headings and bullet points quickly and, for many purposes that's all you really need. However, PowerPoint 2007 has an incredible range of beautiful, subtle visual tricks up its sleeve with which to make text more appealing and, thus, more effective. We'll look at some of those in this section.

INSERTING TEXT
● You can of course, start anywhere and with any slide, but we're going to add some text to the first slide we created earlier.
● We'll begin by clicking the **Insert** tab at the top of the Ribbon Toolbar.

● The Ribbon Toolbar changes to show all of the Insert tools and options.
● Now click on **Text Box** to continue.

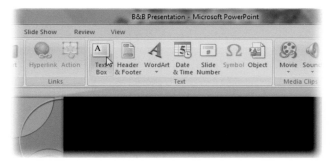

● Move the cursor down to the main slide, select an imaginary top left-hand corner for the text box, click there and then, still holding down the mouse button, drag right and down to make a rectangle.

● This is the text box.

● Now type something into the text box. Here, we're typing **Your adventure begins here… with us.**

FORMATTING TEXT

● Next, click and drag the cursor over the text to highlight it.

● Now move the cursor slightly above the text until the floating toolbar appears.

● Open the drop-down list next to the text size option and choose something bigger. In this example we're going for **36** point–twice the size of the current text.

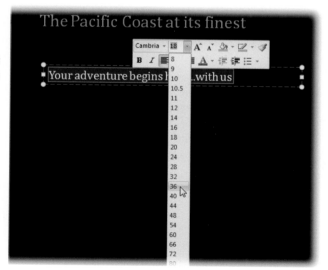

- Increasing the size causes our text to wrap over onto the next line, which we don't want.
- So, grab the little handle on the right-hand edge of the text box and–still holding down the left mouse button–drag it out to the right to increase the size of the box.
- The idea here is to make the text fit on a single line.

- When you think it's large enough, click anywhere on the slide to remove the highlight. If the line still wraps round, try clicking on the left-hand edge and moving that out a little.
- Now let's add some style.
- Click on one of the words in the text line. In this example, we're clicking on the word **here**.

- We're going to add some color to this word, so, start by clicking the **Format** tab in the **Drawing Tools** at the top of the screen.

● Next, move the cursor over to the **Text Fill** command on the toolbar.

● Open the drop-down menu by clicking the arrow there, and choose a suitable color from the palette.

● As with many other PowerPoint formatting options, as you hover the cursor over a particular color, the program will apply it to your selection so you can see if you like it.

● Here, we're choosing light green to match the slide border.

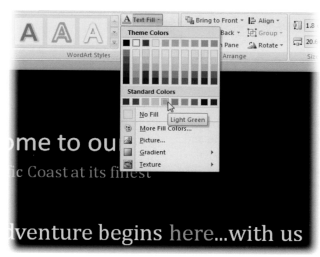

● Now, note that the selection around your text has a dotted line. This means that any formatting will only be applied to whatever is currently selected by the cursor (in the previous steps for example, we selected the word **here**).

● To select all of the text, move the cursor over the dotted line until it turns into a cross with arrows at each point and click again.

● The line turns solid.

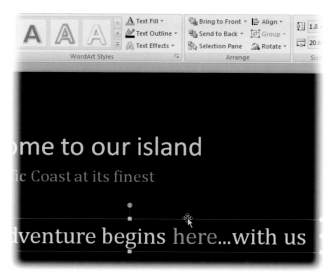

● With everything still selected, move the cursor up to **Text Effects**.

● Click the arrow to open the drop-down menu and choose **Reflection**, then select any one that you like.
● In this example, we're going to select the first one.

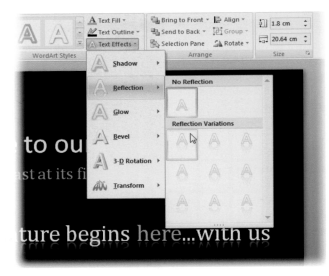

● Finally, with the box still highlighted by a solid line, move it to the bottom of the slide by pressing the ⬇ arrow on your keyboard or by clicking on it and dragging with the mouse.
● Then click anywhere in the slide to finish.

ADDING IMAGES

Even if you don't have access to any original photos, don't use a graphics program, or can't draw, there's nothing to stop you from adding high-quality images to your presentations. We'll cover how to add your own images later in this chapter, but here we're going to look at adding Clip Art. Now, Clip Art has had something of a reputation for producing amateurish results, but, as you'll see in the pages that follow, these days that couldn't be further from the truth.

FINDING CLIP ART

● We're going to add some Clip Art to our first slide.
● We start by moving the cursor over to the **Insert** tab at the top of the Ribbon and clicking it once.

● Move the cursor down to the **Clip Art** command on the toolbar and click there once.

● After a moment, the **Clip Art** task pane will open on the right-hand side of the main window.
● Depending on whether you've used this before, it will either be empty or will have a selection of Clip Art displayed there already.

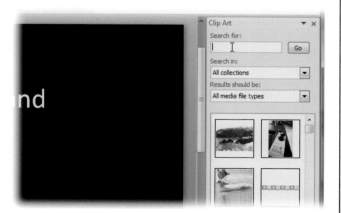

• No matter what's there already, make sure you're connected to the Internet and then type a word into the search box that describes the kind of image you want.

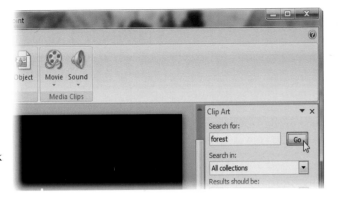

• Here we're going to type **forest**. Leave the rest of the settings as they are and click the **Go** button.

• After a moment, the search will return with whatever images it can find.

• As we didn't change any of the settings, it's found both line drawings and photographs. We're going to select one of the photos of a snowy mountain because we think that'll go well with our slide.

• We just move the cursor over to the photo and click on it once.

ARRANGING CLIPART

• PowerPoint just dumps our chosen photo in the middle of the slide, covering half our text and generally messing things up.

• Fortunately, this is easy to fix. We'll start by grabbing the handle at the bottom right-hand corner with the cursor and then dragging up and inward to make the photo smaller.

● Although smaller, the photo is still covering up our heading, so we'll grab it with the mouse and move it down the screen. In fact, to illustrate another feature we're going to drag it down so it obscures the text at the bottom of the slide. You'll see why in a moment.

● So that we can see both the photo and the text, we're going to change the picture style and arrange things so that it "sits" behind the text.

● We'll start by moving the cursor up to the **Picture Styles** gallery. This time though, we're going to click the bottom arrow.

● PowerPoint opens the entire Picture Styles gallery for us to choose from.

● Move the cursor over each one until you find the one that works best.

● As our slide is dark, we're going to choose the black, double frame.

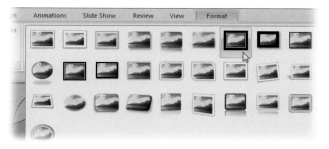

● Finally, move the cursor over to the **Send to Back** option in the Ribbon Toolbar and click it once.

● Click anywhere on the slide to de-select the photo. Here's the result.

● We've managed to insert a photo, re-size it, and then position it behind some text to produce a very effective slide image.

USING SMARTART

● Along with Clip Art and photos, PowerPoint can use special kinds of imagery called SmartArt. These are pre-drawn graphics of a high standard that you can integrate into a slide.

● If you're starting from scratch, simply create a new slide and then, from the **Layout** gallery, select **Title and Content**.

● If you're following us, right click on the third slide in the left-hand column and choose **Layout** from the pop-up menu and then select **Title and Content**.

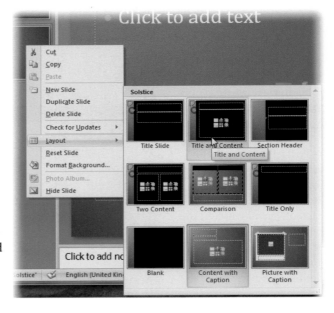

● Type in a title for the slide and then move your cursor down to the little block of six icons in the middle. To find a SmartArt Graphic, select the top right icon by clicking on it.

- The **Choose a SmartArt Graphic** dialog box opens, displaying the range of SmartArt list and diagram options, and descriptive previews, that we saw earlier in Word 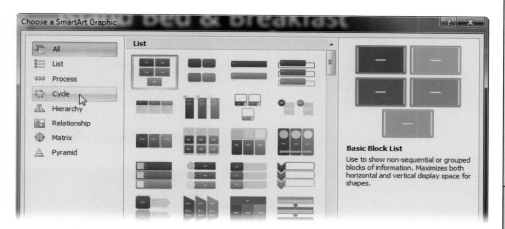. Click the **Cycle** tab in the left-hand column to open that category.

- Then select the first SmartArt graphic in the main window and click **OK** to insert it into the slide.

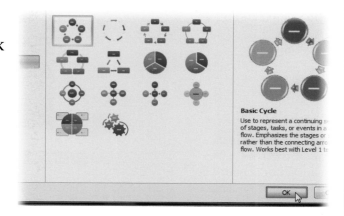

SMARTART GRAPHICS

Experiment with the various types of SmartArt included in the dialog box described above and you won't be disappointed. PowerPoint's ready-made graphics have improved out of all recognition and allow even the least skilled of designers to produce something that's worth looking at. They are particularly good if you want to present photos on a slide in an unusual way.

Choosing a SmartArt Graphic

● As you can see in this example, PowerPoint puts placeholder text inside each circle and adds a little dialog on the left-hand side where we can type in the text we actually want to use. If the pane does not appear, click on **Text Pane**.

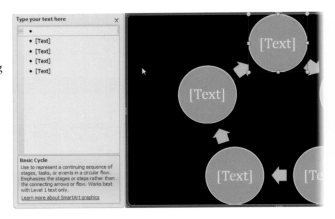

● Next we're going to type in the text for our circles– the idea here is to make our point in graphical fashion. (Later on, we will turn this into a simple animation).

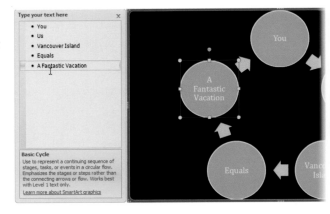

● Next, we'll open the **SmartArt Styles** gallery to make our graphic a bit more modern-looking by clicking the bottom arrow as shown here.

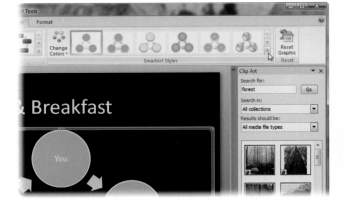

- Move the cursor round the various styles until you find one you like.
- Click on the one you like and PowerPoint will apply it to the graphic.
- We've chosen **Inset**, which gives the circles a pleasant 3D button effect.

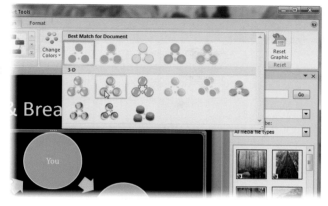

- Click on the main slide to hide the dialog box and remove the selection box, and there you can see the completed slide.
- Text like this can be much more effective than using traditional headings, sub-headings, bullets, and so on.

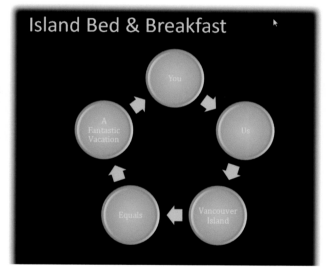

ADDING GRAPHICS

A number of PowerPoint's pre-designed layouts feature the six little insert graphic elements that we described in this section. The first allows you to add a table, the second a chart, the third SmartArt, the fourth a picture already stored on your PC's hard disk, the fifth a piece of Clip Art, and the sixth a media clip (e.g., a sound or movie file). If your slide layout doesn't include any of these, just click the **Insert** tab on the Ribbon and you'll find them.

ADDING NEW ELEMENTS

In this section we'll add a photograph from our hard disc, insert some fancy WordArt, and create an attractive annual temperature chart.

ADDING A PHOTOGRAPH

We've already added Clip Art to a presentation but now we going to insert a photograph that's already stored on our PC's hard disk. You'll see that the procedure is slightly different, although the principle is the same. Having done that, we'll add a treatment and an effect to the frame of the photo, hopefully to enhance its appearance, before going on to incorporate the next element.

INSERTING A PHOTO

● Make sure the third slide is highlighted in the left-hand column and then click the **Home** tab and select **New Slide**.

● Then choose **Content with Caption**.

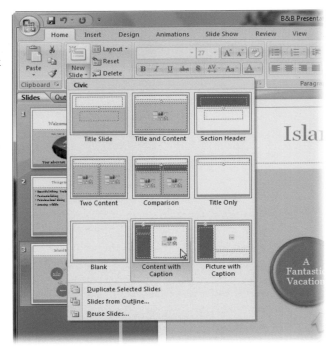

- Add any text content to the new slide by clicking the placeholders and replacing them. Then click the **Insert Picture from File** icon.

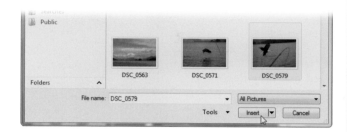

- Use Windows' file commands to navigate to where your photos are stored and click once on the one you'd like to use.
- Then click **Insert**.

FORMATTING THE PHOTO

- You can now re-size and move the photo if you need to. Otherwise, select it and then choose **Picture Shape** from the toolbar.
- Here, we're selecting one of the **Callout** shapes.

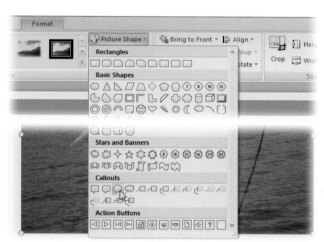

WHY DOES THE PRESENTATION LOOK DIFFERENT?

Rather than use the same slide design throughout this chapter, we thought it would make it more interesting to show off various PowerPoint "looks." So, as we proceed through the chapter, we'll change the design in order to showcase PowerPoint's various design strengths. In each case, the main contents will stay the same and, if we add or change anything, it will only be by using features that we've already seen and explained elsewhere in the chapter.

● Next, add a drop shadow by opening the **Picture Effects** gallery and choosing **Shadow** and then picking one from the drop-down list that appears.

● Here's the finished photo, sized and formatted.

ADDING WORDART

We looked at WordArt earlier, in the chapter on Word , but it's worth looking at again here because it can add real punch to a slide where an "ordinary" typed caption might be lacking. As WordArt is pre-formatted, you can try different styles quickly and easily until you find the one that best suits the design of your slide.

INSERTING WORDART
● Click the **Insert** tab and then open the WordArt gallery by opening the drop-down list as shown here.
● Select a style from the gallery by clicking on it.

● When the WordArt placeholder appears, just type in your own text.

● Click the new text three times in quick succession in order to highlight it, and then change attributes such as the font size or font style if necessary.
● Here we've made it smaller and added italics.

● Finally, drag it down into position.

ADDING A CHART

As PowerPoint is part of the Office suite of programs, this means that you can take advantage of the features included in other Office programs, for example, Excel. The spreadsheet is very good at creating graphs and charts, which makes it a useful partner if you're trying to get information across in a visual way so as to make people pay more attention to it. In this section, we'll add a quick chart showing minimum and maximum temperatures on our island.

OPENING EXCEL

● Start by creating a new slide–we've chosen a simple **Title and Content** slide–and add some text and pictures.
● Click on the **Insert** tab at the top of the Ribbon and click on the **Chart** button.

● The **Insert Chart** dialog box opens, which contains the same extensive range of chart categories and individual chart types that we have already seen in Word and Excel.
● The chart needs to suit the information that you want to display, so choose a chart style and click **OK**.

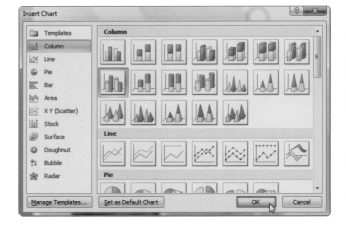

ADDING THE FIGURES

● Excel loads a dummy spreadsheet with placeholder labels and figures. We're going to add high and low annual temperatures. Therefore, we'll only need to chart two of the three columns shown here, so grab the "handle" at the bottom right and drag it in.

● We're going to replace the **Category** labels with months of the year, the **Series** labels with minimum and maximum temperatures, and the **Series 1 and Series 2** figures with real temperature readings. Click in the first cell and start typing.

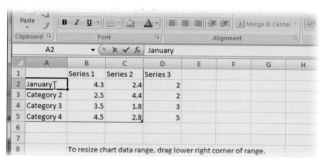

● Here we've completed the spreadsheet and re-sized Excel so you can see the chart in PowerPoint next to it.
● Charts can be re-sized with the mouse if necessary.
● Close Excel when you have finished.

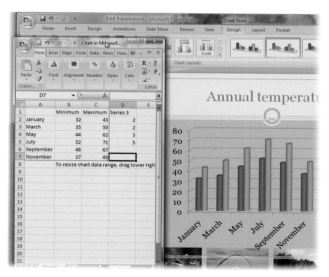

Adding Animation

A good presentation will often also include some movement, and PowerPoint offers various ways to animate text, graphics, photos, and other elements.

Simple Animations

Although the last thing you want is a presentation that's too full of movement, with elements sliding in from all over the place, it's important to add some animation, even if it's only fairly simple. PowerPoint's built-in features allow you, for example, to stagger the appearance of a piece of SmartArt so that you can time any accompanying narration to coincide with the appearance of the various elements. Although it's relatively simple to set up, this kind of attention to detail can help to make a presentation more dynamic and interesting.

ANIMATING SMARTART

● Start by switching to a slide that has some SmartArt on it and then clicking on the **Animations** tab at the top. Note that the **Animate** command next to it is grayed out.

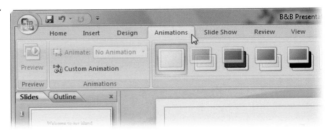

● Click once on the piece of SmartArt on the slide to select it. Check the borders to make sure it's highlighted properly– it's not always obvious.

● With the SmartArt highlighted, open the drop-down menu next to **Animate** and roll the cursor down the various animations options. As you do, PowerPoint will preview each one. Here, the circles are "flying" in from the bottom of the screen.

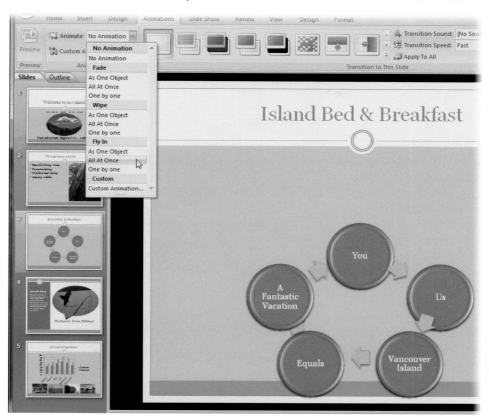

TRIGGERING ANIMATIONS

Although the preview shows the SmartArt circles appearing one by one, when you actually run the presentation, and the SmartArt slide appears, nothing will happen.

That's because PowerPoint animations are set up by default to respond to a mouse click. So, when the slide appears, click the left mouse button to have the first circle appear, click it again for the second, and so on. This makes it easy to synchronize any accompanying narration, because you can control exactly when each part of the diagram appears.

● For something that includes distinct elements like this, however, it might be best to have them appear individually, so we're going to choose to fade them in one by one.

ANIMATING PHOTOS

● Now switch to a slide that has some photos on it.
● Here, we have four photos in a line, but rather than animating them all, we're just going to choose a couple. Click on the first photo to select it.

● Next, we're going to hold down the PC's ⇧ Shift key and select the third photo in the line. Note that both now have selection handles round them.

● Next, move the cursor up to the drop-down list next to **Animate** on the toolbar and click it.
● Now select **Fade**.

● You will now see that the two selected pictures slowly fade into view.

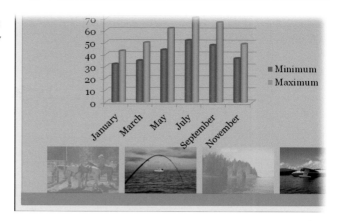

CUSTOM ANIMATIONS

Although PowerPoint's "out-of-the-box" animations are good, there'll be occasions when you'll want to exercise more control over what's going on. Perhaps the timing of when a particular element appears on the screen is especially important, or the order in which elements arrive on screen needs refining. Or you may find that, while it suits the presentation to have certain items appear automatically, you'd like to control others with a mouse click, or perhaps you want to set up animations that include both. In this section, we'll look at PowerPoint's Custom Animations.

STARTING A CUSTOM ANIMATION

● Navigate to a slide that has multiple items on it. We're going to use a bullet list and, if you don't have one, we suggest you spend a moment creating one.
● Make sure the **Animations** tab at the top is selected and then click on the **Custom Animation** button.

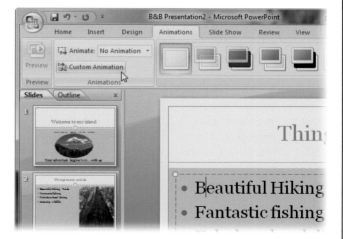

● This opens the **Custom Animation** pane on the right-hand side of the main slide window.

● Before you do anything, make sure that you've selected the first of your bullet points by clicking it.

● Then click on the **Add Effect** button at the top of the **Custom Animation** pane.

● Slide the cursor down the menu and choose **Entrance** and then **Fly In**.

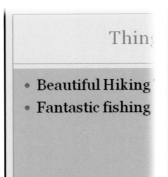

● As soon as you do, PowerPoint plays back the animation, using the defaults shown in the **Custom Animation** pane– starting on a mouse click, from the bottom, and very fast. Too fast, in fact, so we need to change this.

CHANGING THE SPEED

- To slow the animation down, simply open the drop-down list next to **Speed** and select **Medium**.

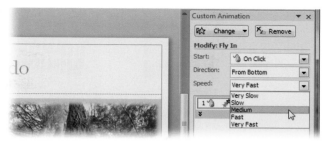

FINE TUNING

- So far we've applied the same animation to all of the bullet points, but it's also possible to set them up individually.
- Start by clicking on the double arrows in the **Custom Animation** pane.

- This opens up a series of boxes, each of which corresponds to a bullet point on the main slide.
- Currently each point has a couple of icons next to it that indicate that an animation is present (that's the moving star) and that it starts when the mouse is clicked.

- Leave the first entry unchanged so that the bullet point doesn't appear until we click the mouse button.
- Open the second drop-down list instead and choose **Start After Previous**.

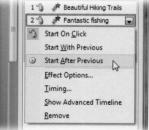

● Note that the first icon next to this action has now changed from a mouse to a clock, indicating the change in animation status.

● Repeat this for the fourth bullet point and then open the drop-down list again and click on **Timing**.

● This opens the **Fly In** dialog box. All we want to do here is increase the delay between the time the third bullet point appears (when we click the mouse) and the fourth automatically sliding up the screen.
● Click the up arrow until the **Delay** setting reads **4**.

● Then click **OK** to close the dialog box.

- Before we move on, it's worth having a look at the controls situated down at the bottom of the **Custom Animation** pane.
- If you don't want the animation to play every time you adjust it, just remove the tick from the **AutoPreview** option.
- To see how the animation will look full screen, click the **Slide Show** button.
- To see the timeline, click the **Play/Stop** button as shown here.

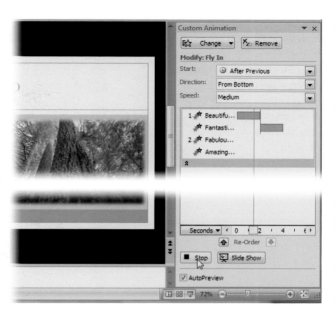

ANIMATION OPTIONS

We've spent most of this section looking at one single style of animation–the entrance. That's because this is the type most people will use most frequently. However, PowerPoint offers plenty of other options, including the ability to control the way items "leave" the slide, as well as controlling their relative styles by adding special effects so they increase in size or spin around or light up like a flash bulb.

ADDITIONAL EFFECTS
- So far, we've only considered those effects that are immediately available from the **Add Effect** button, but PowerPoint has many more available. Check them out by clicking on **Add Effect** and then choose **Entrance** and then **More Effects** from the menu.

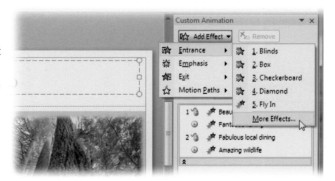

The Timeline

● This opens the **Add Entrance Effect** dialog box where you'll find more than 50 effects that you can preview just by clicking on them in turn.

● When you've found one you like, just click on **OK** to apply it.

● Go back to the **Add Effect** button and click it again. Move the cursor down to **Exit** and you'll see it includes the same options as **Entrance**. Move up one to **Emphasis** and you'll see it's possible to change the font, the size, and style of a heading, as well as making it shrink or grow or even spin into position.

- To see what else can be achieved using the **Emphasis** menu, select **More Effects.**

- This opens the **Add Emphasis Effect** dialog box where, again, there are dozens of special effects from which to choose.
- Audition them by clicking on each in turn.
- Click **OK** to apply one or **Cancel** to return to the main slide view.

THE TIMELINE

Although we've done nothing here that really warrants it, there may be occasions when you need very fine control over the animation elements on a slide, perhaps to have them appearing in time to music that you've added or because there are lots of different animations working together in a complex sequence. If that's the case, make sure the **Custom Animation** pane is open, select one of the items in the list that's being animated (in our example there were four bullet points) and open the drop-down menu. Choose **Show Advanced Timeline** from the menu, and PowerPoint displays a pictorial view of how long each animation lasts, set against a scale calibrated in seconds.

ADDING SOUND

Having created an interesting and informative
visual presentation, you can enhance it even more with
the judicious use of sound, music, and narration.

SOUND EFFECTS

If ever it was important to keep the old adage "less is more" in mind, then it's when you come to the use of sounds–and especially sound effects–in your presentation. There's nothing more distracting than slide shows that are so packed with sounds and effects that the audience can't concentrate on the message that you're trying to get across. Of course, careful use of the occasional effect can genuinely improve the tone of a presentation, adding a touch of light relief or providing atmosphere where necessary; this should be your aim.

CHOOSING THE EFFECT

● We've changed the look of our presentation again, and added a final slide to say "thanks" to our audience for their attention.

● Here we've selected that slide and then clicked the **Insert** tab.

● Move to the **Media Clips** section of the Ribbon, click the arrow under **Sound**, and select the **Sound from Clip Organizer** option.

● This opens PowerPoint's collection of sound effects.

● As we've left the **Search in** settings here unchanged, the program lists sound effects both stored on the PC and on the Internet.

● The first one (**Claps, Cheering**) looks a likely candidate, so we'll click the arrow next to it and then choose **Preview/Properties** from the menu.

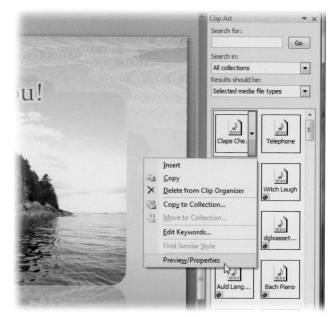

● When the dialog box opens, the sound plays back automatically.

● Click **Play** to hear it again, or use the **Previous/ Next** buttons at each end of the **Refresh** panel to audition other sounds in the clips pane.

● Then click **Close**.

• Use the scroll bar to look through the available sound clips. There are literally dozens of them, and they are not organized in any kind of alphabetical order.

• Once you've chosen the sound you want, select it from the clips pane by clicking on it.

EFFECT PROPERTIES

• When the dialog box opens, choose whether you want the sound to play automatically or when you click the mouse button.

• PowerPoint adds the sound to the slide, and displays a little speaker icon in the center of the slide to indicate it's there.

- You can preview how the slide now looks and sounds by clicking the **Slide Show** tab and then clicking the **From Current Slide** button.
- When the slide runs, it will be obvious that the little speaker icon is quite distracting, sitting there in the middle of the photo.

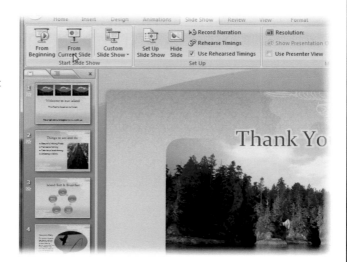

- To hide it, right click on the icon and choose **Send to Back** from the pop-up menu.
- The speaker icon will now be hidden behind the picture so no-one can see it. The sound will still play, however.

Speaker icon indicates that the slide has sound

FINDING SOUNDS

Remember that you can search for specific sounds in the same way that you can search for specific photos or pieces of Clip Art. When the **Clip Organizer** pane is open, simply type in a word that's associated with the kind of sound you're seeking and click the **Go** button. Typing in "nature," for example, returns all manner of interesting sounds of water, animals, the wind in the trees, and so on.

ADDING MUSIC

There's no doubt that music can improve a presentation by helping to set the scene and create an atmosphere, much more effectively than words or even pictures. The trick is to find music that works well with what you're trying to say. We would recommend using a single piece of music that lasts for the entire length of the slide show. This will work well to heighten a contrast or provide light relief.

CHOOSING A TRACK

● Make sure that there's a CD in your PC's drive and then navigate to the first slide in your presentation.

● Click on the **Insert** tab at the top of the Ribbon and then on the **Sound** arrow button. Choose **Play CD Audio Track** from the menu.

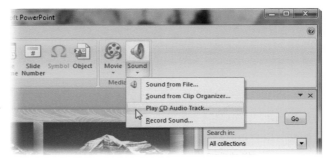

● When the dialog box appears, you can specify where you want the music to start and stop, and whether it should play continuously. You can also hide the music playback icon so it doesn't appear on the screen by ticking the relevant box.

● Click **OK** to confirm your choices.

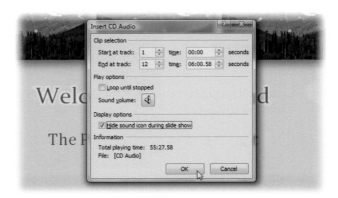

● At the next dialog, choose whether you want the CD to start playing automatically or when you click the mouse button.

SETTING PLAYBACK OPTIONS

● Next, highlight the CD icon in the slide and then move the cursor up to the **Options** tab on the Ribbon Toolbar and click it.

● Currently, if you were to run the slide show, the music would start to play automatically, but stop as soon as you moved on from this slide.

Click on the CD icon to select it

● To get the music to play for the whole presentation, move the cursor up to the **Play Track** command, open the drop-down list there and choose **Play across slides**.

● While we're here, note that from the Ribbon you can also change various settings to do with which tracks play back and when they start or stop.

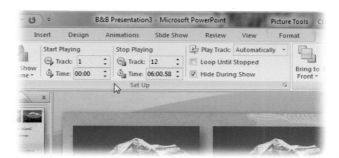

ADDING A NARRATION

When you're there in person, you can obviously present the show yourself, to your own specifications. However, there may be some occasions when your attendance simply isn't possible. It's commonplace these days to have slide shows running unattended at booths and kiosks, and PowerPoint also makes it easy to pack a presentation up into a file that can be e-mailed to someone or sent out on a CD-ROM. By adding a narration, you can ensure that the salient parts of the show are pointed out, even when you're not actually present in person.

PREPARING TO RECORD

● Before you start, make sure that you know what you're going to say. Run through the presentation a few times and make notes.
● Then, when you're ready, connect a microphone to your PC (refer to the manual for how to do this) and then click the **Slide Show** tab and choose **Record Narration**.

● When the dialog box opens, click the **Change Quality** button.

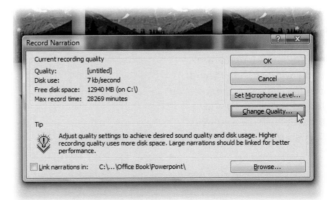

● Open the drop-down list and choose **CD quality**, then click **OK**.

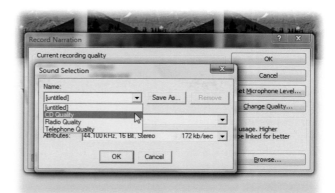

● Next, click the **Set Microphone Level** button.

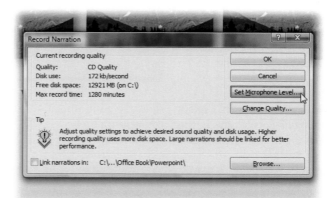

● Using your normal spoken voice, speak into the microphone.

● The aim is to keep the meter in the green, though it's OK if it strays into yellow occasionally.

● Click **OK** when you've finished the test narration.

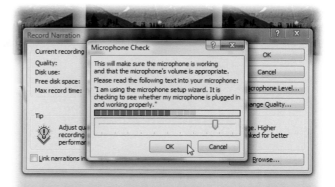

RECORDING

● Finally, get ready. As soon as you click **OK** at the next dialog box, the slide show will start and you need to begin your narration.

● As you speak, remember to make any of the mouse clicks necessary to move from one slide to the next, or to trigger animations and so on.

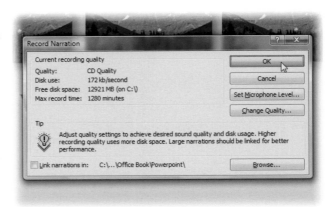

● When the show finishes, PowerPoint asks whether you want to save the narration timings with the slides.

● Click **Save**.

● PowerPoint then displays the Slide Sorter view. In this view, each of your slides is shown as a thumbnail. Underneath each thumbnail, you will see that PowerPoint displays the duration of each slide in seconds.

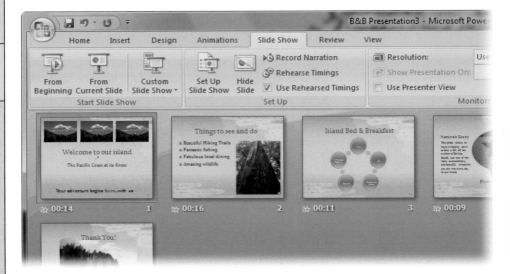

• If you now run the show from the beginning, you'll hear your music, narration, and the applause sound effect at the end. Now is the time to start considering how you intend to distribute your masterpiece. Copying it to a CD is one option.

PACKAGING FOR CD

• Older versions of PowerPoint had a feature called "pack and go," which has been renamed **Package for CD** in the 2007 version. This allows you to copy the whole of your presentation (including all the pictures and sounds) to a blank CD that you can then distribute.

• It can then be viewed on any computer, even one without PowerPoint.

• The option is available in the **Publish** tab when you click on the Office button.

• For full instructions, click on the **Help** button at the top right of the screen and open **PowerPoint Help**.

Adding Video

Having added sounds of different types, it's now time to look at the way PowerPoint handles video. As it turns out, the two processes are very similar.

Using Movie Clips

As we've seen in the previous section, Clip Art has come a long way since its humble beginnings. In fact, as well as photos and sounds, Clip Art also includes animations that can be used to give certain slides a nice quirky appeal. It's important to try to match up any movie clip art that you use with the background of the slide so it doesn't "sit" on top of it like a postage stamp. Fortunately, the choice available to PowerPoint users is wide enough that this shouldn't be too much of a problem.

FIND A MOVIE CLIP

● Start by creating a new slide. Don't worry if it appears after the final slide we created in the previous section—we'll fix that later.
● You can add some text to it if you want.

● Next, click the **Insert** tab at the top of the Ribbon, then on the **Movie** arrow button to open the drop-down menu, and choose **Movie from Clip Organizer**.

● When the Clip Organizer pane opens on the right-hand side, you can search for movie clips.

● As our slide is about horse riding, we're going to search for "horse."

● Key this term into the **Search for** panel and click the **Go** button to start.

● PowerPoint soon returns a selection of small, horse-related, animated Clip Art-style movies from which to make your choice.

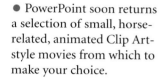

SIZE DOES MATTER

Adding a movie–any kind of movie–to your presentation, is going to increase the overall file size. If it's something that you are going to run from your PC or distribute on a CD-ROM, then this isn't an issue. However, if you intend to send copies of your movie out as attachments to e-mails or perhaps post them on a web page, then it's important to think about how much space they take up. Always keep videos short and sweet and, given the option, save them in Windows Media Video format to save space.

ADDING A MOVIE CLIP

● The third clip in this selection has a pleasant blue background that matches the design we're currently using, so we'll click that once to add it to the slide.

● Once it's on the slide, re-size it if necessary and drag it into position.

● To see what the movie clip looks like, click the **Slide Show** tab and then click **From Current Slide**.

● The slide opens full screen and the little bucking bronco animated clip starts to play immediately.

USING ORIGINAL VIDEO

Shooting your own DVD-quality home movies has never been easier. Digital Video cameras are inexpensive and simple to use, and a modern PC has everything you need to copy and edit your videos, courtesy of the Movie Maker program that's included for free with Windows. PowerPoint can incorporate videos you've shot and edited yourself, and by adding personalized content like this, you can only enhance the message you're trying to get across. This section explains how it works.

INSERTING A MOVIE
● We're going to use the same slide, so click the **Insert** tab. Then click on the **Movie** button arrow and choose **Movie from File**.

● Use Windows' file commands to navigate to the folder where your movie clip is stored.
● Click on it once to select the clip and then click the **OK** button.

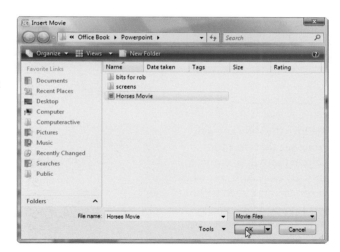

● When the dialog box appears, select whether you want the clip to begin playing as soon as the slide appears or when you click the mouse. Here, we're choosing the latter.

● Spend a moment moving and/or adjusting the size of the video playback window if necessary.

PLAYING BACK THE MOVIE

Then, click the **Slide Show** tab and then choose **From Current Slide**.

● Once the slide appears, you'll see that the little Clip Art movie is animated straight away, as it was when we opened the slide without our home-made movie.

● However, the movie itself won't start playing until we click on it.

● Move the cursor over the movie frame so that it turns into a hand.

The cursor turns into a hand when it's over the movie

- Now click on the still image on the screen, and the movie starts to play back.

- To pause the movie, move the cursor over the screen until it turns into a hand again, and click.
- Click again to continue it.

TOO MUCH SOUND

When you're adding a home-made movie, think about the sound. If you've already got some background music, a sound effect or two, and a narration going on over the top, it might be a good idea to remove the sound track completely using Windows Movie Maker, because there are few things worse than too much sound competing for the audience's attention. If in doubt, keep the movie sound turned way down low or get rid of it.

PRESENTING THE SHOW

So, we've added text, graphics, animations, sounds, and video to our presentation. Now all that's left for us to do is organize our slides and give the presentation itself.

THE SLIDE SORTER

So far we've worked on individual slides in the main slide window and added them to the column on the left. However, PowerPoint has another view–the Slide Sorter view–which allows you to see the entire presentation as if each slide were laid out on a desk, or on the type of light box used by professional photographers. This makes it extremely easy for you to see where slides need to be re-ordered, and also lets you take a view on the overall look and pacing of the slide show.

OPENING THE SLIDE SORTER

● Start by moving the cursor to the **View** tab and then clicking the **Slide Sorter** button.

● Although our test slide show only includes seven slides, you can imagine how useful this view is when you're working on a show containing many more.

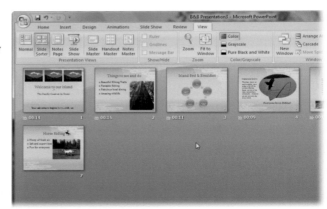

RE-ARRANGING THE SLIDES

● You'll remember that we created a slide in the previous section. Currently it appears after our Thank You slide at the end, so we need to move it forward.

● Just click on it with the cursor and then, still holding down the left mouse button, start to drag it.

● As you move the cursor to the correct position (in this example, one slot before the final Thank You slide), you'll see a vertical orange line indicating where the dragged slide will appear when you let go of the mouse button.

● Let go to drop the slide into position.

● You can move any slide in the show around in exactly the same way.

HIDING A SLIDE

● Here's another neat feature. Let's say you're giving a presentation to a group of people who aren't interested in horse riding. Just right click on the horse slide and choose **Hide Slide** from the pop-up menu.

• Note the slide number at the bottom of slide 6 now has a box round it to indicate that, when the presentation runs, this slide won't appear.

• Remember to reverse the process when you need to.

ZOOMING IN

• Finally, we've actually been operating this show at a reduced size so as to fit more onto the screen.

• In the **Slide Sorter** view, however, it may sometimes be useful to have individual slides displayed on the screen a little larger or even at full size. Move the cursor to the bottom of the screen and drag the slider to the right to increase the size.

• Want to zoom in or out to a specific percentage? Just click on the percentage figure next to the zoom slider and then, when the dialog box opens, type a number into the percentage box. Then click **OK**.

TRANSITIONS

These are the special effects that you see when one slide changes to another. Without transitions, the slides will simply flick one to the next, but with transitions enabled, there are dozens of different wipes, fades, dissolves, stripes, bars, pushes, and covers from which to choose. We could discuss the options endlessly, but there's really no need. It's usually best to stick to one or two different transitions during the course of a show, or it risks becoming too flashy and distracting for your audience.

CHOOSING A TRANSITION

● Click the **Normal** button to return to the main slide view.

● From here, click on the **Animations** tab and then open the Transitions gallery by clicking the arrow as shown here.

NOTES

Below each slide in the main window there is a box where you can type notes. Take the opportunity to type in a few jottings there to remind you of important facts or to develop later into a proper script. If you click the **View** tab, you'll see that there's a Notes page that displays each slide in turn, along with any associated text. You can work on these notes when you're away from the PC.

● Roll the cursor round the various transitions. As you do, you'll see them previewed in the main slide window.

● As PowerPoint has a tendency to set all its animations, including transitions, to **Fast**, it's possible this will be a bit speedy for your liking.

● Just open the drop-down list next to **Transition Speed** on the toolbar and choose **Medium** or **Slow** to see which you prefer.

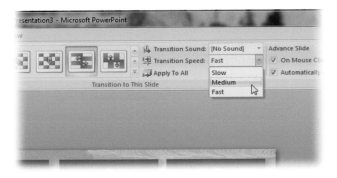

● It's usually best to have the same transition all the way through the presentation so, having chosen one, click the **Apply To All** button.

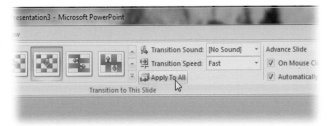

PRINTING

Although PowerPoint presentations are primarily a way to communicate information on the screen, it's sometimes helpful to have handouts to pass round and that your audience can take away. PowerPoint has a wide range of printing features that you can access by clicking the Office button and choosing **Print**. Go here to print out slides, handouts, notes, and so on.

RUNNING THE SHOW

There are various ways to run the slide show. If everything's set up properly as described in the previous pages, your presentation will virtually run itself, unless, of course, you've elected to mouse click between slides. However, there are a few last options that it's well worth covering to help ensure a smooth running presentation and to help your audience get the most out of it.

CONTROLLING THE SHOW

● Having clicked the **Slide Show** tab and chosen **From Beginning**, you can let the show run itself, or right click at any point to take manual control.

● Note that you can jump to a specific slide at any point, apart from slide 6, which is still "hidden."

● Alternatively, you can alter many fundamental show settings by clicking the **Slide Show** tab and then choosing **Set Up Slide Show**. From here you can turn narration and animations on or off, loop the slide show (useful if it's running unattended), show a particular sequence of slides, and so on.

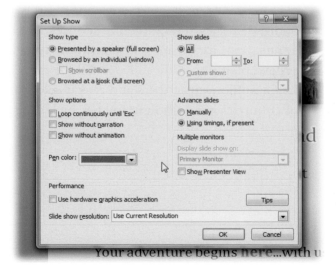

OFFICE LIVE
SMALL BUSINESS

DESPITE ITS NAME, this service is not directly related to the
Microsoft Office suite of programs, although it does
integrate with some of them. Primarily, Office Live
Small Business is a service to businesses that want to have a
fairly inexpensive shop window on the Internet. Relaunched
in a revised form in 2008, with improved web-building tools,
additional sales and marketing services, and a range of extra
applications for business organization, time management, and
project planning, Office Live Small Business now has well over
half a million subscribers and is available in a growing number
of countries in addition to the US, including the UK.

INTRODUCING OFFICE LIVE

Microsoft's Office Live Small Business web hosting service offers a place on the Internet through which small businesses can promote themselves and market their goods and services.

WHAT IS OFFICE LIVE?

For the majority of people looking for a product or a service, certainly in Europe and North America, their first port of call is now the Internet. For larger companies, having a web site has long been a priority, but smaller ones tend, not surprisingly, to hold back from making what appears to be sizeable commitment of time and/or money. The need to have an Internet presence is, nonetheless, there, and Microsoft has developed Office Live Small Business to meet that need.

THE OFFICE LIVE PAGE
● This service, which is free for the first year of usage in its basic form, provides the means for small businesses to set up and maintain their own web sites, as well as offering a bundle of sales, marketing, and business management tools. The web address of Office Live Small Business is **http:// smallbusiness.officelive. com**. To find out more, click on the **Learn more** link.

WHAT'S ON OFFER?

- Each of the blue headings on the Learn More page is a link to a fuller explanation, so click on these to find out.

- At the heart of the Office Live service, Microsoft offers the web space, the domain name, and the web site building tools to help any small business build and maintain its own web site.

- Office Live also includes up to one hundred business e-mail accounts, software for managing contacts, documents, and projects, as well as access to a workspace that can be shared with colleagues and customers.

- All this is free for the first year, after which there is an annual fee that depends on where you are located. (UK company domain names with a co.uk suffix are free for two years.)

- At an additional cost, Office Live offers the tools for businesses to use online sales and marketing techniques, and to make sure that the business's presence is advertised through search engines.

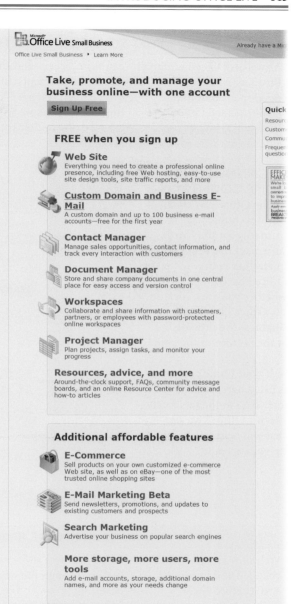

NOT TO BE CONFUSED WITH...

As well as Office Live Small Business, Microsoft has developed an online facility–called Office Live Workspace–where users can store, access, and share files and documents. In this chapter, when we use the term Office Live we are referring to the Small Business web hosting service only. To find out more about Office Live Workspace, visit **http://workspace.officelive. com**.

LOCATING YOUR HOME COUNTRY

● The Office Live Small Business home page is primarily for the North American market. If you are in another region served by Office Live (or to find out whether you are), click on the **Office Live Small Business Worldwide** link at the bottom of the panel.

● If your home country is listed here, click on the link to go to the regionally specific Office Live site that will help you to set up your account.

A CHANGE OF SCREEN

Web sites are always being changed and improved, and Microsoft will undoubtedly continue to refine the pages you see when you visit Office Live Small Business and when you go through the steps of setting up a web site. The web-building tools will themselves, no doubt, change over time. There are also differences between regional sites. For these reasons, the screens that we show here may not always correspond exactly with those that you see online.

FINDING OUT MORE

● Before committing yourself to signing up to Office Live, you will obviously want to find out as much as you can about what it offers you and your business. The Microsoft site provides a thorough overview of all aspects of the service.

● Click on each of the links in the top right corner to discover detailed articles on a range of Office Live topics.

● The **Frequently asked questions** link is a good route to take if you want to delve more deeply into what Office Live is, what benefits it offers you, the commitments you enter into, and issues of privacy and support.

● Click on any of the questions that has a small "+" sign next to it to see the detailed answer.

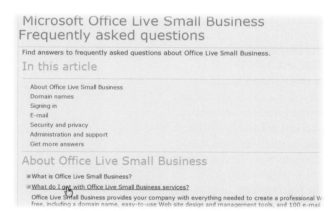

● The **Small Business Resource Center** contains practical advice on setting up your web site for your particular needs, design tips, and seminars on sales, marketing, promotion, and management.

● Click on the links to open further pages.

SIGNING UP

**If you've decided that Offfice Live Small Business is
a service that offers what you need in the way of a web site,
start the process by signing up.**

CREATING AN ACCOUNT

Signing up should be a fairly straight-forward process. All you need in order to start from scratch is a functioning e-mail account and your credit card details.

If you already have a Windows Live ID, then it's even easier. Just make sure you know your password, and you can sign up to Office Live using the same ID.

BEGINNING THE PROCESS

● Once you've found out all you need to know about Office Live Small Business, checked out the fine print, and satisfied yourself that this is for you, return to the home page and click on the **Sign Up Free** button.

● Unless you already have a Windows Live identity, fill in the **Your e-mail address** panel with your existing address and click on **Create**.

● You will then be led through a series of simple steps that involve filling in your name and address, credit card details, the kind of business you have, and the size of the business.

● At the end of the process, a dialog box will appear informing you that have set up your Office Live Small Business account.
● To go to the account, click on the blue button.

Congratulations!
You've completed signing up for Microsoft Office Live Small Business

Click **Go to my account** to set up your account in minutes with a Web site, e-mail accounts, business applications, and more.

Go to my account

GETTING STARTED
And here we are. This is your personal Home page, and if you are going to make the most of Office Live, then you will be coming here quite often.
● When you open the page, the Getting Started panel occupies the top half of the screen. When you no longer need this, you can hide it by clicking on the tab at the bottom right.
● As you can see in the top right corner, we have been assigned an Office Live web address. This has been chosen on the basis of the information about the company and the nature of its business that we keyed in during the signing in process.
● You may consider that your business needs its own independent domain name, in which case your first task is to click on the **Get a Web address** link.

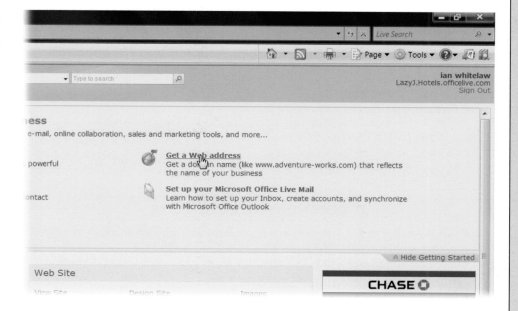

CHOOSING A DOMAIN NAME

● In the screen that opens, type in the domain name you want to register and click on **Check availability**.

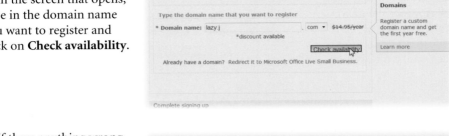

● If there anything wrong with your proposed domain name, an error warning will alert you to this and you can then correct it.

● Even if there is nothing wrong with the domain name, you may not be the first person to think of it, in which case the availability search will return a message saying that it is unavailable.

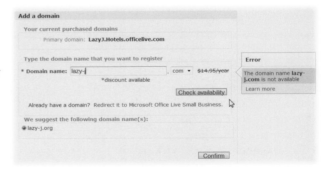

IT DEPENDS WHERE YOU LIVE

Note that if you live in a country that is not listed in the Office Live Worldwide page, you may not be able to register a domain name through Office Live. You can, however, register a domain name through a registrar and then redirect it to Office Live by clicking on the link at the bottom of the **Add a domain** panel.

● In which case, you'll need to keep on trying.

● Here, we're spelling out the company name to see if that name is available.

● We've found a domain name that works.

● If you want to carry on the search for the perfect domain name, click on **Back,** but if you're happy with your choice, click to confirm and complete the registration process.

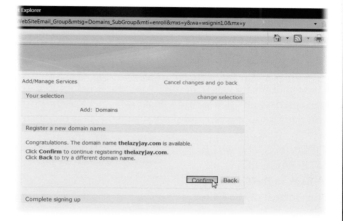

● In the next screen you will be asked to fill in your contact information, and when you've done this, the registration is complete.

● The domain name will become active 24 hours later.

CREATING A WEB SITE

If you've survived the form filling, you can now look forward to the fun of actually creating your own web site using the Office Live web-making tools and building blocks.

GOING TO YOUR WEB SITE

It's time to get creative and start work on your web site, and if that sounds daunting, it needn't. The great thing about Office Live Small Business is that, once you've registered, your site is already there. All you need to do is go in and put your own information, images, documents, and other elements into the pages. The tools that are supplied make that easy–and enjoyable–to do. In this section we're going to demonstrate the principles of working on the opening Home page.

OPENING THE WEB SITE PAGE EDITOR

● Back in the Getting Started area of the Office Live page, click on **Create a business Web site**.

● If your web browser is set to block pop-ups, at this point you may be asked to allow pop-ups temporarily, or always allow pop-ups from this site, which you may want to do.

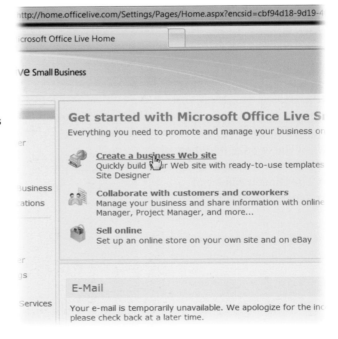

ttp://home.officelive.com/Settings/Pages/Home.aspx?encsid=cbf94d18-9d19-4

icrosoft Office Live Home

ve Small Business

Get started with Microsoft Office Live S
Everything you need to promote and manage your business or

Create a business Web site
Quickly build your Web site with ready-to-use templates
Site Designer

Collaborate with customers and coworkers
Manage your business and share information with online
Manager, Project Manager, and more...

Sell online
Set up an online store on your own site and on eBay

E-Mail
Your e-mail is temporarily unavailable. We apologize for the inc
please check back at a later time.

- You will now have the first view of your site's **Home** page. The company name has been placed in the header area, there's a vaguely appropriate image in the top left corner, and the whole page is laid out with placeholder text, good advice, and placeholder images in numbered zones.
- We've clicked and dragged our cursor across the words **Home Page**, which were orange and are now highlighted in blue, and the **Page Editor** tab is open at the top of the page.

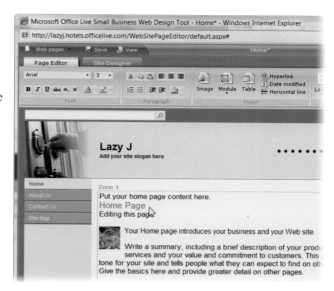

THE PAGE EDITOR TAB

The web design tool kit consists of two tabs at the top of the page, somewhat like the Ribbon in Office 2007. Each of these comes to the front when you click on certain elements in the page, or you can click on a tab to open it. In this section, we're going to work our way along the Page Editor tab and see what the tools do.

MANIPULATING TEXT

- Looking closely at these, we get a sense of déja vu. The **Font** and **Paragraph** tools are basically the same as those in Word, and they work in the same way. We will look at the other tools as we need them.

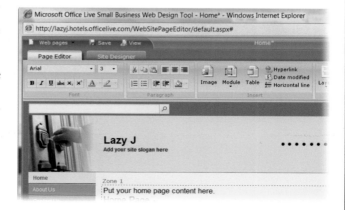

● To change the font of the selected text, click the arrow on the right of the top left panel and select a font from the drop-down menu.

● To change the font size, click on the arrow at the end of the panel that has the number **3** in it.
● Each available font size has a number, and we're selecting number **5 (18pt)**.
● Using the **Font** and **Paragraph** tools, we can work our way through the placeholder text, replacing and restyling it to create our personal business message.

WORKING WITH IMAGES

● We want to include some of our own images on the page, images stored on the hard disc of our computer, so click on the first picture box to highlight it and then click on the **Image** button in the **Page Editor** toolbar.

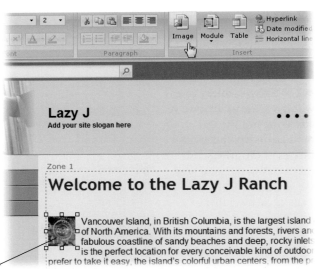

The picture box has been selected

- The **Insert an image** dialog box opens, with a message saying, not surprisingly, that there are no images in our Image Gallery, which is where images must be stored for use in our pages. We can start the uploading process from here, or it can be done in the Image Gallery itself.
- We're going to click **Cancel** and then go to the page that is already behind our web page–the **Page Manager**.

THE PAGE MANAGER

- From here we can go to any of our web site pages, edit or delete them, visit the Office Live Resource Center, or, as we are going to do, view the Image, Document, or Template Galleries.
- Click on **Image Gallery**, which can be found at the top of the **Web Site** panel.

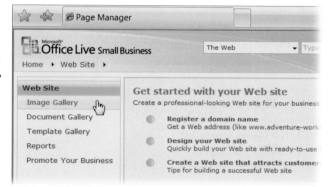

- The **Image Gallery** opens with the message that we've already seen.
- Click on **Upload** to add images to the gallery.

INSTALL IMAGE UPLOADER

The first time that you do this, the **Image Uploader** dialog box appears, telling you that before you can upload, you must download the necessary software.

● Click on **Download** and then follow the instructions to install the software on your computer.

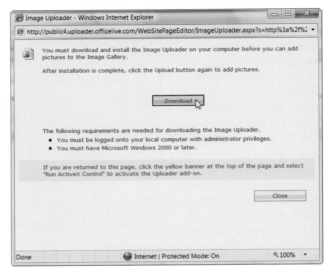

UPLOADING TO THE GALLERY

● Once the Image Uploader program has been installed, clicking on the **Upload** button in the Image Gallery opens the **Image Uploader** window. Here you can navigate through the folders on your hard disc to find the images you want.

● Click to place a tick in the check box on any image you want to upload to your site.

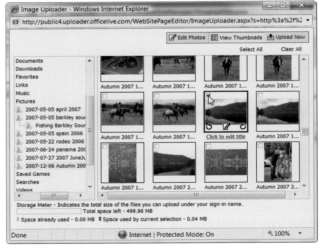

● When you have selected the pictures you want, click on the **Upload Now** button at the top of the box.

● The **Upload Progress** dialog box opens.
● If you have selected a great many photographs, or if the images are high resolution and the files are large, this may take a while.

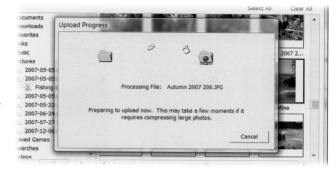

● The selected pictures appear in the gallery.
● To delete an image from here, place a tick in the check box on the image and then click on **Delete**.
● We are now ready to place an image on our web page, so we'll return to the Home page.

PLACING AN IMAGE

● With the picture box on the web page still selected, click again on the **Image** button, and this time the **Insert an image** box has something to offer.
● As the instruction in the dialog box says, select an image and click **OK**.

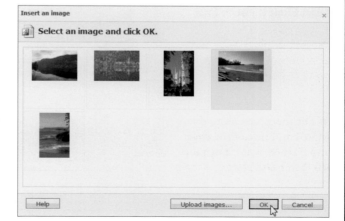

- The image appears full width on the web page.
- Click once on the picture to select it, and handles appear with which you can resize the image.
- Click on the image to drag it to a new position.

- To make the text flow around the image in this position, right click on it and select **Float Left** from the pop-up menu.

- To position the image on the right and the text on the left, right click again and select **Float Right**.

- The image moves to the right-hand side of the page, and the text flows down the left-hand side of it.

IMPORTING MODULES

● Moving along the Page Editor toolbar, we come to the **Module** button. This provides access to ready-made features that can be incorporated into your web page. Make sure you have clicked in a Zone, so that the module can be placed on the page, click on the **Module** button, and select from the drop-down list.

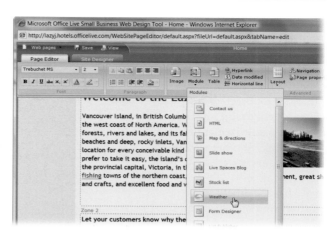

● The **Weather** feature, for example, allows you to insert a live weather report and a four-day forecast for the location of your choice.

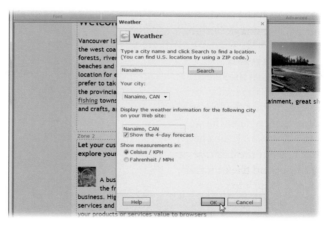

INSERTING A TABLE

● Clicking on the **Table** button opens the **Create a Table** dialog box, where you can choose a table type, specify the color scheme and the dimensions, and insert it on your web page.

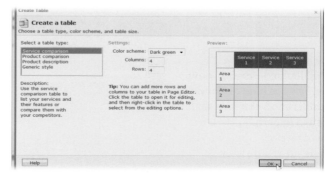

INSERTING A HYPERLINK

● It may well be in the interests of your business to promote or recommend others, or to direct your customers to useful sources of services or information. Having links to other web sites on yours is a great way to do this.

● We have highlighted the word **fishing** in the text, and we're going to turn it into a hyperlink to a friend's fishing charter web site by clicking on the **Hyperlink** button.

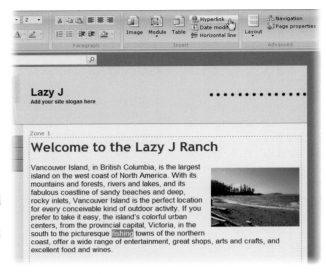

● The **Insert link** dialog box opens on the screen.
● Click on the radio button to specify that the link is to a web site, type in the web site address, tick the check box to open the link in a new window, and click on **OK**.

● The word that we highlighted–**fishing**–now appears in blue text and is underlined, showing that it is a hyperlink. We'll test what it does when we visit our site a little later 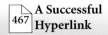.

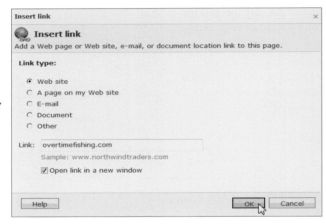

A Successful Hyperlink

CHOOSING A PAGE LAYOUT

● Now we're going to jump to the **Advanced** group of tools and click on the **Layout** button. The **Page layouts** drop-down menu offers the choice of five different ways to lay out the zones on the current page.

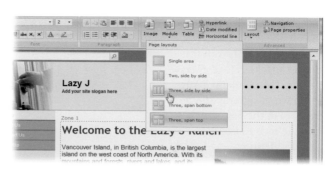

THE NAVIGATION BUTTON

● The last button that we're going to click on in the Page Editor toolbar is the **Navigation** button.

● The **Navigation** pane that opens enables you to change the order in which pages are shown in the navigation bar on your web pages, and to alter the relationships between pages in your web site.

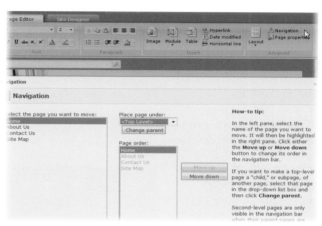

THE SITE DESIGNER TAB

So far, we have mainly been using tools that only affect aspects of the page on which we are working. In this section we are going to discover the tools on the **Site Designer** tab, which make changes that apply to all the pages or to the whole site. To get started, click on the **Site Designer** tab, next to the Page Editor tab.

CUSTOMIZING THE HEADER

● We'll start at the left-hand end of the tab, so click on the **Header** button.

● The **Customize Header** dialog box opens. Here, the two lines of text in the header appear in two separate panels. The company name given when signing up appears in the first panel, and the second holds placeholder text.

● Both panels have font formatting tools with which to change the style of the text if you wish to do so.

● We have keyed in our company slogan in the second panel and we're clicking on **OK**.

● Note that this same dialog box pops up if you just click in the header itself.

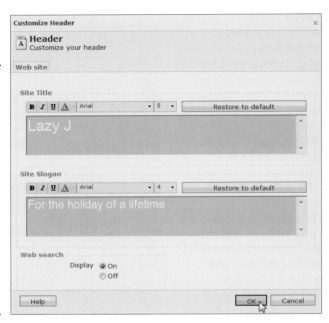

INSERTING A COMPANY LOGO

● Clicking on the **Logo** button opens the Image Gallery that we saw earlier.

● If you have previously uploaded a company logo in a suitable file format (such as a .jpg or .gif file), you can now bring it into your web pages at the top of each page or next to the company title, and specify the size it should be.

SMALL IS BEAUTIFUL

When planning images for use in your web pages, it's best to make sure the file sizes are small, for several reasons. Large or high resolution pictures not only take longer for you to upload–they also take longer to appear on screen when visitors open your pages in a browser. You also have a limited amount of storage space, unless you wish to pay for more.

CHOOSING A THEME

● The image that adorns the left-hand end of the header comes from Office Live's range of Themes.

● Click on the button to open a drop-down list of categories and click on one to view the selection of images it contains.

● When you find a picture that suits your company's image, click on it in the right-hand panel.

● Your chosen picture appears in the header.

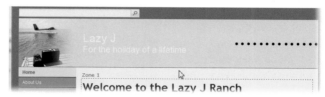

CHOOSING A HEADER STYLE

● Clicking on the **Style** button reveals a panel of alternative header layouts.

● In each one you can see the relative positions of the Theme image, the company title, and the slogan. Click on one to select it.

● It may be hard to imagine how each one will look on the page, but you can keep clicking on the **Style** button, choosing a different one, and seeing it action until you find the one you want.

THE NAVIGATION BUTTON

● We've seen a button called **Navigation** on the **Page Editor** tab, but this one is for positioning the navigation buttons to take us to other pages in the site.

● At the moment, they are located on the left of the page, but we can choose alternative positions. Here we are selecting **Top & Left**.

CHANGING THE COLOR THEME

● The **Color** button opens a list of color theme palettes very much like those that we have seen in Word and other Office programs.

● The current color theme is **Chocolate**, and we are changing this to **Iris**.

● As with the header layout, you can keep experimenting until you discover the one you like. There are 35 color themes, so you should be able to find one to suit your company image.

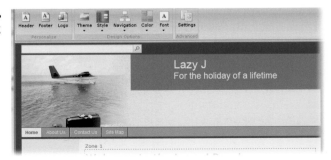

CHANGING THE SITE FONT

● By default, the font for all the text in your site is **Arial**. The **Font** button allows you to change this to one of six other fonts. Here, we are selecting **Trebuchet MS**.

● This change causes the text to reflow slightly, so choices like this should be made early in your web building process to avoid having to fit text twice.

ADVANCED SITE OPTIONS

● Clicking on the **Settings** button opens the **Advanced site options** dialog box in which you can choose to set the page width to **100%** instead of a fixed number of pixels, which widens the page to occupy the full width of the screen.

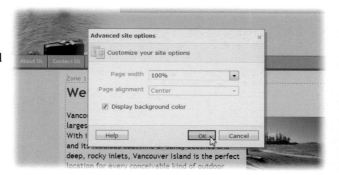

SEEING YOUR HANDIWORK

- Speaking of viewing, it's about time we took a look at our page as others will see it, rather than in the **Web Site Page Editor** view, so we're going to click on the **View** button at the top of the page.

- Before the page can be viewed in our browser, we need to confirm that we want to save all the changes that have been made.
- Click on **OK**.

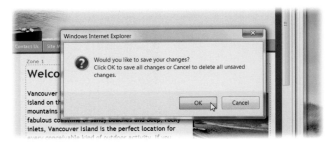

- We've still got a long way to go, but here we see our Home page in full screen view. We can now quit the browser, safe in the knowledge that our work on the site has been saved.

- As we have been working in a deliberately reduced window, this page looks rather different, and you may choose to work on a full screen window for that very reason.

- We can't resist checking to find out whether the hyperlink we created really works, so we're now clicking on the underlined word **fishing** in the text to see what happens.

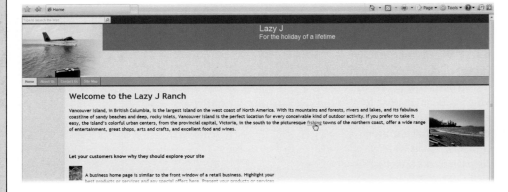

A SUCCESSFUL HYPERLINK

● The web site to which we made the link duly opens over the top of our page in a new window, as we requested in the **Insert link** dialog box. Success!

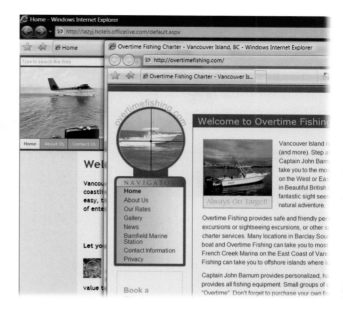

TOO LATE TO GO BACK?

● Let us suppose that you have spent some time working on your web site, saved the changes, and you regret what you've done.

● Fortunately, you can choose to revert to an earlier version by going to the **Page Manager** screen, clicking on the **Site actions** button, and choosing **Restore Site** from the drop-down menu that appears.

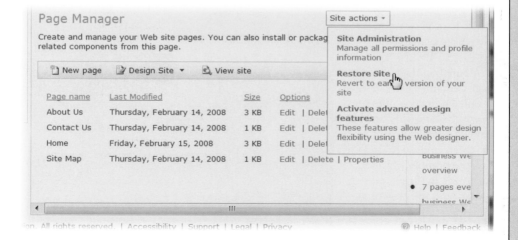

BUSINESS TOOLS

In addition to the web space and the tools to build and maintain your own web site, Office Live also offers a range of programs and facilities to help you manage your business.

WEB SITE PERFORMANCE

It's all well and good for your company to have a web site, but is it being visited? You need to know how your web site is performing, and to understand how you can increase the numbers of visitors to your site. Through the web site reports and the advice that it makes available, Office Live helps you to do both.

PERFORMANCE FIGURES

● When you go to Office Live (**http://home.officelive. com**) and log in, the Home page immediately offers you detailed and up-to-date information about how your web site is faring.

● Click on **View reports** to see what's available.

● A panel on the left of the page contains tabs that open detailed reports on the sites from which visitors came to your site, the keywords used in search engines to find the site, the number of times each page in the site was visited, and the browsers and operating systems that our visitors were using.

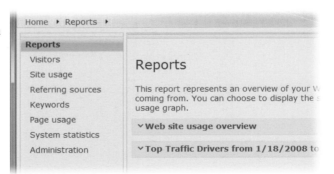

- The main part of the **Reports** page gives us a **Web site usage overview** report that shows us how many visits have been made to our site so far this year.
- By clicking on various links on this page we can find out more about what these statistics tells us, or what steps we can take to increase the number of visits.

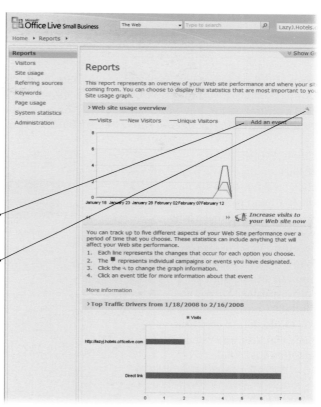

Events can be added to the graph

The options icon opens a range of display choices

- The **Add an event** button opens the **New Event** dialog box in which we can add campaigns and events to the graph in order to gauge what effect they've had on the number of visits.
- By clicking on the options tool icon, we are given the choice of five different performance options that we can choose to view in this overview report, and the time scale displayed.

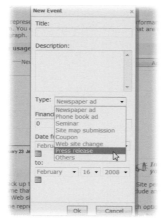

STAYING CONNECTED

With Microsoft Office Live Mail and Contact Manager, you can make Office Live a central part of how you manage your business correspondence and customer relations. If you have your own custom domain (which you can set up from the Home page), you can also create branded company e-mail addresses.

OFFICE LIVE MAIL

- Back on the Home page, click on the **E-Mail** tab in the left-hand panel.
- From the page that opens, you can set up your e-mail accounts and download Windows Live Messaging. You can also download software called Microsoft Outlook Connector and then use Outlook to access your mail, contacts, and calendar in Office Live Mail.

CONTACT MANAGER

- This program, which can be activated free by subscribers to Office Live, allows you to organize your company's contacts and customer information in an online database, and can be used as part of an e-marketing strategy.

- If you already use Outlook to manage your contacts, these can be imported into Office Live Contact Manager.

BUSINESS APPLICATIONS

● **Business Applications**, which are currently free to Office Live users, include **Document Manager**, which provides an online location for storing and sharing documents, and **Team Workspace**, where work colleagues can collaborate on events and tasks.

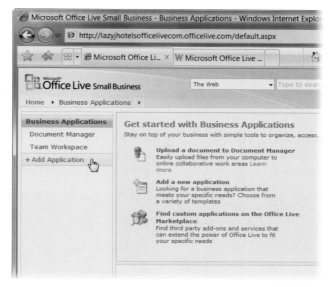

● Further applications can be added from a range of categories, including project, time, and business management programs.
● Click on any of the categories to see the list of available programs.

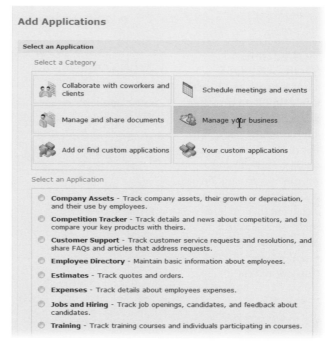

SALES AND MARKETING

For small businesses who want neither the expense nor the hassle of setting up online sales and marketing operations for themselves but need these services, Office Live offers, for a fee, a **Sell Online** and a **Promote Your Business** facility.

SELLING ONLINE

● **Store Manager** is a facility that turns your web site into an e-commerce base, helping you advertise your products and then sell them through eBay, using simple templates and secure transactions.

PROMOTING YOUR BUSINESS

● **adManager** and **E-mail Marketing Beta** provide two ways of promoting your company name. The first of these provides a means of purchasing Internet advertising linked to keywords on popular search engines, to lead purchasers to you. The second is for organizing e-mail newsletters and promotional campaigns.

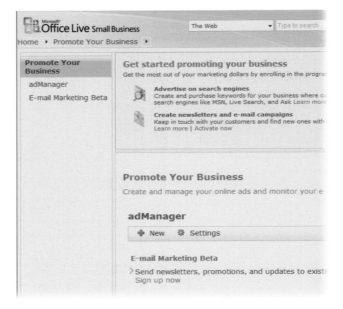

PLENTY OF ADVICE

Many of the areas that Office Live brings to the small business owner can seem intimidating to the uninitiated, from web site building to search advertising. The Small Business Resource Center (**http://smallbusiness.officelive.com/ ResourceCenter**) not only supplies thorough explanations, but it also offers advice on small business topics that extend beyond the Internet issues.

ARTICLES AND ONLINE SEMINARS

● Go to the bottom of the **Small Business Resource Center** window and click on the **Articles** link.

● In the page that opens, you will find an extensive list of articles on topics ranging from using online marketing to working from home, as well as detailed discussions of all aspects of web design.

● The link below the Articles link on the Small Business Resource Center window–**Web Seminars**– opens a broad catalog of on-demand online video seminar categories covering a wide spectrum of small-business-related subjects.

Articles and Insights

- Articles
- Web Seminars

Community and Support

- Blogs and Discussions

Web site design

- Updating your site: Tips for a tweak or a facelift
- Tips for an effective 'Contact Us' page
- Engaging content can turn clicks into sales
- 12 things you shouldn't publish on your site
- A one-page Web site may be all you need
- Usability mistakes every site should avoid
- 5 reasons to have a Web presence now

Microsoft

Office Live Seminars

Microsoft Office Live Web Seminars bring you some of today's most dynamic business authorities sharing insight and advice on topics important to small business success.

Browse Topics

Starting a business
Find out what it really takes to launch a business today, from developing your business plan to securing financial backing.

Exploring franchise opportunities
Learn the fundamentals of franchising and why many of today's most successful entrepreneurs choose this business model.

Winning "her" way
Hear how women-owned businesses are building successful enterprises their way and about the strategies that are paying off for them.

GLOSSARY

ACTIVE CELL
In Excel, the cell with the black border around it on a worksheet or, in a selected block of cells, the white cell. When you type, the characters appear in the active cell as well as in the Formula bar.

ANIMATION
Creation of moving elements within a presentation.

APPLICATION
Another term for a piece of software, usually a program.

ATTACHMENT
A file that is "attached" to an email message.

AUTO FILL
Auto Fill is used to copy a cell's content and/or format into a block of adjacent cells, or to create a data series by dragging the fill handle.

BLOG
Short for web log, this is a kind of diary stored on a webpage.

BORDER
A decorative effect that can be added to surround paragraphs of text or groups of cells.

CELL ADDRESS
The location of an Excel cell as defined by the column and row it is in–for example, A5 or H23.

CELL CONTENTS
The text, numerical value, or formula that you have entered into a cell. You can check the contents of a cell by selecting it and looking in the Formula bar above the worksheet. If a cell contains a formula, then what appears in the cell on screen is different from what the cell contains. What appears on screen is the value of the cell that has been calculated by the formula it contains, which is shown in the Formula bar.

COMPRESSION
The act of reducing the size of a file by using software to "compact" it.

DIALOG BOX
A rectangular window that appears on the screen and prompts you for a choice or reply, usually with buttons, such as **OK** or **Cancel**.

DOCUMENT
A file containing user data, such as text written in Word.

DOWNLOAD
The process of file-transfer from a remote computer to your own computer.

DV
Stands for digital video, the format used by almost all home movie cameras.

DVD
Stands variously for Digital Video Disc or Digital Versatile Disc and has replaced CD-ROM as the preferred medium for storing backups as well as home movies.

E-MAIL (ELECTRONIC MAIL)
A system for sending messages between computers that are linked over a network.

FILE
A discrete collection of data stored on your computer.

FILE NAME EXTENSION
Letters added to the end of a file name that indicate what type of file the document is, e.g. .docx (a Word document).

FONT
The typeface in which text appears onscreen and when it is printed out.

FORMAT PAINTER
A tool for applying an existing character or paragraph format to another part of a document.

FORMULA
In Excel, an expression entered into a cell that calculates the value of that cell from a combination of constants, arithmetic operators, and (often) the values of other cells in the worksheet.

FORMULA BAR
The white bar above the worksheet that always shows the contents of the active cell.

FUNCTION
In Excel, a defined operation or set of operations that can be performed on one or more selected cell values, cell addresses, or other data. Functions are incorporated into formulas. Excel functions include the function SUM, which returns the result of adding a range of values.

GIF (GRAPHICS INTERCHANGE FORMAT)
A widely used file format for web-based images.

HANDOUT
Printed version of a slide presentation given to the audience to accompany the presentation.

HARD DRIVE/HARD DISC
The physical device on your computer where programs and files are stored.

HOME PAGE
The first page you see when you arrive at a web site, typically containing a welcome message and hyperlinks to other pages.

HTML (HYPERTEXT MARK-UP LANGUAGE)
The formatting language used to create web pages. HTML specifies how a page should look onscreen.

HYPERLINK
A "hot" part of a web page (e.g., text, image, table) that links to another part of the same document or another document on the Internet.

ICON
A graphic symbol used on screen to indicate the function of a tool or command.

INDENT
The indent shifts part of the text, or just the first line in every paragraph, across the screen.

INSERTION POINT
A blinking upright line on the screen. As you type, text appears at the insertion point.

INSTALLING
The process of "loading" an item of software onto a hard drive. *See also* Uninstalling.

JPG
A graphic file format used on many websites for storing photos, thanks to the way in which it preserves quality while reducing file size.

NUMERICAL VALUE
In Excel, a number, date, time, percentage, or monetary amount.

ON LINE
Connected to the Internet.

ORGANIZATION CHART
A hierarchical chart, often used to illustrate the chain of command within a company.

PLUG-IN
A program that adds features to a web browser so that it can handle files containing, for example, multimedia elements.

PRESENTATION
A series of linked single-screen slides viewed in sequence.

PROGRAM
A software package that allows you to perform a specific task on your computer (also known as an application).

RADIO BUTTON
Small onscreen button within an application that visibly turns on and off when clicked with a mouse.

RESOLUTION
The density of the pixels that make up an image on a computer screen or the dots that make up an image, measured in pixels or dpi (dots per inch).

RESIZING
Dragging the edges of an object to alter its size.

RANGE
A block of cells in Excel.

RIBBON
Easily accessible toolbar format, common to several Microsoft Office 2007 programs.

RULER
Indicator at the top and left of the screen, with marks in inches or centimeters like a real ruler. Rulers also show the indents and margins of the text.

SCROLL
To scroll is to move up or down a document or screen.

SCROLL BARS
Bars at the foot and on the right of the screen that can be used to move around the document.

SELECTED CELLS/SELECTION
An area of an Excel worksheet that has been highlighted, using the mouse, for an action or command, such as copy or clear, to be performed on it.

SELECTING
Highlighting files or folders to enable you to perform certain activities on them.

SLIDE
A single screen from a presentation.

SLIDE SHOW
Screen view in which a PowerPoint presentation can be viewed as a whole.

SLIDE SORTER
Screen view in which all of the slides in a presentation can be viewed in thumbnail form.

SOFTWARE
A computer needs software to function. Software ranges from simple utilities to immense computer games.

STATUS BAR
The small panel at the foot of an open window that displays information about the items located there.

TASKBAR
The panel at the bottom of the desktop screen that contains the Start button, along with quick-access buttons to open programs and windows.

TIFF
Tagged Image File Format. A file format that retains a high level of information in an image, therefore suited to images that contain a lot of detail.

WEB BROWSER
A program used for viewing and accessing information on the web.

WEB SITE
A collection of web pages that are linked together, and possibly to other websites, by hyperlinks.

WINDOW
A panel displaying an open document on screen.

WORKBOOK
A collection of worksheets.

WORKSHEET
A grid of cells in which you can enter and manipulate data.

WORLD WIDE WEB (WWW, W3, THE WEB)
The collection of web sites on the Internet.

INDEX

ACKNOWLEDGMENTS

Dorling Kindersley would like to thank the following:

John Barnum, Overtime Fishing (www.overtimefishing.com);
Joan Larson, Creekside Studio (www.joanlarson.com);
Russ Heinl (www.heinlaerialphotography.com);
Donald Lovegrove (www.vancouverisland.com/www.britishcolumbia.com); and
Rob Burgess-Webb, Mount Washington Alpine Resort (www.mountwashington.ca)
for permission to reproduce web site screenshots and images.

Dawn Cambrin, Gibsons, BC, Canada, for the index.

Microsoft Corporation for permission to reproduce screens from within
Microsoft® Windows® Vista Ultimate™ Edition, Microsoft® Office OneNote® 2007,
Microsoft® Office Outlook® 2007, Microsoft® Office Word 2007,
Microsoft® Office Excel® 2007, Microsoft® Office PowerPoint® 2007,
Microsoft® Office Live Small Business, Microsoft® Internet Explorer, .

Microsoft® is a registered trademark of Microsoft Corporation
in the United States and/or other countries.

*Every effort has been made to trace the copyright holders of all materials used
in this book. The publisher apologizes for any unintentional omissions and would
be pleased, in such cases, to place an acknowledgment in future editions.*

All other images © Dorling Kindersley.
For further information see: **www.dkimages.com**